THE
UNJUST
STEWARD

Wealth, Poverty, and
the Church Today

UNJUST STEWARD

Wealth, Poverty, and the Church Today

Miguel Escobar

Forward Movement
Cincinnati, Ohio

Library of Congress Control Number: 2022938684

Scripture quotations are from the New Revised Standard Version of the Bible, copyright ©1989 the National Council of the Churches of Christ in the United States of America.

Psalm quotations are from *The Book of Common Prayer.*

Cover and interior illustrations by Jason Sierra

Author photo by Ron Hester

All rights reserved worldwide.

#2645

ISBN: 9780880285117

© 2022 Forward Movement

Forward
Movement

inspire disciples. empower evangelists.

For my family

Table of Contents

Foreword

It is impossible to live an authentic Christian life without wrestling deeply with issues of wealth and poverty. As the biblical scholar Walter Brueggemann has noted, it is "unmistakably clear that economics is a *core preoccupation* of the biblical tradition."[1] Similarly, the church historian Justo González has observed that questions of economic and social order were "*central*" to the "life of the early church."[2]

And yet most of us are blissfully unaware of this fact. Many Christians in twenty-first-century North America suffer from a collective amnesia about the centrality of issues of wealth and poverty in the Christian tradition. We forget that we minister to Jesus Christ whenever we feed the hungry, give drink to the thirsty, and clothe the naked. And we forget that we will be called to account for our actions—or inaction— at the Last Judgment.[3]

This is precisely why *The Unjust Steward* by Miguel Escobar is such an important work for our time. Escobar helps us to reclaim our theological heritage with respect to issues of wealth and poverty. Like the eucharist, this book is a reminiscence, or *anamnesis*, of a past that continues to have deep relevance to our lives today.

Within the pages of this volume, you will discover many treasures about the issues of wealth and poverty in the Bible and in the early church. You will encounter reflections on the Lord's Prayer, Saint Luke's Gospel, and the Pauline epistles. You will also hear the voices of ancient teachers such as Justin Martyr, Antony of Egypt, John Chrysostom, Gregory of Nyssa, and Augustine of Hippo.

But this book is not just an excellent teaching resource about the Bible and the early church theologians. It will also help you to draw important connections between your life and these ancient texts. Escobar's powerful reflection upon his own social location and life journey serves as a model for our own theological reflection. And the discussion questions and "A Next Step" suggestions at the end of each chapter are a great way to move from reflection to action.

To that end, this book also addresses the important intersections between wealth and poverty and contemporary issues such as gender inequality, the COVID-19 pandemic, anti-Blackness, sexual racism, predatory lending, and modern-day slavery. As such, this volume will be a useful resource to those who are interested in intersections of economic justice with liberationist, postcolonial, and queer theologies.

Finally, this book is a wonderful resource for Episcopal parishes and seminaries that wish to engage more deeply with the theological and ethical dimensions of wealth and poverty. Miguel Escobar is a faithful Episcopalian who has served in a variety of contexts in the Episcopal Church, ranging from the Office of the Presiding Bishop to Episcopal Divinity School at Union Theological Seminary. As such, Escobar's work reflects the deep commitment of the Episcopal Church to issues of economic justice.[4]

To paraphrase Augustine of Hippo, pick up this book and read it. You are sure to find many riches within.[5]

The Rev. Patrick S. Cheng, JD, PHD
Visiting Professor of Anglican Studies
Episcopal Divinity School at Union Theological Seminary

Endnotes

1 Walter Brueggemann, *Money and Possessions* (Louisville, KY: Westminster John Knox Press, 2016), xix (emphasis added).

2 Justo L. González, *Faith and Wealth: A History of Early Christian Ideas on the Origin, Significance, and Use of Money* (Eugene, OR: Wipf and Stock, 1990), xii (emphasis added).

3 See Matthew 25:31-46 (the Parable of the Sheep and the Goats).

4 See, for example, General Convention Resolution 2018-B026, which embraces the United Nations' Sustainable Development Goals, which begin with "End poverty in all its forms everywhere" as the basis for the Episcopal Church's policy and action on development.

5 Augustine of Hippo, *Confessions* XIII.xii ("*tolle lege, tolle lege*").

Introduction

In summer 2010, I presented a short workshop on Christian stewardship practices in Hendersonville, North Carolina. This presentation took place during a conference for Latino Episcopalians, an event conducted almost entirely in Spanish. The twelve or so attendees who gathered in the conference room that day were clergy and lay leaders of Spanish-speaking congregations.

As was often the case, my presentation began with a discussion of "stewardship" and the "stewardship of God's abundance" as the theological framework for congregational fundraising. For those who may not be immediately familiar with this term, Christian stewardship refers to the idea that all of us are called to be faithful and prudent managers of the abundance that God has entrusted to our care. This sense is then applied to everything from annual fundraising campaigns (frequently called stewardship campaigns) to the responsible management of a congregation's savings and endowment. In short, stewardship means leaders of congregations and other church institutions are called upon to be the faithful managers of God's abundant resources.

With all this in mind, I dutifully arrived that day with slides outlining the tenets and practices of how most mainline congregations do their annual fundraising, practices undergirded by this theology of stewardship—*mayordomía* in Spanish—in which all Christians are called upon to be stewards—*mayordomos*—of all that God has given us. Just a few slides in, however, I noticed that a couple of those gathered around the room appeared both skeptical and perplexed. Eventually, one of the attendees explained to me that the Spanish word I was using for steward, *mayordomo*, had profoundly negative associations where he was from, so much so that he would never want to be considered a *mayordomo*. *Mayordomos* were the people who had exploited people like him and his family, the property/business manager-in-charge who squeezed out every cent they could from the blood and sweat of their workers. There were nods around the room as people recognized that "stewardship" was a very strange term for me to use as it was so closely associated with exploitation and injustice.

Failing to grasp the gravity of his statement, I thought that the point he was raising was simply a matter of translation, and so we began to discuss other words that would work instead. In the years since, though, I've come to see the responses I met that day less as a matter of translation and more as a faithful memory of the kinds of characters stewards actually are. Who is the steward in Jesus's time? What is stewardship?

This gulf in perspective became especially clear as I began learning more about the history of *mayordomos* in Latin America. Across many parts of Latin America, on the vast colonial estates called haciendas, the *mayordomo* was the head administrator in charge of making the plantations, mines, and factories profitable. Whereas the owners of haciendas typically lived off-site in major urban areas, the *mayordomo* lived on-site, and it was their job to roughly rend and report profits back to the *patrón*. On the haciendas, *mayordomos* regularly used physical punishment, violence, and debt bondage to attain their profits. Even in twentieth-century Bolivia, for instance, in studies on the labor practices of the hacienda system prior to 1952, there are examples of *mayordomos* whipping workers and threatening expulsion from the estate.[1] The means by which this profit was made and the disconnection of the owner from the lives of the people who were impacted by the decisions of "good stewardship" are central to issues of wealth and poverty in the church today.

As I began to dig deeper into this issue of stewardship, I soon discovered many others who have questioned the wisdom of this doctrine and where it came from. Writing in the 1930s, the American theologian Reinhold Niebuhr strongly criticized mainline Christianity's adulation of the steward and stewardship. Niebuhr traced the origins of this doctrine to the influence of business leaders in mainline Protestantism during the industrial buildup between the two World Wars.[2] In "Is Stewardship Ethical?", a short article he wrote for the *Christian Century* in 1930, he critiques stewardship as an exasperatingly naïve framework that allows the church to avoid asking the more difficult questions about sources of wealth, including the exploitative practices through which such wealth was made. Instead, he argues, stewardship does little more than "sanctify power and privilege as it exists in the modern world by certain concessions to the ethical principal."[3]

Niebuhr gives the example of "the pious businessman" who is both honest and generous to his church, two virtues that "give him the satisfaction of being a Christian."[4] Yet this pious businessman "regards his power in his factory much as kings of old regarded their prerogatives. Any attempt on the part of the workers to gain a share in the determining of policy, particularly the policy which affects their own livelihood, hours, and wages, is regarded by him as an attempt to destroy the divine order of things."[5]

Niebuhr contends that stewardship is an inadequate theological framework for how the church talks and thinks about money, asserting that the call to be a good steward does nothing to challenge the pious businessman to fulfill his broader moral obligations to his employees: "There is not one church in a thousand where the moral problems of our industrial civilization are discussed with sufficient realism from the pulpit to prompt the owner to think of his stewardship in terms of these legitimate rights of the workers."[6] Niebuhr challenges the church to find a better approach for thinking about wealth and poverty, a theological vision that not only asks critical questions about sources of wealth but also recognizes "how necessary and ultimately ethical are the restraints of an ethical society upon man's (sic) will to power and his lust for gain."[7]

What would it mean, then, to begin to look beyond stewardship as a way of thinking about wealth and poverty? To start, I believe we should first return to what is considered to be one of Jesus's most perplexing teachings, that of the parable of the unjust steward found in Luke 16:1-13. The situation described in this parable matches almost exactly the exploitative arrangement of the Latin American haciendas described above, and it once again raises the larger question of how mainline Christianity came to embrace the role and character of the steward.

Luke's parable of the unjust steward describes a steward that would have been familiar to the dozen Latinos gathered in the workshop on that day as well as Reinhold Niebuhr writing in the 1930s. The story Jesus tells takes place on a vast agricultural estate, one in which a landowner and his property/business manager, an effective steward, have pressed workers into significant debt and debt bondage. Biblical scholars note that the steward in this story is likely a "first slave," or a man who has been freed from slavery for the sole purpose of serving as a manager and overseer of the slaves, day laborers, and tenant farmers who were made to work the land.[8]

One day, the rich landowner suspects his first slave—the steward—of squandering his wealth. Before any proof or defense can be offered, the landowner fires this steward, at which point the steward panics and must come up with a plan for his survival.

His plan is a curious one. Whereas previously the good steward had extracted wealth from those he had overseen, the steward now begins to send his master's wealth flowing in reverse. He does this by using his master's wealth to remit the debts of the slaves, day laborers, and tenant farmers who were indebted to the master. Biblical scholars note these debts were so large that they were likely the debts of entire villages.[9] We learn the steward does this in the hope of later being welcomed into these laborers' homes after news of his dismissal becomes widely known.

Surprisingly, the steward's decision to use the landowner's wealth to remit debts ends up being praised by both the master and Jesus. Jesus concludes this parable by appearing to praise fiscal imprudence and immorality, a shocking fact that has perplexed interpreters for millennia: "And I tell you, make friends for yourselves by means of dishonest wealth so that when it is gone, they may welcome you into the eternal homes" (Luke 16:9). Jesus goes on to say that like the steward, his followers must ultimately choose who their master is in life: "No slave can serve two masters; for a slave will either hate the one and love the other, or be devoted to the one and despise the other. You cannot serve God and wealth" (Luke 16:13).

Who is the steward, and what is the injustice being described, then? At the outset of the parable, the steward's actions are fundamentally exploitative. His expected role is to extract wealth from the land and those working it in order to maximize returns and profit. It is telling that the steward finds his safety and salvation only when the money begins to flow in reverse, in an act of economic jubilee. "Following the money" in this parable is key here as the steward finds his salvation by acting in the opposite way he is expected to, an act of anti-stewardship.

All of this may seem like quibbling over terminology yet I am convinced it goes deeper than that. It is striking to me that even as secular cultural institutions such as the Metropolitan Museum of Art return major gifts from the Sackler family (justly condemned for their pharmaceutical company's leading role in America's opioid crisis) and colleges and universities across the nation are divesting their endowments from fossil fuels, the church's idolization of "the steward" and "stewardship" prevents it from having serious conversations about where its wealth is coming from and at what great cost.[10] The exploitative character of the steward and the rapacious logic of stewardship prevails. I've now personally observed multiple instances in which the principle of "sound stewardship" has served as the rationale for church organizations *not divesting* their endowments from fossil fuels. In each instance, the argument was eerily reminiscent to the actions of the unjust steward at the outset of the parable, wherein effective stewardship meant extracting the maximum returns on behalf of the organizational masters, never mind the exploitation of the land and the poor involved in this decision.

This suggests to me there is something fundamentally unjust about stewardship. I've come to believe this idea of stewardship—derived from the Roman *latifundia*, carried through to the Latin American hacienda, forged in the stealing of indigenous people's lands and the institution of slavery, and later championed by wealthy industrialists— is far too limited a framework for engaging the broader moral obligations that Christians have on issues of wealth and poverty.

My friend and colleague, the Very Rev. Dr. Kelly Brown Douglas, dean of Episcopal Divinity School at Union, speaks and writes regularly about theology's role in broadening the moral imagination. This book is an attempt to do just that: to broaden and deepen the conversations taking place about wealth and poverty in the church today.

In order to do this, I question "stewardship" as one of the main ways mainline Christianity talks and thinks about wealth and poverty. Though I am not a New Testament scholar, I have been struck by how often the gospels describe the steward as a dubious character. In addition to the parable of the unjust steward, a steward again appears at the wedding at Cana (John 2:1-12). There, the chief steward is baffled by the bridegroom's choice to serve the good wine last: "Everyone serves the good wine first, and then the inferior wine after the guests have become drunk. But you have kept the good wine until now" (John 2:10). As the chief steward is considering cost savings, Jesus is transforming water into wine. Whereas the unjust steward exploits the land and people, Jesus is praising the one who remits debts, an act of economic jubilee. The steward is repeatedly presented, then, as a foil to the way of Jesus.

Second, in keeping with this notion of broadening the moral imagination, this book highlights some of the other ways Christianity has wrestled with issues of wealth and poverty in its past. I have done this is by looking at 24 instances in which Christian thinkers dealt directly with issues of wealth and poverty over the first five centuries. The result is a series of snapshots that begin to tell the dramatic and conflicted story of how the church transitioned from the radical message of Jesus toward theological doctrines that served to justify the building up of vast institutional wealth. It is a stark transformation. On one end of this story, we have Jesus instructing a rich man to sell his possessions and give all his wealth to the poor (Matthew 19:16-30; March 10:17-31; Luke 18:18-30), and on the other, we have Augustine urging the wealthy to direct their donations to him, as opposed to the poor, as he embarks on a vast church building campaign: "Your bishop may not lack for clothes or need of a roof above his head. But perhaps he is building a church. You cannot see into the empty coffers of your leader; but you certainly can see the empty shell of his building as it goes up... May God grant that I do not say this in vain."[11]

I should add here that this is not an entirely tragic story. Between Jesus and Augustine, there are many encouraging and inspiring moments along the way. For even as the church moved on from the witness of its founder, there were leaders and movements who sought to reconnect the church back to its Jesus's radical vision. Their voices and practical advice—frequently offering a *via media* between Jesus's teachings and the value of the church as an institution—are deep wells from which to draw strength and encouragement for ministry today.

Acknowledgments

While the idea of this book has been germinating since I led that workshop in 2010, the research and writing of this book truly began in the first months of the COVID-19 pandemic. Indeed, this book was begun in the first weeks of isolation in April 2020 and concluded during another ten-day isolation period at the beginning of January 2022, the latter the result of finally contracting the virus. The chaos of the pandemic, the vast poverty and inequality that it exacerbated and exposed, as well as the racial reckoning caused by the murder of George Floyd in late May 2020, all infuse the chapters of this book.

As I set about gathering my notes in April 2020, I did so in the hope that it would be able to be well-used by congregational leaders. My goal was to write 24 accessibly written reflections, any of which could be read and discussed in congregational settings. As you will see, I've included discussion questions and a practical next step as aids to foster group conversation. A four-week discussion series could easily be organized by selecting four chapters that are particularly relevant to one's community. My hope is that chapters help lead to robust discussion in community by offering new insights and images with which to think about wealth and poverty.

Finally, I want to say thank you to several people who were key in the writing of this book. First to Ben, my husband, who steadfastly encouraged and supported me as I immersed myself each day on this project, even as this often meant taking over the living room of our one-bedroom apartment during the pandemic. I lean on Ben's love and support daily. Secondly, I am grateful to the many friends and colleagues who encouraged me in this project and who were willing to read and offer their feedback on early drafts. These include Mark Beckwith, Thomas Cannell, Patrick Cheng, Gary Commins, Kelly Brown Douglas, Mary Foulke, Bill Franklin, Scott Gunn, Jeffrey Lee, Sandra Montes, Steven Paulikas, Richelle Thompson, and Joseph Wolyniak. This circle also included several students and recent graduates of Episcopal Divinity School at Union including Carl Adair, Mary Barber, Nicole Hanley and Maryann Philbrook. It is oftentimes said that writing is lonely work, and this felt especially true while writing in a pandemic, yet the thoughtful feedback, insights, and words of encouragement I received from this group meant that this book was written in community. To say "thanks" doesn't quite suffice for the depth of gratitude I have for their friendship and support.

Endnotes

1 Stephen M. Smith, "Labor Exploitation on Pre-1952 Haciendas in the Lower Valley of Cochabamba, Bolivia," *The Journal of Developing Areas,* Vol. 11, No. 2 (1977): 227–244.

2 David King, "Beyond Abundance: Is Stewardship Ethical?" *Word & World*, Vol. 38, No. 3 (Summer 2018).

3 Reinhold Niebuhr, "Is Stewardship Ethical?", *The Christian Century*, April 30, 1930, 555.

4 Niebuhr, "Is Stewardship Ethical?", 555.

5 Niebuhr, "Is Stewardship Ethical?", 555.

6 Niebuhr, "Is Stewardship Ethical?", 556.

7 Niebuhr, "Is Stewardship Ethical?", 557.

8 Bruce J. Malina and Richard L. Rohrbaugh, *Social-Science Commentary on the Synoptic Gospels* (Minneapolis, Minnesota: Fortress Press, 2003, Second Edition), 292.

9 Malina and Rohrbaugh, *Social-Science Commentary*, 292.

10 A charming profile of America's thirtieth wealthiest family, the Sacklers, *Forbes* magazine notes that "Nearly all 50 states have filed lawsuits against Purdue and Sackler family members for their alleged roles in the opioid crisis." forbes.com/profile/sackler/?sh=615973da5d63

11 Peter Brown, *Through the Eye of a Needle: Wealth, the Fall of Rome, and the Making of Christianity in the West, 350-550 AD* (Princeton, New Jersey: Princeton University Press, 2012), 355.

REVERSAL AND KOINONIA

No slave can serve two masters;
for a slave will either hate the one
and love the other,
or be devoted to the one
and despise the other.
You cannot serve God and wealth.

—Luke 16:13

1 Dreams
of Reversal

In 1996, my grandfather, Eusebio Castilleja, lay dying of skin cancer in his bedroom. I was fourteen years old and seated with my siblings at my grandparents' kitchen table, trying in my own teenage way to grasp the meaning of what was taking place and watching as my parents, aunts, uncles, and cousins took turns saying their goodbyes.

On the one hand, death by cancer was nothing new. Like so many migrant farm laborer families, varieties of cancers seemed to bloom undetected and unchecked until it was far too late. Some of my fondest memories from childhood are the result of long car rides from our home outside San Antonio, Texas, to the tiny East Texas town of Rosebud—population less than 2,000— where I played wildly with my siblings and cousins outside as my parents, aunts, and uncles mourned relatives indoors. In my memory, those trips mostly involved climbing trees, running from cows, tasting honeysuckle, and steeling myself for the eventual moment when I'd have to kneel and kiss my deceased relative on the forehead. My grandfather's death, however, was the first time that death-by-cancer had touched someone I had known well, a person I loved and admired deeply.

My maternal grandparents, Eusebio and Cruz Castilleja, immigrated from Monterrey, Mexico, in 1954 and settled in San Antonio's West Side in a small home on Delgado Street. Each summer, they'd pack up their six children, including my mother, for a long drive from San Antonio to family farms outside of Krakow, Wisconsin, to work as migrant farm laborers. My father's family had a similar pattern, although he remembers spending summers picking cotton near Houston, Texas. Decades later while on a road trip to Galveston beach, I remember my dad pulling the car over by the side of a cotton field so his children could see what it felt like to extract the pillowy fibers from the razor-like leaves. I remember the sharpness of the thorns, and my siblings and I held on to our cotton through the rest of the trip.

The experiences and humiliations of those fields ended up as the seeds of the stories I'd grow up hearing around family dinner tables. Long after my parents, aunts, and uncles had moved on to office jobs and professional careers, family gatherings included unbearably long story-telling sessions—usually led by an uncle—about what had taken place during those years. My family was lucky in that we were able to leave the fields behind within a generation. And though there were family members who didn't wish to dwell on that past, the stories would flood out whenever there was a funeral, and there was an unending stream of funerals.

On one of the long car trips back from a funeral in Rosebud, I remember my parents talking about why so many people in our family were dying from cancer. They had just overheard other family members—perhaps distant cousins or an aunt twice removed—talking about the connection between the cancers and the pesticides they were exposed to in the fields. My father recalled crop dusters dropping pesticides directly on them as they worked below. Like poisonous snow, I remember thinking. Part of why I remember that conversation so distinctly is that it led me to worry about whether that poison could be transmitted from generation to generation, from skin to skin. Was the poison eating away at me already?

In 1996, the same year of my grandfather's death, a study on the prevalence and cultural attitudes toward cancer among migrant farmworkers affirmed much of what my parents were describing on that car ride back from Rosebud. After confirming that seasonal and migrant workers are at elevated risk for lymphomas and prostate, brain, leukemia, cervix, and stomach cancers, the study describes the way cancers are understood and described among impacted families: "In regard to cancer, an intense fear of the disease coupled with fatalism regarding its treatment and course were found to be pervasive among the migrant workers who participated in the focus groups. Cancer was nearly synonymous with death, an association that likely reflected the experience that migrant workers have had with cancer." The economic drivers behind this exposure to pesticides were also explored. When asked why a participant continued to work in the fields when he knew full well the risks of exposure to pesticides, he responded: "If I refuse to go into the field, there are many others who would be happy to do it so their families could eat."[1]

As I sat in my grandparents' home and my grandfather lay dying, different strands that I had intuited about the way the world worked were coming together. His cancer was a striking lesson in the intertwined nature of poverty and vulnerability to disease. Poisonous snow had fallen from the sky onto the skin of my grandfather and closest relatives. Who flew the plane and what were they thinking? Did they know what would eventually happen to the people below? Did they even see us as human beings? An understanding of the universe as an ultimately cold and cruel place closed in. But then, my depressed daydreaming was interrupted by the sudden presence of a priest.

What I recall is a knock, a hubbub among my aunts, and then suddenly, the presence of a Roman Catholic priest in my grandparents' house, a holy outsider in my family's deepest moment of mourning. He was quickly escorted from the front door to my grandfather's bedroom, where he performed the Last Rites.

Being something of a veteran of Roman Catholic funerals, I'd certainly seen priests and understood at a basic level why one had just knocked on the door. But at fourteen, I found myself asking a deeper set of questions that I'm still reflecting on today. Why, really, had a priest suddenly appeared? What did my Mexican grandparents' faith have to say about what was happening? And why was it that the church was one of the only institutions that showed up when so many others failed to?

A year or so later, I was riding my bike through the quiet country roads surrounding my family's home in the Texas Hill Country. As a result of seeing the priest walk through the doorway of my grandparents' home, I'd begun a slow, careful reading of the gospels of Matthew and Luke, one that involved copying out by hand significant chunks of the gospels per day to absorb the text more fully. I had recently come across the *Magnificat* in the Gospel of Luke and, strange teenager that I was, decided to commit it to memory. As a result, particular lines kept floating to mind as I rode my bike up and down the gentle slopes that early evening. "My soul magnifies the Lord…He has brought down the mighty from their thrones, and lifted up the lowly…He has filled the hungry with good things, and sent the rich away empty" (Luke 1:46-55).

These lines were unlike any version of Christianity that I had experienced up to that point. The small Texas town I grew up in was thoroughly controlled by an aggressively white, Christian fundamentalism that was somehow both ridiculous and terrifying at the same time. A politicized version of Christian fundamentalism was growing in strength and force across the country throughout the 1990s, something I experienced firsthand as I watched friends disappear into homeschooling or become transformed from decent and funny kids into radical evangelists who joined their parents in trying to ban books from the school library.

By the time I graduated from the local, public high school, Christian students had staged walkouts of Biology II when evolution was taught; an English teacher was fired for teaching the novel *Snow Falling on Cedars* because it had a scene of interracial sex and discussed Japanese internment camps; our principal led the school in the Lord's Prayer before football games with impunity; and motivational speakers had been regularly brought in to exhort us to follow Jesus lest we burn in hell.[2] In middle and high school, bleached blond teenagers participated in Young Life rallies, held hands in a circle each morning for prayer around the flagpole, and casually dropped comments regarding the immorality of interracial relationships because "God forbids man from laying with animals."[3]

What I didn't realize then but am painfully aware of now is that I was witnessing what the journalist Katherine Stewart has described as the rise of radical Christian nationalism, a highly organized movement centered on the fabrication that the American republic was founded as a Christian nation. This radical movement asserts that legitimate government rests on adherence to the doctrines of a specific religious, ethnic, and cultural heritage, a white nationalist Christianity whose defining fear is that the nation has strayed from the truths that once made it great.[4] Stewart intentionally uses the term "radical" because this version of white Christian nationalism pretends to work toward the revival of "traditional values" while contradicting and undermining the long-established principles and norms of democracy.[5]

Thankfully, I was mostly excluded from much of this on account of being Latino, a nerd, and very gay. Yet I watched closely as this version of Christianity created holy cover for cruelty toward those on the margins, and it is impossible to describe how much work it has taken to undo the fear, shame, and self-hatred that I internalized from those years. My primary experience of Christianity, therefore, had been this soul-crushing expression of white, fundamentalist conservatism, with cruel, so-called Christians mocking anyone who deviated from this norm.

Because of this, it felt—in fact, it oftentimes still feels—like a betrayal to open the Bible, a text that is thoroughly owned by those who are committed to terrorizing the lives of LGBTQ+ communities and people of color. And yet my curiosity ultimately got the better of me. What did the text actually say? How did this same text galvanize both the white Christian nationalist movement that I actively feared as well as lead a Roman Catholic priest to show up to honor the dignity of my grandfather at his deathbed? I was—and remain—fascinated by such contradictions.

What I discovered in my careful reading of the gospels was a world of agricultural images and miraculous stories that was a great deal more like the world described around my immigrant grandparents' kitchen table than the bleached blond Christianity that gathered around the flagpole for prayer. The Bible held stories about day laborers and outcasts, people who were desperately sick seeking a miraculous cure; there were stories of people who were persistently hungry, had been robbed and left to die, or were begging on the side of the road, as well as stories of people who had been humiliated and then lifted up.

While it wasn't clear to me at the time, I now realize that I was responding to one of the peculiarities of the gospels themselves. In *Christianity: The First Three Thousand Years*, historian Diarmaid MacCulloch writes, "Biographies were not rare in the ancient world and the Gospels do have many features in common with non-Christian examples. Yet these Christian books are an unusually 'down-market' variety of biography, in which ordinary people reflect on their experience of Jesus, where the powerful and the beautiful generally stay on the sidelines of the story, and where it is often the poor, the ill-educated and the disreputable whose encounters with God are most vividly described."[6] The gospels are about the lives of *gente humilde*, as my family might say.[7]

Further, in addition to these stories being about "the poor, the ill-educated, and the disreputable", the gospels also expressed a longing for the world to be turned upside down. In Luke's version of the Beatitudes, for example, not only does Jesus say that it is the poor, the hungry, those who are weeping, and those who are hated who are blessed in God's kingdom, but also Jesus proceeds to pronounce woes on the rich, the well-fed, those who are laughing now, and the currently adulated. Jesus hopes for a great reversal.

Reading those words, my teenage soul joined generations of people who have found strength and courage in both halves of Luke's Beatitudes, both the positive affirmations of the poor as blessed as well as the less frequently cited pronouncement of woes on the "powerful and beautiful people" who make the lives of the poor miserable. As I delved more deeply into the Old and New Testament, I discovered that God's anger frequently flashes like lightning bolts on a hot Texas summer afternoon, and very often this anger is directed at the way the poor are being humiliated and mistreated. God angrily asks, "What do you mean by crushing my people, by grinding the face of the poor?"[8] What do we mean by this, indeed? It was a life-changing revelation to realize that my sorrow, and yes, profound anger, at the way the world was ordered might also be connected to God's dream of justice, and that many of the biblical stories were pointing toward a great reversal.

The stories and images of God's impending reversal are one of Christianity's gifts, a balm and source of hope to all those who are living with a boot on their neck. There are two halves to this gift, both an affirmation of the dignity of the poor as well as warnings to the rich, those who are well-fed, those who are laughing now, and those who are well-praised. Even so, in an effort to be welcoming to all, mainline Christianity has often tended to only focus on the positive affirmations found in the gospels while ignoring Jesus's harsh warnings toward the powerful and wealthy. Truthfully, I've heard more than a few sermons reduce the gospels to the message of "follow your joy." Yet these exclusively positive takes are forever running up against the starker vision of the gospels, including Jesus's encounter with the rich young ruler—a story that appears in Matthew, Mark, and Luke—in which Jesus states that it is easier for a camel to go through the eye of a needle than for a rich man to enter the kingdom of heaven.

In the 24 years since I began my furtive reading of the gospels, I've learned a great deal more about what drove this vision of reversal. I've realized that pressure speaks to pressure, including across millennia.

In *Loving the Poor, Saving the Rich*, early church historian Helen Rhee describes the intense socioeconomic pressures of the period just prior to and inclusive of Jesus's ministry. Called the Second Temple Period in Jewish history, this period is typically bracketed as taking place between 516 BCE and 70 CE during the time when the Second Temple in Jerusalem existed before it was destroyed by the Romans in retaliation for ongoing revolts. Rhee notes that this time in Jewish history was one of intense pressures, the result of foreign domination from the Persians, Greeks, and Romans, as well as a time of harsh living conditions for the masses.[9]

Rhee writes, "In first-century Palestine, the social scene betrayed the concentration of wealth in the hands of a small elite group (the landed aristocracy) and the general impoverishment of the majority of the population (the landless peasants). The tension between the wealthy landed minority and the peasant landless majority goes back to the late monarchical period, but throughout the Second Temple period and especially during Herod's rule, the situation grew increasingly worse through the continuing economic oppression and confiscation of the land by the rich and powerful. Creation of huge estates through the exploitation of the land and through mortgage interest produced a growing number of landless tenants or hired laborers in the very land they had once owned. And the coalition between the great landowners and the mercantile groups over the monopoly of the agricultural goods made the peasant workers' lot more difficult to endure."

Rhee goes on to describe this period as having "the firm imprint of feudalism" wherein the pressures on the lives of the poor were immense. Other compounding factors such as overpopulation and over-cultivation of the land, natural disasters, and increasing tributes and tithes all combined to force "the already poor majority into the arduous struggle for unfortunate survival in a highly stratified society."[10]

In addition to setting the stage for social upheaval and rebellion, the pressures of the Second Temple Period also resulted in a particular vision, tone, and framework about what God's justice would one day look like. The visions of God's justice in literature from this period, including 1 Enoch and the Psalms of Solomon, echo throughout the New Testament, especially in the gospels of Matthew, Mark, and Luke, the Book of Revelation, and the Letter of James. Over and over again, one finds poor people looking toward a final, apocalyptic struggle between the righteous and the wicked, one in which the righteous are the victimized poor and the wicked identified as the powerful rich.

Rhee concludes that "this eschatological conflict between the righteous poor and the wicked rich involved the 'great reversal' of their earthly fortunes on the last day," and that "in this political and socioeconomic climate, the early followers of Jesus believed that, with the coming of Jesus, the eschatological new age had indeed dawned."[11]

While these themes of the "pious poor and oppressive rich" and "great reversal" are interwoven throughout all four gospels, they are especially present within the Gospel of Luke.

In addition to the *Magnificat* (Luke 1:46-55), Jesus announces his mission as proclaiming good news to the poor (Luke 4:18-19) and tells followers to invite "the poor, the crippled, the lame, and the blind" to banquets (Luke 14:13, 21). Luke's version of the Beatitudes includes a series of woes to the rich (Luke 6:20-26) and mocks the rich fool who stores up his wealth in barns (Luke 12:16-21). There is also, of course, the story of the rich young ruler, told in Matthew, Mark, and Luke, and how it's easier for a camel to go through the eye of a needle than for a rich man to enter heaven. Indeed, the rich who are to be praised are people like Zacchaeus the tax collector who gives half his wealth away and promises to repay four times the amount he has defrauded of others (Luke 19:1-10). We also encounter the "unjust steward" who halves the debts of his master's servants, a small sign of God's Jubilee and, perhaps, the closest thing Luke has in terms of a constructive pathway forward for making use of "dishonest wealth" (Luke 16:9).

In addition to these examples, perhaps the most vivid depiction of God's reversal in the Gospel of Luke is the one that takes place between Lazarus and the rich man. Theologian M. Douglas Meeks describes this parable as a vivid illustration of the coming reversal and the need for repentance among the rich and powerful for their treatment of the poor.[12]

Luke 16:19-31 tells the contrasting lives and fates of the beggar Lazarus and a rich man. Characteristic of the way that the gospels view society from the bottom up, this story names the beggar (Lazarus) while the rich man remains a generalized figure. We are told the rich man "was dressed in purple and fine linen" and "feasted sumptuously every day" while Lazarus lay at the rich man's gate "covered with sores," hoping to "satisfy his hunger with what fell from the rich man's table." Jesus tells his listeners that such was Lazarus's poverty that even the dogs would come to lick Lazarus's sores.

Death comes for both Lazarus and the rich man, but even in death, social distinction prevails. Whereas the rich man is properly buried, Lazarus dies at the rich man's gates. The first hearers of this story would likely have known that beggars like Lazarus often ended up being buried in mass graves. It is only in the eternal life that their fortunes are finally reversed. Meeks states, "But, though not even decently buried, Lazarus ('God helps') now sits at the table with Abraham in God's eschatological household. In contrast, the rich man, properly interred, experiences that hell that the poor Lazarus had known in his lifetime."[13]

In a passage that is as frightening to the rich as it would have been soothing to the first listeners of this parable, Jesus continues by telling how the rich man who is now in hell calls out to Abraham: "Father Abraham, have mercy on me, and send Lazarus to dip the tip of his finger in water and cool my tongue; for I am in agony in these flames." But Abraham responds, "Child, remember that during your lifetime you received your good things, and Lazarus in like manner evil things; but now he is comforted here, and you are in agony." God's justice is revealed in this reversal; a great chasm has been set between the rich man in hell and Lazarus in paradise, and the worldly order has been turned upside down.

In the ancient heart of Christianity is a deep longing for God's reversal of rich and poor. Its depiction of "the righteous poor and oppressive rich" and God's preferential option for "the least of these" continues to represent something new, countercultural, and strange, both in ancient Rome and today. The historian (and my former professor) John Anthony McGuckin writes, "It was a widespread belief in Hellenistic society that the (often wretched) disparity of lot was simply how things were in the greater cosmic order. Imbalances were not injustices. The attitude (still prevalent today, of course, as an often-unvoiced supposition in many venues) was at the core of pagan Roman ideas on wealth and status."[14] In contrast, "the gospel's very different approach to entitlement (based on what was a ridiculous idea to wider Greco-Roman society—that all men and women were equals as the consecrated images of God on earth) was a veritable clash of civilizations."[15]

As I will describe over and over again in this book, the United States's cultural attitudes toward the poor are not so different from the ancient Roman views. Indeed, in our recurring depictions of "the unworthy poor"—think Ronald Reagan's "welfare queen" of the 1980s—we oftentimes even outdo the ancient Romans in disparaging the character of the poor. In my work with activists such as the Rev. Dr. Liz Theoharis of the Poor People's Campaign and David Giffen of New York's Coalition for the Homeless, I'm frequently reminded of how countercultural it still is to say that society should have compassion for people struggling at the bottom of the socioeconomic ladder. When meeting with Dr. Theoharis, for instance, I've often noticed that she has a large poster behind her that reads simply, "Fight Poverty. Not the Poor." And in meeting with David Giffen, I have heard him speak many times about the important role faith leaders can play at neighborhood community meetings by simply reminding those gathered that the 60,000-plus people who live in the New York City shelter system, including 21,000 children, are people too, not trash that can be discarded. Both of these activists are forever pushing up against a culture, one that was alive and well in ancient Rome and continues to thrive today, that justifies inequality by dehumanizing the poor. Horrifically, people who claim Christianity are frequently leading the way in this regard. Yet the ancient heart of Christianity is a different story altogether.

To insist that society should have compassion for its most vulnerable members remains a surprisingly countercultural statement, particularly in a highly stratified society like the United States. Part of my hope in this book is to encourage Christians to embrace this understanding and not be ashamed of the Bible's central message of reversal. This "clash of civilizations" will turn up over and over again as we explore how Christianity wrestled with issues of poverty and wealth over its first five hundred years. One of the most remarkable features of early Christianity—and a powerful witness to us today—was the belief that wealth represented a dangerous form of spiritual temptation and injustice, that the poor are in fact blessed by God, that God still comes to us in "the least of these."

In the 25 years since my grandfather's death, I've completed an undergraduate degree in religious studies, traveled to Mexico and lived with nuns, completed my Master of Divinity at Union Theological Seminary, and have worked for the Episcopal Church for 14 years. Nevertheless, those origin stories remain foundational to who I am and how I've come to understand the promise and challenge of what it means to be a person of faith today. These seeds were planted early, and it has only recently occurred to me just how early this began. Long before my grandfather's death, long before I began my furtive reading of the gospels, I was already being shaped by the Gospel of Luke's focus on the reversal of the rich and poor, insiders and outsiders, and one in which God shows up in surprising ways. I simply didn't realize it at the time.

The Christmas traditions many of us are familiar with come from the gospels of Luke and Matthew, but it is Luke especially that plays with the themes of power and powerlessness at every turn. It is in Luke, for instance, that we learn of Mary giving birth to Jesus in a manger, wrapping him in bands of cloth, and laying him down "because there was no place for them in the inn."[16]

For many, these stories have become so familiar that the shocking nature of this message—that God's only Son was born into destitution, a member of one of the lowest castes in his society—is lost. And yet, as a child, it wasn't lost on me. This is not because of any particular insight on my part but because of the shared insights of a family that heard these stories through the lens of immigration and migrant field labor.

When my maternal grandparents were alive, Christmas meant celebrating Mexican-American traditions like *Las Posadas*, a sung tradition that dramatizes Mary and Joseph's exhausting search for refuge and a place to give birth to Jesus. Led by my maternal grandparents, we would divide our family into two parts: half the family would sing the role of Mary and Joseph, and the other half would sing that of the reluctant innkeeper.

At the outset, a weary Joseph says, "In the name of heaven, we ask you for shelter, as my beloved wife can no longer walk." The innkeeper, who voices society's response to the poor at every turn, responds, "There is no room for you here. Keep on going ahead. I will not be opening my doors, for you are likely scoundrels and thieves." It is only slowly, and very reluctantly, that the innkeeper becomes aware of who Mary and Joseph truly are, a lengthy push and pull that finally gives way to the innkeeper opening his heart and home.[17]

Year after year, we sang this. Year after year, I absorbed, perhaps unconsciously, how the words intersected with my family's search for a place in this country. Since then, I've learned that all of us— including the wider church—have the capacity to play both parts: sometimes we align ourselves with those seeking safety and refuge; other times, we are the stubborn innkeepers with stony hearts. At the end of singing *Las Posadas*, my family would line up to kiss the foot of the baby Jesus who was nestled amidst straw in a large nativity scene. I now know that something remained with me in seeing my venerable grandparents, parents, aunts, and uncles bending down to kiss the foot of a child king born into utter poverty.

Discussion Questions

How is the theme of God's reversal of the rich and poor, powerful and powerless a part of your own faith? Is this something you identify with and long for? Is it something to be feared?

What does a Christianity that embraces this vision of God's reversal look like? What sort of actions and ministries would this entail? What would this feel like for the most vulnerable? How would it feel for those who hold positions of power?

How was wealth and poverty, the rich and the poor, spoken of in your family? How do you see "the poor" being depicted in US culture, including immigrants, the homeless, people on welfare?

Does it surprise you that in the parable of the rich man and Lazarus, only Lazarus is named in scripture while "the rich man" remains a generalized figure? What would it mean for the church to advocate for the dignity and humanity of those who society regularly and broadly dismisses as "the poor"?

A Next Step

Learn more about the Mexican tradition of *Las Posadas*, a sung liturgy that dramatizes Mary and Joseph's search for refuge and a stony-hearted innkeeper's refusal to offer a place for them in the inn. The innkeeper initially gives voice to society's fear and revulsion toward the poor, accusing Mary and Joseph of being thieves and scoundrels. Only slowly does he realize their true identity. Reflect on how you see these dynamics playing out in society today. Where is God in this story?

Endnotes

1 Paula M. Lantz, Laurence Dupuis, Douglas Reding, Michelle Krauska, and Karen Lappe, "Peer Discussions of Cancer Among Hispanic Migrant Farm Workers," *Public Health Reports,* Vol. 109, No. 4 (July-August, 1994): 512-520.

2 Associated Press, "*Snow Falling on Cedars* booted from Port Orchard schools," *The Lewiston Tribune*, May 3, 2000.

3 Presumably referencing Leviticus 18:23.

4 Katherine Stewart, *The Power Worshippers: Inside the Dangerous Rise of Religious Nationalism* (New York: Bloomsbury Publishing, 2000), 4.

5 Stewart, *The Power Worshippers*, 6.

6 Diarmaid MacCulloch, *Christianity: The First Three Thousand Years* (New York: Penguin, 2011), 77.

7 This roughly translates to "humble, poor folks."

8 Isaiah 3:15.

9 Helen Rhee, *Loving the Poor, Saving the Rich: Wealth, Poverty, and Early Christian Formation* (Michigan: Baker Publishing Group), loc. 1001 (Kindle).

10 Rhee, *Loving the Poor, Saving the Rich*, loc. 1001 (Kindle).

11 Rhee, *Loving the Poor, Saving the Rich*, loc. 1001 (Kindle).

12 M. Douglas Meeks, "Economics in the Church Scriptures," in *The Oxford Handbook of Christianity and Economics*, ed. Paul Oslington (Oxford: Oxford University Press, 2014), 9.

13 Meeks, "Economics in the Church Scriptures," 9.

14 John Anthony McGuckin, *The Path of Christianity: The First Thousand Years* (Westmont, Illinois: IVP Academic, 2017), 1026.

15 McGuckin, *The Path of Christianity*, 1026.

16 Luke 2:7.

17 Ironically, the innkeeper in *Las Posadas* does the opposite of what the Gospel of Luke describes and eventually offers a room at the inn. "Enter now you holy pilgrims, holy pilgrims! Please receive this little place. Although this inn is so poor, I offer it with my heart." This is a surprising turn as it contradicts the story of the gospel. It is almost as if *Las Posadas* cannot bear the harshness of Luke's description.

2 The Lord's Prayer as Song for a Hungry People

A song by the Dominican singer Juan Luis Guerra can teach us a lot about reading the Old and New Testaments. On one level, the song "Ojalá que llueva café" is joyful and upbeat; it could even be mistaken for a charming tour of Dominican food. In it, Guerra sings "May it rain coffee in the countryside…a whole torrent of yucca and tea…May autumn bring, instead of dry leaves, salted pork and a newly planted field of sweet potatoes and strawberries."[1]

With his soft yet insistent voice, Guerra sings of a vision of miraculous abundance: downpours of cheese, honey, and hills of wheat—images of such abundance that they are almost biblical in nature. This song also serves as a kind of prayer. While the first word of the song, *ojalá*, is often translated as "may it be," this doesn't quite convey the depth of this Spanish word. *Ojalá* is one of those many Spanish words that reflect Arabic's 700-plus years of influence on the language, as *ojalá* is derived from "O Allah." To begin a song with *ojalá*, then, is to call out to God: "O God, may it rain down coffee in the countryside."

Yet for all the miraculous food pouring down, if you listen closely, the song is actually about hunger. In the award-winning music video for "Ojalá," Guerra's descriptions of freshly planted fields of sweet potatoes and strawberries play over occasionally graphic images of Dominican children and gaunt elderly fieldworkers turning beautiful black eyes toward the sky in the hopes of a downpour of food. His song is a prayer for God to rain down coffee "so that the people in the countryside don't have to suffer so much," longing for a day that "the children may sing."

The first time I heard "Ojalá que llueva café," I was struck by how similar Guerra's vision of this downpour of coffee, yucca, plantains, and grain sounded to many of the ways the Bible speaks about food. When the Bible describes manna falling from heaven (Exodus 16:1-36; Numbers 11:1-9) or the specificity of the wandering Israelites' longing for the fish, cucumbers, melons, leeks, and garlic of their Egyptian enslavers (Numbers 11:5), or of Jesus's feeding of the five thousand with just a few loaves and fishes (Matthew 14:13-21; Mark 6:31-44; Luke 9:12-17; John 6:1-14), I now hear Guerra's prayer for the Dominican countryside in the background. These biblical images are miraculous songs of abundance, yes, but the underlying beat is that of hunger.

It is easy to forget or dismiss the reality of hunger, especially for those who have never experienced food scarcity and the way it shapes the stories of the Bible. As a result, we may be missing some of the deepest meanings of the recurring, miraculous images of food and meals in the Old and New Testaments. How would we read the scriptures differently if we took into account that these texts spring forth from a hungry people?

A frequently overlooked example of this is right in the Lord's Prayer. Embedded within this most familiar of prayers is Jesus's request for God to "give us this day our daily bread," a petition so well-known and repeated so regularly that many are surprised to learn this familiar phrase contains a linguistic mystery.

The difficulty occurs in the seemingly untranslatable Greek word *epiousios*, a word rendered as "daily" but which isn't exactly that. In fact, *epiousios* doesn't appear anywhere else in Greek literature outside the gospels of Matthew and Luke. It is likely a Greek neologism for a word first uttered by Jesus in Aramaic. Like a copy of a copy, the English translation of *epiousios* to daily is a fuzzy translation of a Greek word that was itself trying to approximate a word or idea that may have been new or unusual in Aramaic.

There are many different translations of the word *epiousios*, with particular schools of thought and theology backing each one. One unwieldy attempt is from the Latin Vulgate in the late sixteenth century, which translated *epiousios* as "supersubstantial." This interpretation is still preferred by a few who insist that Jesus was clearly referring to the "extra substance" found in the sacrament of the eucharist. Nevertheless, "give us this day our supersubstantial bread" has never quite caught on.[2]

So what might an accessible rendering of *epiousios* be? While scholars continue to debate this, two plausible renderings are "Give us this day an extra portion of bread" or "Give us bread for today and for tomorrow."[3] Since I am neither a linguist nor a biblical scholar, I will avoid weighing in on which of these I think is exactly right. I am, however, interested in trying to grasp the deeper meaning of these two interpretations, the spirit of the words. I believe this requires thinking along the same lines of "Ojalá que llueva café" and recalling how these words were first spoken in a landscape marked by hunger, with the threat of famine looming on the horizon.

I've heard the Lord's prayer said at banquets and reception dinner tables where it seemed that no one attending had ever worried about their next meal. I've also said this same petition in homeless shelters and at a house for undocumented refugees, where the people holding hands around the table had experienced and survived persistent hunger. The very same words—and particularly this petition for "daily bread"—landed differently, depending on the stomachs of the people in the room. How could it not?

Therefore, when trying to grasp what these translations mean, it's worth remembering the interpretive power of a hungry stomach. Some basic questions come to mind for consideration. Were the first hearers' stomachs full or were they empty? Were most getting enough to eat on a regular basis or were the people listening to Jesus consistently worried about their next meal? I have found that reflecting on such questions adds a new dimension to this petition for bread, to the Lord's Prayer, and to the many stories of meals and miraculous abundances of food that occur so regularly within the Bible.

Significant historical evidence shows that Jesus, the writers of the gospels of Matthew and Luke, and many in the first Christian assemblies were teetering at the edge of subsistence and were, in fact, survivors of regular and persistent hunger. While farmers had strategies for mitigating food shortages caused by bad weather and political calamity, the region of Galilee experienced regular famines—

periods of extreme scarcity of food—approximately every 20 years. The cultural memory of a season of severe hunger was never too far away, then. It is likely that many who would have first heard Jesus's petition for "an extra portion of bread" or "enough bread for today and tomorrow" were themselves struggling with food insecurity, shortages, and that they carried the generational memories of times when hunger had become devastating starvation. The question is: how might this have influenced their hearing of this petition?

What follows is a meditation, then, about this familiar petition for bread embedded in the Lord's Prayer. As it turns out, Jesus wasn't just praying for "daily bread" but quite literally for something more.

As already discussed in chapter one, the gospels are rare examples in Greek literature in which it is "the poor, the ill-educated, and the disreputable whose encounters with God are most vividly described"; they are texts about *gente humilde*, stories that speak about encounters with God from the underside of history.[4] Therefore, to understand how Jesus speaks about food, we have to dig into the broader landscape of wealth, poverty, and hunger that characterized this time period.

Roman society was marked by stark inequality with an imperial and aristocratic elite (1-3 percent), a middle group with moderate surplus resources (7-15 percent), and a vast group of "the poor" who were either stable near subsistence (22-27 percent), at subsistence (30-40 percent), or below subsistence and therefore lacking necessary food, shelter, and clothing (25-28 percent).[5] It is therefore estimated that 75-90 percent of the Roman world lived close to subsistence level—near, at, or below—and were struggling for survival and sustenance on a daily basis.[6] For this group, "life expectancy was low (life expectancy at birth was somewhere between twenty and thirty and probably closer to twenty). Nutritional deficiencies were widespread."[7] This vast group of "the poor" was also particularly vulnerable to natural disasters, including droughts resulting in periodic food shortages and disease.

These figures apply to the Roman Empire generally. When looking at the particular region where and when Jesus's ministry took place, scholars such as Helen Rhee and Bruce Longenecker describe a geographical region groaning under the weight of increasing socioeconomic pressures. During Jesus's time and in the period just leading up to it, overpopulation and over-cultivation of the land, natural disasters, and increasing tributes and tithes combined to force "the already poor majority into the arduous struggle for unfortunate survival in a highly stratified society."[8]

Survival for this poor majority frequently hinged on whether or not one had access to land. While some would have been fortunate enough to own small farms, a significant number would have been tenant farmers renting their land "from 'absentee landlords' (often at exorbitant cost and for short periods of time), or were slave-tenants tasked with the responsibility of extracting the yields of the land for the landowner."[9] Just prior to the first century, a growing number of tenant farmers faced the bitter task of working the very land their families had once owned, having been forced by increasing tithes, taxes, and other socioeconomic pressures into selling their ancestral lands and now sending surpluses to the absentee landowner.[10] The day laborers who Jesus spoke about regularly faced an even harsher lot, for "when workers were 'a dime a dozen', there was little to prevent the urban elite from maximizing the percentage of their 'top-slice' by exploiting their rural workers, through the assistance of a business manager, and to the point of leaving them with nothing more than the bare resources needed for the most basic form of living—a case of 'living just enough for the city.'"[11]

Droughts, political instability, and warfare made this landscape ripe for famine, a dangerous threat that forever loomed on the horizon. "In the biblical traditions, famine is placed among the most well-known ills together with pestilence and sword in a kind of negative triad," writes Morten H. Jensen, in a fascinating study on the climate, agricultural, and political conditions of first-century Galilee.[12] He describes the delicate balance of the right types and levels of precipitation needed to yield crops in this region, how severe hunger was caused by a confluence of drought and political instability, as well as the indelible impression made by recurring famines on the biblical tradition:

> The Hebrew Bible is replete with references to famines—at the time of Abraham, Isaac, and Joseph (Genesis 12:10; 26:1; 41:54; 43:1), under David and Solomon (2 Samuel 21:1;

1 Kings 8:35-40), in the days of Elijah and Elisha (1 Kings 17:1-
24; 2 Kings 4:38; 8:1-3), and others. Often God is described as
the protector against famine (Psalm 37:19; Ezekiel 34:29) or
as the one inflicting famine as punishment (Leviticus 26:26;
Deuteronomy 28:22-24; 32:24; 2 Samuel 21:1; 1 Kings 17:1;
Psalm 105:16; Isaiah 14:30; 51:19; Jeremiah 11:22; 14:11-
18; 24:10; 42:13-17; Amos 4:6-8; 8:11-14; Sirach 39:29 and
others). Nehemiah 5:1-5 is especially interesting, describing
the people's complaints about being forced to mortgage fields,
vineyards, and houses in order to acquire grain during the
famine (5:3).[13]

While the New Testament refers to famine less frequently, it remains a
threatening image in apocalyptic material (Mark 13:8; Revelation 6:8;
18:8), in references to famines in the Hebrew Bible (Luke 4:25; Acts
7:11), in the story of the prodigal son (Luke 15:14), and the hunger that
led to Barnabas and Paul's famine relief visit and Jerusalem Collection
(Acts 11:27-30).[14] Beyond the biblical texts, there is external historical
evidence of four or five famines just before and during the first
century in Galilee. "The known famines of 25/24 BCE, 38/39 CE, 45/46
CE (besides the local famine in Jerusalem in 69 CE) cohere well with
modern data, which indicate that famine occurs as regularly as every
twentieth year."[15]

The impact of famine on these communities is hard to overstate.
Margaret Atkins and Robin Osborne write in *Poverty in the Roman
World* that "times of dearth divided communities between those who
had and those who had not managed to fill their storehouses" and
that urban dwellers fared especially poorly. The price of food soared
during times of scarcity as landowners refused to release grain from
their storehouses into the urban markets. Such was the desperation
that "individuals were no doubt tempted to sell themselves or their
children into slavery—a practice legislated against by Solon in Athens
but still encountered by Augustine."[16]

Given this historical account, it is likely that Jesus himself, the writers
of the gospels of Matthew and Luke, and many in the first Christian
assemblies struggled with getting enough to eat on a recurring
basis and that many in the first Christian communities had a direct
experience—and shared cultural memory—of a period of prolonged
hunger in their lives. Jesus's ministry took place among the poor
who were struggling on a day-to-day basis for survival. Jesus and

his disciples (Matthew 8:20), the Jerusalem Church (Romans 15:26; Galatians 2:10), and the Pauline communities (1 Corinthians 1:26-27; 2 Corinthians 8:1-2) belonged to the "lower socioeconomic stratum and 'the poor' in varying degrees; and they regularly described experiencing oppression and maltreatment by the rich and powerful in one way or another (cf. Luke 12:11-12; Acts 4:1-3; 8:1-3; 12:1-4; 2 Corinthians 11:23-27; Hebrews 10:32-34)."[17]

Of course, it is one thing to say that many in the first Christian assemblies had a direct experience of prolonged hunger in their lives, and it is another to begin to unpack what that means. To do this, I want to leap across centuries and look at one of the first scientific studies about what semi-starvation does to people.

In the 1940s, a groundbreaking study called the Minnesota Starvation Experiment examined the physiological and psychological effects of semi-starvation. Led by Ancel Keys, this study provided insights on how to feed and rehabilitate the emaciated civilians of previously German-occupied Europe.[18] Basic facts about hunger were unknown at this point, including how many calories a starved person needed to recover. This made the planning and logistics of the rehabilitation efforts challenging.

To find the answers to these questions, 36 male conscientious objectors, primarily from Peace churches, volunteered to participate in this grueling study. Over the course of the study, through regular food reductions, participants lost approximately 2.5 pounds per week until most had lost fully 25 percent of their original body weight. Reductions and additions in calories were made using single slices of bread. As bread slices decreased, participants rapidly developed "sunken faces and bellies, protruding ribs, and edema-swollen legs, ankles, and faces" and other problems such as anemia, neurological deficits, and skin changes.[19]

Significantly, food became a ritualized obsession and came to occupy the center of participants' lives. One study participant, Richard Willoughby, was interviewed many decades later when he was in his eighties and still recalled how "eating became highly ritualized" and another, Harold Blickenstaff, described how "food became the one central and only thing really in one's life."[20]

One finding from the three-month rehabilitation period proved especially important for the post-war relief plan and also has special resonance with that strange term *epiousios* in the Lord's Prayer. Keys and his colleagues discovered that the semi-starved participants continued to physically deteriorate even when they had been returned to their previously normal levels of caloric intake. They found "no appreciable rehabilitation can take place on a diet of 2,000 calories a day. The proper level is more like 4,000 daily for some months." In other words, the starved needed at least two days' worth of bread in order to begin to recover the destroyed tissues—bread enough for both today and tomorrow.

Knowing this ultimately influenced how much food was distributed in post-war relief efforts. It also brings me back to some of the rooms where people who have experienced prolonged hunger have been gathered for a meal. It makes me wonder whether there wasn't some profound wisdom borne of the experience of hunger embedded in Jesus's request for an extra portion—or for today and tomorrow's portion, right now.

In late March 2020, as the infection and mortality rates of COVID-19 steadily increased and the situation in my home city of New York became dire, I found myself hoping the COVID-19 pandemic would somehow "pass over" my friends and family. This prayer for a "pass over" came spontaneously to me as the deadliness of the pandemic became clear. It occurred to me then that as a result of COVID-19, I knew at a much deeper level what Passover meant than I had just a few weeks prior. This was not an intellectual understanding but a bodily one, a knowing rooted in the experience of having watched the fog of death settle on my city and hoping against hope the angel of death would pass over the households of my loved ones.

Similarly, I'm wondering if part of the difficulty of interpreting *epiousios* is that its meaning is tied to the experience and fear of hunger and is one of the many instances in which the wealth of full stomachs prevents many first-world interpreters from grasping the deepest meaning of the gospel text.

This petition for daily bread—or rather, for enough bread to last a family for today and tomorrow—is especially important for faith leaders to bear in mind given that the number of people living in extreme poverty in the world has increased for the first time in 25 years. The sharp rise in people living on less than $1.90 a day was caused in 2020 by a combination of factors, including the COVID-19 pandemic, climate change, and conflict. In a report on the devastating year of 2020, the World Bank writes that "poverty reduction has suffered its worst setback in decades," and it now estimates that between 88 and 115 million people will be pushed into poverty, with the hardest hit regions being South Asia and Sub-Saharan Africa.[21] Against this new global landscape, it matters greatly, then, that Jesus's words were spoken, heard, and first repeated by people in similar situations, people who experienced persistent hunger and for whom the memory and threat of famine loomed large. To hope, work, and pray for people to have enough bread for today and tomorrow is still the work of Christianity.

Discussion Questions

Does it matter to you that the word "daily" is likely not an accurate translation of the unique Greek term *epiousios*? Why or why not?

How might hunger—or an empty stomach—be a factor in understanding what references to meals and bread mean in the Old and New Testament?

Many people across the country and world experience periods of food insecurity and hunger. Have you had this experience? What is your reaction to the possibility—indeed, likelihood—that Jesus and many of his earliest followers shared in this experience?

Hunger is often treated as a spiritual metaphor, but we should also reflect on it as a bodily reality. What would it mean to reread the many instances of food and meals in the gospels as stories told by and for a hungry people?

Can you imagine including a creative translation of the Lord's Prayer into your own faith practice? How would you render this line? Here's my own creative version: *Give us this day so much we have leftovers. Give us so much that we have to put foil on full plates.*

A Next Step

Take time to learn about the prevalence of hunger in your area (town, city, diocese). Learn the geographical areas and populations where hunger is concentrated and explore some of the major systemic causes. In my home of New York City, the systemic causes of hunger include low wages, unemployment, the location of grocery stores, lack of affordable housing, and expensive healthcare cutting into families' food budgets, as well as a weakened safety net and nutritional assistance program. Partner with organizations addressing both immediate hunger and the systemic causes of hunger in your community.

Endnotes

1   Watch the video at: youtube.com/watch?v=uJimpth-yNs.

2   MacCulloch, *Christianity*, 89.

3   MacCulloch, *Christianity*, 89.

4   MacCulloch, *Christianity*, 77.

5   Rhee, *Loving the Poor, Saving the Rich*, loc. 80 (Kindle).

6   Rhee, *Loving the Poor, Saving the Rich*, 5, 11.

7   Margaret Atkins and Robin Osborne, *Poverty in the Roman World* (Cambridge, England: Cambridge University Press, 2009), 4.

8   Rhee, *Loving the Poor, Saving the Rich*, loc. 1001 (Kindle).

9   Bruce W. Longenecker, *Remember the Poor: Paul, Poverty, and the Greco-Roman World* (Grand Rapids, Michigan: Wm. B. Eerdmans Publishing, 2010), 23.

10 Longenecker, *Remember the Poor*, 24-25.

11 Longenecker, *Remember the Poor*, 24-25.

12 Morton H. Jensen, "Climate, Droughts, Wars, and Famines in Galilee as a Background for Understanding the Historical Jesus," *Journal of Biblical Literature*, Vol. 131, No. 2 (2012): 320.

13 Jensen, "Climate, Droughts, Wars, and Famines in Galilee," 320.

14 Jensen, "Climate, Droughts, Wars, and Famines in Galilee," 320.

15 Jensen, "Climate, Droughts, Wars, and Famines in Galilee," 323.

16 Atkins and Osborne, *Poverty in the Roman World*, 5.

17 Rhee, *Loving the Poor, Saving the Rich*, 35.

18 Leah M. Kalm and Richard D. Semba, "They Starved So That Others Be Better Fed: Remembering Ancel Keys and the Minnesota Experiment," *The Journal of Nutrition,* Vol. 135, Issue 6 (June 2005): 1347-1352.

19 Kalm and Semba, "They Starved So That Others Be Better Fed," 1347-1352.

20 Kalm and Semba, "They Starved So That Others Be Better Fed," 1347-1352.

21 "Poverty and Shared Prosperity 2020: Reversals of Fortune," (Washington, D.C.: World Bank, 2020), 5.

3 Wealth's Purpose in the Gospel of Luke

Because Jesus and his followers were poor—indeed, perpetually teetering on the edge of hunger—he had a great deal to say about the wealthy and how their wealth should be used. One of the places this occurs is in what many consider to be his most complex and unsettling parable, that of the unjust steward in Luke 16:1-13. The Unjust Steward ends up being a touchstone for many later Christian thinkers, including myself, and is therefore the title of this book.

Told briefly, the parable of the unjust steward is about a rich landowner who suspects his property/business manager, the steward, of squandering his wealth. The rich man fires his steward, at which point the steward panics and must figure out a plan to survive after the dismissal by his master. The steward's plan is surprising. He decides to use his master's money to remit the debts of his master's debtors. He does so in the hopes of later being welcomed into these debtors' homes after news of his having been fired becomes widely known (news traveled much more slowly then).

The surprising twist in this parable is that the rich landowner then undergoes a change of heart. Bizarrely, the steward's decision to use the landowner's wealth to remit debts isn't seen as another example of the steward's squandering. Instead, his actions result in the landowner's praise. Jesus concludes this winding parable by appearing to praise fiscal immorality, a fact that has perplexed interpreters for millennia: "And I tell you, make friends for yourselves by means of dishonest wealth so that when it is gone, they may welcome you into the eternal home" (Luke 16:9).

If you are confused at this point, you are not alone. Part of the confusion may come because the parable is intentionally and playfully vexing. My friend and colleague, Dr. Patrick Cheng, notes how this strange and intriguing parable ultimately "queers" traditional notions of stewardship. Studying the parable of the unjust steward requires us to enter into a world wherein none of characters stick to their societally ordained roles and where miraculously absurd things happen. The steward, whose role had been to roughly extract harvests and collect debts from the tenant farmers who worked his master's land, finds his safety and salvation by sending the money flowing in reverse, back to the people he was collecting from. The rich landowner, who at the outset is furious at the steward for squandering his property, ends up praising that same steward for giving money away. And then there is Jesus who ends up encouraging a kind of holy profligacy, urging us all to use the "dishonest wealth" of masters to make friends for ourselves among the poor. What does any of this mean?

There are countless theories about how readers should approach this parable, perhaps more so than any of the other strange stories Jesus told. One imaginative approach comes from Anglican priest Richard Dormandy, who observes that this parable falls between two other stories of rich men. The three parables of the prodigal son, the unjust steward, and the rich man and Lazarus fall one after the other and are tied together by the themes of profligate mercy and unexpected forgiveness of debts and revolve around the question of how wealth is supposed to be used.[1] Dormandy argues that we're actually dealing with a single story about rich men and their wealth told in three parts.

In this three-part story in the Gospel of Luke, we first hear about a rich father who uses his wealth to celebrate the return of his wayward son. This is immediately followed by the story of the rich landowner and his unjust steward who uses his master's wealth to release tenant farmers from debts. Six verses of commentary from Jesus follow, including Jesus's blunt statement that "You cannot serve God and wealth," which then sets the reader up for the final story of the rich man who dresses in fine clothes, throws feasts for himself, and fails to see the desperation of Lazarus at his gate. Unlike the first two stories that center on the forgiveness of both sins and debt, there is no forgiveness or mercy shown in the third story to the rich man who ignored Lazarus at his gate. The rich man's agony becomes a pointed warning and a final lesson about the consequences of keeping and using wealth for one's self alone and not seeing the suffering of the poor all around us.

In the parable of the prodigal son, the father is described as a wealthy landowner who employs many hands (Luke 15:17) and has property to divide between his two sons (Luke 15:12). The younger of the two sons spends all his inheritance in travel and dissolute living, including on prostitutes, if we are to believe the later complaints of his older brother. When a severe famine befalls the land, this newly poor prodigal son must hire himself out to one of the citizens of that country. Even this is not enough to save him from starvation, however, and he ends up becoming so desperately hungry that he becomes jealous of the food of the pigs he is tending: "He would gladly have filled himself with the pods that the pigs were eating; and no one gave him anything" (Luke 15:16). He is in a similar position to the desperation of Lazarus who "longed to satisfy his hunger with what fell from the rich man's table" (Luke 16:21). At this low point—notably, one that is all about the dangers of an empty stomach—the prodigal son recalls that even his father's hired hands were given something to eat. He returns to his father, begs for forgiveness, and asks to be treated as one of his father's hired hands so he can at least have enough food to survive (Luke 15:18-19).

Many of Jesus's parables hinge on an unexpected turn, and the parable of the prodigal son is no exception. Instead of accepting the prodigal son's proposal to become a hired hand, the father welcomes his son back with open arms and—twist!—begins spending even more money to celebrate his prodigal son's return. The father's generosity is both striking and disturbing. Having already given his youngest son half of his property, which was quickly wasted, the father now gives this same son a ring for his finger, sandals for his feet, and orders a fatted calf to be killed for a feast, "for this son of mine was dead and is alive again; he was lost and is found!" (Luke 15:24).

It is only now that the true conflict in the parable appears. The dutiful older brother who has stayed with his father all these years suddenly steps forward and complains bitterly about his father's excessive generosity toward his younger brother. "Listen! For all these years I have been working like a slave for you, and I have never disobeyed your command; yet you have never given me even a young goat so that I might celebrate with my friends. But when this son of yours came back, who has devoured your property with prostitutes, you killed the fatted calf for him!" (Luke 15:29-30). The responsible older brother sees his rich father's forgiveness, many gifts, and throwing of a feast for his wayward younger brother as incautious, irresponsible, and profoundly unfair. The parable concludes with the father telling his dutiful and responsible son, "Son, you are always with me, and all that is mine is yours. But we had to celebrate and rejoice, because this brother of yours was dead and has come to life; he was lost and has been found" (Luke 15:31-32).

Jesus ends up praising the father's promiscuous generosity and turns prudency on its head by making the dutiful and responsible son the antagonist of this story. And Jesus criticizes the responsible older brother for measuring out his love with the same scrupulosity as he wished his father managed their money. Dormandy notes that the wealthy father "earns the disapproval of his firstborn firstly, for giving half his wealth away to the prodigal younger brother, and then for wasting even more on the boy when he returns home. This sets us up for the parable of the unjust steward, which itself raises the question of 'what is waste?' 'How should wealth be used?' and 'How do we make right judgments?'"[2]

The second story in this cycle is that of the unjust steward, which like the prodigal son, centers on themes of searching for a safe home and forgiveness (including the forgiveness of debts) and concludes with Jesus once again appearing to praise imprudent generosity.

Jesus's story begins by talking about another "rich man" who learns that his steward was squandering his property (Luke 16:1). Right off the bat, we know that this is similar to the parable of the prodigal son in that this story too has to do with the squandering of wealth. This rich man demands the steward give an account of his management but then, in anger, fires the steward before any such account can be given (Luke 16:2). The steward is shocked and afraid. He finds himself at a low point, similar to the situation faced by the prodigal son when he had squandered all the property entrusted to him. The steward asks himself, "What will I do, now that my master is taking the position away from me? I am not strong enough to dig, and I am ashamed to beg" (Luke 16:3). Like the prodigal son, the steward must now come up with a plan to ensure his very survival.

A bit of historical context adds richness to the steward's situation. Stewards were frequently born a slave in the master's household before they were raised into their positions of relative power. As a steward, he would have been treated by his master as "first slave," or his master may have made him a freedman to serve in this important role.[3] Stewards, therefore, occupied a precarious and much-hated role in the hierarchy of the Roman estate. In the biblical account then, the steward's authority as "first slave" and property/business manager depends on his ability to squeeze profits from the very people he has come from: tenant farmworkers and other slaves. Much like the prodigal son, he is facing a return journey home: finding a safe home after his dismissal means humbly returning to the very people he has come from and betrayed over all those years, those whom he has exploited for decades on behalf of his master.

Stewards were a critical part of the economic infrastructure that ratcheted up the pressure on tenant farmers and slaves. The steward held a "representative nature" and was "able to manage the principal's many financial responsibilities just as if the owner were present, since the principal's confirmation accompanied the financial decisions made by the administrator."[4] It was well within the steward's power to increase or reduce debts, and the typical response to debt-holders was strikingly harsh: "In addition to expulsion from an estate, there were three courses of legal action that landlords could take against their debtors: property confiscation, imprisonment, and debt bondage (Matthew 18:23-24; cf. Matthew 5:25-26//Luke 12:58-59)...Many extant leasing contracts from early Roman Egypt in fact contain declaration clauses indicating not only that a steep interest rate would be added to all late payments (e.g., 50 percent), but also that the landlord would have the right to take action against both the tenant's person and property should the lessee continue to default."[5]

When we hear the steward, then, frantically wondering what he will do now that he no longer has his master's support, realizing that he isn't strong enough to dig, we should bear in mind that among the first hearers of this parable are those on the underside of this exploitative arrangement, including tenant farmers, slaves, and day laborers. More than a few likely smile to themselves with a sense of revenge, knowing the dangerous mess the steward now faces.

The decision the steward subsequently makes is a desperate attempt to ensure a safe home among those he had formerly exploited. In an act of anti-stewardship, the steward begins to summon his master's debtors and release them from their debts, thereby returning wealth that had been unjustly extracted. Speaking to a debtor who owes a hundred jugs of oil, the steward tells him, "Take your bill, sit down quickly, and make it fifty." To another who owes wheat, "Take your bill and make it eighty." Biblical scholars have noted the debts described here are extraordinary, so high as to have possibly been the accumulated debts of entire villages.[6]

I recently came across a striking painting portraying this moment by the contemporary Russian artist Andrei Nikolaevich Mironov.[7] In it, an elderly steward who is, indeed, no longer strong enough to dig, sits at his work desk, peering intently at statements of debts. Dressed warmly in fine clothes, the steward points to a few lines on the paper—presumably an amount of debt—and appears to be explaining how these debts would be reduced to a young man who is looking over the shoulder of the elderly steward. The drama of the entire painting is reflected in the young man's face for he looks on with a mixture of incredulity, wonder, and relief as the debts he, and possibly his entire village, once carried are now released.

The look on the young man's face speaks to the fact that debt remittance is one of the most ancient signs and symbols of God's liberative action at work in the world. As we will discuss in a later chapter on Christianity's ancient views on predatory lending and debt, the Old Testament describes debt as similar to the slavery experienced by the Hebrew people in Egypt (Leviticus 25:35-38). These texts hold that the release of the poor from the entrapment of debt is akin to God's freeing the Hebrew people from slavery. In the New Testament, release from debt is deeply interwoven into the very fabric of Jesus's proclamation that he has come to bring good news to the poor (Luke 4:18a). Freeing oppressed people from the enslavement of debt is described here and in many other parts of the Bible as one of the holiest uses of wealth.

Interestingly, Jesus's parable of the unforgiving servant (Matthew 18:21-35) reinforces this same theme. In this challenging parable, we hear of a servant whose own debts are graciously forgiven but who is ultimately condemned to torture because he refuses to forgive the debts owed to him. "You wicked slave! I forgave you all that debt because you pleaded with me. Should you not have had mercy on your fellow slave, as I had mercy on you?" (Matthew 18:32-33). Here again we are to understand that God is liberating his servants from debts, and we are to do the same.

Returning to the parable of the unjust steward, with the steward's release of his master's debtors, the parable enters into a different emotional landscape. In a miraculous turnaround, the cruel landowner experiences a change of heart, and we learn "his master commended his dishonest manager because he had acted shrewdly." The turn that takes place next is a reminder of how part of the power of parables lies in their ability upset expectations. In this case, the surprise commendation of the master sets up Jesus's observation that "the children of this age are more shrewd in dealing with their own generation than are the children of light" and concludes with Jesus's scandalous counsel to "make friends for yourself by means of dishonest wealth so that when it is gone, they may welcome you into the eternal homes" (Luke 16:8-9). Like the parable of the prodigal son, the point may be that wealth—even the dishonest wealth of an exploitative landowner—is intended to be used for God's purposes, returned to the people it had been extracted from, especially for the remission of debt and the freeing of communities trapped in economic slavery.

Jesus concludes by commending the steward for knowing what to do with dishonest wealth and therefore knowing who the true master is that he should serve: "If then you have not been faithful with the dishonest wealth, who will entrust to you the true riches? And if you have not been faithful with what belongs to another, who will give you what is your own? No slave can serve two masters; for a slave will either hate the one and love the other, or be devoted to the one and despise the other. You cannot serve God and wealth" (Luke 16:11-13). Jesus insists it is better to serve God than wealth and that even unjustly gained wealth must be turned toward God's liberative purposes.

Whereas the first two parables explore how wealth is to be used, the final parable of the rich man and Lazarus is a warning about what awaits the rich who fail to use their wealth accordingly. Unlike the father of the prodigal son, we surmise that the rich man uses his wealth for himself and his household alone. Jesus describes this rich man as one "dressed in purple and fine linen and who feasted sumptuously every day" (Luke 16:19). Indeed, amidst his refinery and feasting, the rich man is blind to the poor man, Lazarus, who languishes at his gate and longs "to satisfy his hunger with what fell from the rich man's table."

Death comes for both Lazarus and the rich man, but whereas the rich man is properly buried, Lazarus dies at the rich man's gates. In death, God's justice brings about a reversal of their fates, and it is the rich man who ends up languishing and tormented in the afterlife. The rich man joins the prodigal son and unjust steward in experiencing a low point—and in needing an act of mercy to turn his fate around. But in this case, no mercy is forthcoming. Abraham responds to the rich man's request for mercy by saying that it was far too late now and that a great chasm had been fixed (Luke 16:25-26). Abraham replies to the rich man's continued pleading by saying that Moses and the prophets had warned him and his brothers to act differently throughout their lifetimes, yet they ignored such warnings while they were alive and feasting. Therefore, the rich man is to now suffer in death the torment that Lazarus experienced in life.

Through the parables of these three rich men, a few themes emerge about how wealth should be used. Wealth, including wealth gained by unjust means, is to be harnessed in the here and now; there is no use waiting to use riches until after one's death. This idea is supported by the parable of the rich fool who Jesus condemns for simply storing up his wealth in larger and larger barns (Luke 12:13-21).

But if we are to use wealth in the here and now, it must be for something more than just purple cloth, fine linen, and feasting for ourselves and household alone. Like the father of the prodigal son, we are to use our wealth in acts of generosity and mercy that might appear irresponsible and even imprudent to many—that is, holding "great banquets" with saints and sinners, the dutiful and the prodigal, and for banquets in which "the poor, the maimed, the blind and the lame" are invited. Whether speaking of the good wine at the wedding in Cana (John 2:1-12), the expensive nard poured over Jesus's feet (John 12:3), or a costly feast for a prodigal son, Jesus repeatedly praises celebrations that look to the rest of the world like unwise squandering of wealth. What would it mean to embrace this vision?

In the parable of the unjust steward, a story that zeroes in on what actually constitutes waste and squandering, readers are advised to return unjustly gained wealth and use it for the merciful remission of debt and the freeing of the poor from economic slavery. This connects Jesus's ministry to one of the most ancient signs and symbols of what God's liberation looks in real life—namely, the freeing of the poor from the slavery of debt. The steward ultimately finds his salvation in an act of anti-stewardship, and Jesus praises the way the repentant steward makes the monies flow in reverse, using dishonest wealth to make friends among the poor. This theme is picked up again in Jesus's praising of Zacchaeus, a tax collector who is granted salvation when he gives half his possessions to the poor and pays those he has defrauded back four times as much.

Finally, in the parable of the rich man and Lazarus, Jesus offers a warning to those who retain such wealth and use it only for themselves and their kin—namely, that the threat of God's great reversal awaits them if they do not change their ways. The wealthy have the opportunity to demonstrate acts of generosity, mercy, and the forgiveness of debts in this lifetime alone, but they cannot count on such acts of mercy from God if and when they fail to do so in this lifetime.

Discussion Questions

Contrary to almost every received tradition that equates mature faith with the sound stewardship of financial resources, Jesus repeatedly urges incautious generosity, merciful celebrations, and seemingly irresponsible acts of aiding those in need. In the parable of the unjust steward, he even goes so far as to urge the use of "dishonest wealth" for the remittance of those oppressed by debt. What is your reaction to this seemingly unscrupulous side of Jesus?

The parable of the unjust steward is one place in the gospels where we encounter a steward. A somewhat kinder version of this role appears in John 2:1-11 as part of the miracle of the wedding at Cana. Even there, however, Jesus is once again represented as upending the steward's carefully managed expectations: "Everyone serves the good wine first, and then the inferior wine after the guests have become drunk. But you have kept the good wine until now" (John 2:10). What is Jesus's relationship to stewards and stewardship? Does this surprise you?

Having read over these various stories, what do you think Jesus is telling us wealth is for? How might this impact the way that you use your wealth on a day-to-day basis?

Many congregations have a "stewardship season" to raise funds for the annual operating budget. Can you imagine your congregation centering its main discussion of money on a different character than the steward? How would your congregational life be changed if it celebrated a season dedicated to the good Samaritan (Luke 10.25-37), or Zacchaeus (Luke 19:8-9), or to the unjust steward? What would be gained and what might be lost in making this change?

A Next Step

In the United States, much wealth—including generational and institutional wealth—can be traced to the unjust exploitation of the poor, including the "original sins" of the stealing of land and the economic institution of slavery. As we will discuss in the next chapter, in twentieth-century America, generational wealth created through home ownership was frequently the result of racist federal government policies such as redlining, reverse redlining, and neighborhood racial covenants, which has led to vast disparities in who has inherited wealth today.

What would it mean to be like the unjust steward and redirect portions of this dishonest wealth toward the communities from whom this wealth has been extracted through exploitation, injustice, and racist policies? I know of some congregations that have literally enacted the parable of the unjust steward by redirecting portions of their community's wealth toward the alleviation of medical debt. Many individuals, congregations, and institutions are now divesting from the fossil fuel industry. Still others are discussing focused acts of reparations. What would this look like in your life and community?

Endnotes

1 Richard Dormandy, "Unjust Steward or Converted Master?" *Revue Biblique*, Vol. 109, No. 4 (2002): 512–527.

2 Dormandy, "Unjust Steward or Converted Master?", 514.

3 Malina and Rohrbaugh, *Social-Science Commentary on the Synoptic Gospels*, 292.

4 John K. Goodrich, "Voluntary Debt Remission and the Parable of the Unjust Steward (Luke 16:1-13)," *Journal of Biblical Literature*, Vol. 131, No. 3 (2012): 547–566.

5 Goodrich, "Voluntary Debt Remission," 554.

6 Malina and Rohrbaugh, *Social-Science Commentary on the Synoptic Gospels*, 292.

7 Andrei Nikolai Mironov, "Parable of the Unjust Steward," 2012, commons.wikimedia. org/wiki/File:Parable_of_the_Unjust_Steward._A._Mironov.jpg.

4 Paul on Eucharist and Economic Justice

In August 2004, I boarded an Amtrak train for a three-day trip from Texas to New York to begin studying for my Master of Divinity degree at Union Theological Seminary. It was a life-changing journey as I've called New York my home ever since. The train eventually brought me to Penn Station to begin my studies at Union, and after a tumultuous year of adjusting to life in the city, I began trying to find a faith community to belong to.

Over that first year of seminary, I had come to realize I could no longer remain in the Roman Catholic church. The revelations about the child sex abuse scandal that the *Boston Globe* began publishing in 2002 as well as the prospect of spending any more time arguing for what I consider to be "the basics" such as women's ordination and acceptance of LGBTQ+ people led me to realize that I needed to go elsewhere to find a community that shared my values. And so, on a bright and clear Sunday morning, I headed north from Union Theological Seminary into West Harlem to check out a small, racially diverse Episcopal congregation that several other students had been telling me about.

I didn't know what I was getting myself into when I walked through the red doors of St. Mary's Episcopal Church for the first time, but I immediately sensed something different about this community of faith. I now know I was entering into the story of a congregation that has been a place of hope and justice-seeking for people living in West Harlem for almost two centuries.

Early on, the then-rector of the parish, the Rev. Dr. Earl Kooperkamp, told me stories about the DNA of the congregation. St. Mary's of Manhattanville began as a mission parish of the wealthier church of St. Michael's of Bloomingdale on what is now 99th Street. St. Mary's became the first free Episcopal church in New York City, meaning that it abolished pew rentals in 1831.[1] The charging and renting out of pews was a controversial source of income for Anglican, Catholic, and Presbyterian churches at the time because of the way this practice made class divisions painfully apparent, with the wealthy paying more to reserve the better pews. St. Mary's had begun charging pew rentals in 1829 but quickly realized it was more trouble than it was worth given the meager returns. This meant that in 1831, St. Mary's became the first free-pew church in New York City, and this idea and spirit of St. Mary's as a place where people of many different socioeconomic backgrounds could come together in equality was still evident in 2005 when I quietly took my seat in the back of the church.

Another of Fr. Kooperkamp's stories was about a far more recent event—and often told with a mischievous smile. This story was about a "Pothole Communion" service that took place in the early 1990s. Thankfully, parts of this service were captured on film by the director Jonathan Demme, who created a documentary about his cousin, the then-rector of St. Mary's, the Rev. Bob Castle. *The New York Times* would later describe Fr. Castle as "an obdurate whirligig fulminating against the establishment."[2]

The scene in *Cousin Bobby* begins mysteriously with a quiet shot of St. Mary's sanctuary with some commotion at the altar. Only gradually does it become clear that six young Black and Latino men, in military uniform, are lifting the altar to ceremoniously carry it outdoors. The carrying of the altar from the sanctuary into the street was part of a liturgical procession replete with processional cross, offering baskets, and all the items necessary for celebrating an outdoor eucharist. But rather than going to a park or beach, they set the altar in the middle of 125th Street and Old Broadway, in West Harlem, right beside a community health clinic and close to the police precinct offices. From that intersection, Fr. Castle preached—yelled, really—about the need for a traffic light and how long they'd been asking the city to install one. He pointed to a gigantic pothole in the street and told the young boy holding the heavy processional cross to take it to its very edge. Fr. Castle cried out, "For one month we have been trying to get the city to repair that hole... We have come to say that we are good people. We are poor, we are Black, we are Hispanic, but we are good people. And we demand what is right for us, and we will take nothing less than justice. And there will be no peace until there is justice."[3]

St. Mary's history as the first "free church" in New York and the memory of this Pothole Communion Service infused the place with a different sort of spirit. In 2005, congregational leadership included people experiencing homelessness as well as those with multiple graduate degrees. Columbia students sat in the pew and listened as lectors with elementary school educations read the lessons. St. Mary's was the first place I came to know people experiencing homelessness by first and last name, not as people on the other side of a soup kitchen line but as fellow parishioners, choir members, and as members of the parish council. It was also where I, a recently arrived New Yorker studying behind the cloistered walls of a seminary, began to receive an entirely separate education about how this city of extraordinary wealth treats its poor.

The first time I came across the term "Stop-and-Frisk," for instance, wasn't at Union Seminary or even in a news article about the policy. Rather, it was in a sermon by Fr. Kooperkamp. As was oftentimes the case, he would ascend the creaky wooden stairs of the pulpit to deliver, without notes, a fiery condemnation of what was then a still relatively new policy whereby New York City's Police Department systematically harassed young Black and Latino men across the city.

This program, which operated from 2002, peaked in 2011, and officially ended in 2014, resulted in more than 5 million people being stopped-and-frisked over the course of twelve years, with the overwhelming majority being young Black and Latino males between the ages of 14 and 24.[4] The New York Civil Liberties Union stated that "at the height of stop-and-frisk in 2011 under the Bloomberg administration, over 685,000 people were stopped," meaning that many Black and Latino males were stopped on multiple occasions in a single year. This policy continued for more than a decade, across multiple mayoral administrations, despite it being known early on that in nearly 9 out of 10 cases, stopped-and-frisked New Yorkers were found to be completely innocent. The policy was therefore a known failure if measured against its purported goals but successful when understood as part of a larger campaign of harassment against Black and Latino young men.

Although I would come to read many articles about Stop-and-Frisk over the course of those twelve years, the place I really learned about its impact was at church. It was through periodic sermons and, more importantly, through the responses of the mothers and grandmothers in the congregation that I learned how this harassment campaign was felt and experienced in families. It was by watching the fathers of the congregation sit up and applaud when their frustration was voiced in both sermons and prayers, a recognition of how dangerous this policy of harassment was for their sons and grandsons. This showed me how the prophetic is pastoral and how policies directly impact families in ways that can only be learned in-person and in community.

As I have wandered about the church since then, I have oftentimes met people who describe themselves as having a eucharistic piety, a profound relationship to Christ's body as it is present in the consecrated bread and wine of the Lord's Supper. I'd like to believe I have a eucharistic-focused spirituality as well, although in truth, who gathers around the table has always seemed to me to be just as important as the elements on the altar itself.

At St. Mary's, while standing in line to receive communion, I would reflect on the fact that the line was composed of people from very different backgrounds: people both housed and homeless, people of immense security and privilege as well as those living right on the edge of the abyss. In this, the congregation was one of those rare spaces in American society where people of radically different socioeconomic backgrounds came together for a common meal. I came to believe this diversity was a transformational aspect of the eucharist, and so it is striking, then, to see how this socioeconomic diversity is also emphasized in some of the earliest available writings about the Lord's Supper.

The way we celebrate communion—who is included and who is not—has been a point of contention since the earliest days of Christianity. In many of his first-century writings, the Apostle Paul expresses fury at how the Lord's Supper is being celebrated in Corinth. In Paul's eleventh chapter of 1 Corinthians, Paul chastises the community for the way the wealthy separate themselves out from the poor. He sees the eucharist as profoundly connected to the lives of the poor and insists that the Lord's Supper is a time for bridging socioeconomic divides.

Paul was a leader of the first generation of Christians and is considered to be the most important person in the history of Christianity after Jesus. Paul was a Greek-speaking Jew from Asia Minor who was born about the same time as Jesus (c. 4 BCE). Until about the middle of his life, he was a member of the Pharisees and a persecutor of the nascent Christian movement. Paul participated in the stoning of Saint Stephen and afterward "made havoc of the church" by searching out Christians and handing them over to prison and death.[5] Then, while on his way to Damascus, Paul had a vision in which Christ rebuked him and told him he was destined to take the Christian faith to the Gentiles.

This vision of Christ changed the trajectory of Paul's life. After traveling to Arabia for what appears to have been an initial unsuccessful mission, Paul's missionary journeys took him to the eastern Mediterranean and finally to Rome, where he died sometime in the mid-60s CE.

Historian Diarmaid MacCulloch writes that "entering Paul's theological world in his letters is rather like jumping on a moving merry-go-round: the point of entry hardly matters. It is an intensely painted set of portraits of how a Christian community works and what a Christian community signifies."[6] Paul's attempts to persuade the early Christians to see and do things his way reveals just how difficult it was for people rooted in the Greco-Roman culture to assimilate Paul's understanding of the Christian message and its implications for personal and community life. And it appears this was especially true in a city like Corinth.

Paul's first letter to the Corinthians includes a series of responses to news he received through "Chloe's people" about various conflicts that emerged within the Corinthian community after he left. This includes a conflict that is the result of divisive practices around the Lord's Supper.

In 1 Corinthians 11:17-34, Paul is furious because he has learned that the wealthy are separating themselves out from the poor during the Lord's Supper. It is within this context of chastising the wealthy that the first historical reference to the words of institution occurs: "For I received from the Lord what I also handed on to you, that the Lord Jesus on the night when he was betrayed took a loaf of bread, and when he had given thanks, he broke it and said, 'This is my body that is for you. Do this in remembrance of me.' In the same way he took the cup also, after supper, saying, 'This cup is the new covenant in my blood. Do this, as often as you drink it, in remembrance of me.' For as often as you eat this bread and drink the cup, you proclaim the Lord's death until he comes" (1 Corinthians 11:23-26).

As familiar as these words are to Christians—indeed, a version of these words is repeated most Sundays across many churches—far less familiar is the surrounding conflict between the wealthy and the poor. Specifically, in this passage, Paul accuses the wealthier Corinthians of bringing their own food and drink to the assembly, separating themselves out from those who are poor and hungry, and eating their separate meal among members of their own social class.[7]

In *Remember the Poor*, Bruce Longenecker describes Paul's indignation as tied to "a situation in which economic factors of corporate identity were being overlooked by some Jesus-followers." Paul is fierier in his own words and forcefully condemns the way the Lord's Supper has become yet another opportunity to display social division and class status. Paul's voice seems to break with bitter sarcasm when he writes, "Indeed, there have to be discriminations among you, for only so will it become clear who among you are distinguished."[8]

The notion of a congregation composed of the rich and poor and sharing a meal was as challenging a concept then as it is now, yet this breaking down of caste was clearly part of Paul's overall vision. In his letter to the Galatians, Paul writes about what Christ means for social divisions: "There is no longer Jew or Greek, there is no longer slave or free, there is no longer male or female, for all of you are one in Christ Jesus."[9] Almost two millennia later, the antebellum abolitionist US Senator Charles Sumner would say something similar as he fought against segregation in the Boston school systems: "The separation in the Public Schools of Boston, on account of color or race is in the nature of Caste, and on this account is a violation of Equality. Caste makes distinctions where God has made none."[10] Both then and now, this vision of God's equality at the table cuts against the grain of caste-based societies.

The recipients of Paul's letter were most likely surprised by Paul's indignation as class-specific dining was a widespread practice in the Roman Empire. In a passage written around the turn of the second century, the Roman magistrate Pliny the Younger describes a dinner host who assigned three different levels of food and wine in keeping with the three levels of social orders present at the same table. "One was for himself and me; the next for his friends of a lower order (for you must know, he measures out his friendship according to the degrees of quality); and third for his own freed-men and mine."[11] There is also historical evidence of clubs and associations serving different types of meals and drink to different levels of donors.[12] Separating by caste status at meals, therefore, was as widespread and seemingly acceptable in early Christianity as the more recent American practice of segregation and the zoning of neighborhoods by wealth and race.

Nevertheless, Paul's fury at the wealthier Corinthians leaps off the page. He is furious at how such separation humiliates those who are hungry and have nothing to eat. As discussed in a prior chapter, Jesus himself, the writers of the gospels of Matthew and Luke, and many in the first Christian assemblies likely had a direct experience of a period of prolonged hunger in their lives, and so the wealthy choosing to separate themselves out from those who had nothing to eat at the Lord's Supper is a particularly egregious act.[13]

Paul angrily condemns such segregation: "When you come together, it is not really to eat the Lord's supper. For when the time comes to eat, each of you goes ahead with your own supper, and one goes hungry and another becomes drunk. What! Do you not have homes to eat and drink in? Or do you show contempt for the church of God and humiliate those who have nothing?"[14] It is with this searing condemnation in mind that we should reconsider Paul's warning in 1 Corinthians 11:29 that the Corinthians eat and drink judgment against themselves when they fail to "discern the body."[15]

A great deal has been made over the centuries about Paul's statement that one must discern the body during the eucharist, and I am not so foolish as to protest the tidal wave of later thought that insists this refers to the real presence of Christ in the bread and wine. What I will say is that, in addition, we should consider how this phrase occurs between Paul's chastisement of the wealthier Corinthians and his statements on the church as the body in the next chapter. There, Paul writes that the most vulnerable parts of the body should be treated with greater honor. In using this phrase, Paul is reminding the Corinthians that they should be able to discern both the strongest and most vulnerable members of the church body when approaching the table for the Lord's Supper, for "the eye cannot say to the hand, 'I have no need of you', nor again the head to the feet, 'I have no need of you.' On the contrary, the members of the body that seem to be weaker are indispensable, and those members of the body that we think less honorable we clothe with greater honor, and our less respectable members are treated with greater respect; whereas our more respectable members do not need this."[16] [17] Andrew McGowan observes: "Discerning the body—not only the body of Christ identified with the bread, but the body thus constituted by those who shared the bread—was the condition for celebrating a meal worthy to be thought of as 'the Lord's'(1 Corinthians 11:27–29; cf. v. 20)."[18]

I therefore believe it is very much in the spirit of Paul to ask critical questions about how Christians celebrate the Lord's Supper today. When planning or attending a service, we should ask ourselves:

- To what extent does this eucharistic service represent the coming together of people across socioeconomic divisions, particularly the wealthy and the poor? Or is this an example of the wealthy having separated themselves from the poor for a status-specific meal?

- To what extent would Paul be able to "discern the body" at this communion service, including those he describes as the most vulnerable and least respectable/honorable? Or does this represent the one part of the body saying to another, "I have no need of you"?

Of course, the tendency of the wealthy to separate themselves out from the poor is alive and well within both broader US society and mainline Christianity. We live in a period of unprecedented inequality, and all too often these disparities are reinforced, rather than countered, by the makeup of our churches and the priorities of our ecclesiastical institutions.

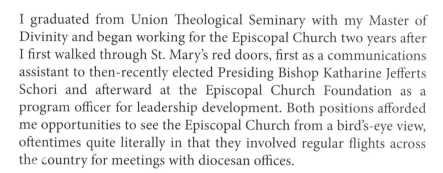

I graduated from Union Theological Seminary with my Master of Divinity and began working for the Episcopal Church two years after I first walked through St. Mary's red doors, first as a communications assistant to then-recently elected Presiding Bishop Katharine Jefferts Schori and afterward at the Episcopal Church Foundation as a program officer for leadership development. Both positions afforded me opportunities to see the Episcopal Church from a bird's-eye view, oftentimes quite literally in that they involved regular flights across the country for meetings with diocesan offices.

In 2016, my colleague, the Rev. Ronald Byrd, and I made a visit to an Episcopal diocesan office in the Midwest and were shown a map that I'll never forget. The map was divided into colored zip codes, and within the various zip codes, I could see little crosses representing the locations of existing Episcopal congregations. A few zip codes were shaded pink to represent the wealthiest neighborhoods in the city, whereas others were shaded yellow to represent the poorest. Perhaps it isn't surprising to learn that the wealthiest zip codes had a cluster of Episcopal congregations and the poorest zip codes had very few, if any at all.

I was being shown this map because the diocesan staff member I was meeting with saw this as a major concern, and she was working hard to plant and sustain Episcopal communities of faith in those zip codes that hadn't been "on the map" of prior generations. Nevertheless, when one asks how it could possibly be that the Episcopal Church has remained more than 95 percent white and among the wealthiest of denominations amidst the rapidly changing demographics of the United States, we should bear these maps of socioeconomic segregation in mind.

In this midwestern city, and many others across the United States, dioceses engaged in concerted church planting campaigns after the end of World War II. Both where diocesan leaders chose to locate those new churches and which of those churches still remain standing reflect a long-standing preferential option for wealthy enclaves. However, this is not just the story of the Episcopal Church but rather part of a broader pattern of segregation among mainline churches; these structural patterns baked into cities mean that the observation by the Rev. Martin Luther King Jr. still remains true: Sunday is the most segregated time in America.

Richard Rothstein's book, *The Color of Law: A Forgotten History of How Our Government Segregated America,* is a key text for understanding just how much effort has gone into segregating communities by wealth and color in the United States, patterns that make the status-specific dining practices of the Roman Empire look benign in comparison. Rothstein's work traces how racial disparities in homeownership were created through redlining, reverse redlining, restrictive covenants, and other legal policies, all of which contributed to the generational wealth gap between whites and people of color that we see today.

Rothstein goes into some detail about the role of racially restrictive covenants and the specific role of churches. Community associations— very often with the support of their neighborhood congregations— embedded racial exclusion clauses into home deeds on the grounds that home values dropped when people of color moved into neighborhoods. The mainline churches nestled in these communities frequently had a significant organizing role in these racial exclusion covenants. Rothstein cites one example in which a Roman Catholic priest in a wealthy Chicago suburb was an outspoken, driving force behind the creation of its racially restrictive covenant, and he goes on to describe how a single racially restrictive covenant was executed by religious institutions on Chicago's Near North Side, including the Moody Bible Institute, Louisville Presbyterian Theological Seminary, and the Board of Foreign Missions of the Methodist Episcopal Church.[19]

As it happens, the same midwestern city I visited a few years ago now has a racial covenant tracking project, and there is a dissertation waiting to be written by one day overlaying the map of where Episcopal congregations are currently situated and the emerging map of which neighborhoods had racial covenants.

Mainline Protestants and Catholics need to have a more developed understanding about why so many congregations fail to come together across socioeconomic divisions, including some deep reflection on both economic inequality and racial housing segregation. The fact that my own denomination of the Episcopal Church is more than 95 percent white is the result of a preference for building in historically white and wealthy enclaves as much as it is of insensitivity in personal interactions. This is a banal but insidious story of systemic decisions about how and where the church has invested its resources, including decisions about where we choose to plant congregations and which congregations we choose to sustain amidst institutional decline. Consider your own town or city: a similar diocesan map would likely show an over-investment in the historically white and wealthy enclaves and relative absence in "ghettos." Knowing full well the charged weight of that term, Rothstein insists on using it when referring to the poorest neighborhoods where racial/ethnic minorities were systematically crowded into by federal policies.

In light of Paul's description of the Lord's Supper as a time for coming together across socioeconomic divides, I've long wondered how one "discerns the body" at, say, a eucharist service aboard a cruise ship or at a summer resort chapel aimed at resort attendees but not at the people who work the low-wage jobs that support those spaces. I've wondered about how one "discerns the body" at gatherings intended exclusively for wealthy congregations?

How, I wonder, are these not examples of the same status-specific dining that Paul rails against in 1 Corinthians? Paul's bitter words come to mind: "Indeed, there have to be discriminations among you, for only so will it become clear who among you are distinguished."[20] Yet few question the validity of the eucharists that take place at these services, so why bring these socioeconomic criteria up at all?

The first historical reference to the Lord's Supper in 1 Corinthians 11:17-34 suggests socioeconomic implications to this meal that have long been downplayed, if not ignored. Paul chastises the wealthy for separating themselves out from those who have nothing to eat and insists this is contrary to the spirit and purpose of the tradition he has received. Paul continues to hope for a Lord's Supper and Christian community that is embracing and representative of the whole body. As we look at our own communities, it is easy to imagine that Paul, writing today, would be even fiercer in his condemnation.

Discussion Questions

In 1 Corinthians 11:17-34, Paul angrily accuses the wealthier Corinthians of bringing their own food and drink to the assembly, segregating themselves out from those who are poor and hungry, and eating a version of the Lord's Supper among members of their own social class. Why do you think this made Paul so angry?

Sunday after Sunday, Christians hear a version of the words of institution as part of the eucharistic liturgy. "For I received from the Lord what I also handed on to you, that the Lord Jesus on the night when he was betrayed took a loaf of bread, and when he had given thanks, he broke it and said, 'This is my body that is for you. Do this in remembrance of me.' In the same way he took the cup also, after supper, saying, 'This cup is the new covenant in my blood. Do this, as often as you drink it, in remembrance of me.'" For as often as you eat this bread and drink the cup, you proclaim the Lord's death until he comes" (1 Corinthians 11:23-26). The earliest historical record of these words comes from this very passage in which Paul is chastising the Corinthians for socioeconomic segregation. Knowing this now, how might you hear these words differently at eucharistic services?

Reflect on the Lord's Supper/eucharistic services that you are a part of. What do you think Paul might say about the makeup of those communities of faith? Knowing that Sunday continues to be, as the Rev. Martin Luther King Jr. pointed out, the most segregated time in America, are there eucharists that you attend that represent a coming together across race, caste, and socioeconomic divides?

A Next Step

Consider who is present and who is missing at your regular eucharist service. Recognizing the deep, systemic causes of exclusive communities, including the long history of locating and resourcing Episcopal congregations in white and wealthy neighborhoods, is the first step to beginning to move toward Paul's vision of a Lord's Supper that is reflective of the full body of Christ. To what extent does your congregation's eucharistic service represent the coming together of people across socioeconomic divisions, particularly the wealthy and the poor? Is it another example of the wealthy separating themselves from the poor for a status-specific service? To what extent are you able to "discern the body" at this communion service, including those whom Paul describes as the most vulnerable and least respectable/honorable? Or does this represent one part of the body saying to another "I have no need of you"?

Learn your community's story of redlining, reverse redlining, and racial covenants: My parents grew up and I was born in San Antonio, Texas, one of the cities that concentrated (or "ghettoized" to use Richard Rothstein's preferred word) Latinos/Hispanics into the West Side (a flood plain), and Blacks and African Americans into the East Side through redlining, reverse redlining, and racialized covenants. Learning the history of how the city came to be divided reshaped my understanding of how poverty works in America and how resources become allocated inequitably in different parts of cities. The history of how your community was segregated is an important one to learn. For individuals who have historic homes and congregations, one exercise is to closely examine the deeds of the home or rectory to see if there is a racial exclusion clause included. The Minneapolis Mapping Prejudice Project reflects one city's collective attempt to map where these racial exclusion clauses existed, many of which are still embedded in home deeds.[21]

Endnotes

1   stmarysharlem.org/history.

2   N.R. Kleinfeld, "Old Friends, New Foes: President and a Preacher; One 60's Activist Runs Columbia; One Fights It," *The New York Times*, May 31, 1996.

3   *Cousin Bobby,* Directed by Jonathan Demme (Madrid, Spain: Tesauro,1992).

4   "Stop-and-Frisk in the de Blasio Era," ACLU of New York, 2019 Report, March 14, 2019.

5   Donald Attwater and Catherine Rachel John, "On Paul," in *The Penguin Dictionary of Saints* (New York: Penguin, 1996), 258.

6   MacCulloch, *Christianity*, 102.

7   Malina and Rohrbaugh, *Social-Science Commentary on the Synoptic Gospels*, 109-111.

8   1 Corinthians 11:19, New Oxford Annotated Bible, Third Edition.

9   Galatians 3:28.

10 Isabel Wilkerson, *Caste: The Origins of Our Discontents* (New York City: Random House, 2020), 24.

11 *Pliny Letters,* tr. William Melmoth, rev. W. M. L. Hutchinson (London: Heinemann, 1915), Book 2, VI.

12 Gerd Theissen, *The Social Setting of Pauline Christianity: Essays on Corinth*, ed. and trans. John H. Schultz (Philadelphia: Fortress Press, 1982) as cited in *The Tapestry of Early Christian Discourse: Rhetoric, Society and Ideology* by Vernon K. Robbins (London: Routledge, 1996), 115-118.

13 Rhee, *Loving the Poor, Saving the Rich*, 5, 11.

14 1 Corinthians 11:20-22.

15 1 Corinthians 11:29.

16 1 Corinthians 12:21-24.

17 Interestingly, this notion of the mystical body of Christ would become central to the theology of Dorothy Day and Peter Maurin of the Catholic Worker Movement, for "it meant that the stronger members of the body had an obligation to care for the weaker ones." From John Loughery and Blythe Randolph's *Dorothy Day: Dissenting Voice of the American Century* (New York City: Simon & Schuster, 2020).

18 Andrew B. McGowan, *Ancient Christian Worship: Early Church Practices in Social, Historical, and Theological Perspective* (Ada, Michigan: Baker Academic, 2016), 31.

19 Richard Rothstein, *The Color of Law: A Forgotten History of How Our Government Segregated America* (New York City: Liveright, 2012). See chapter on IRS Support and Compliant Regulations.

20 1 Corinthians 11:19, New Oxford Annotated Bible, Third Edition.

21 Visit mappingprejudice.umn.edu to learn more.

5 Paul's Compensation and Solidarity with the Poor

If mainline Christianity's structures have reflected a long-standing preference for wealth, theology from the margins has often pointed in the exact opposite direction. Indeed, one of the most important theologians of the twentieth and twenty-first centuries is a Peruvian Roman Catholic priest whose experiences of poverty and physical illness in childhood, as well as his ongoing solidarity with the poor, has led him to articulate that which first-world theologians and biblical scholars have often failed to see: namely, the overarching biblical thrust, theme, and witness of God's preferential option for the poor. I believe this theologian's insights are key for reading Paul's letters and particularly when considering Paul's complex discussion of compensation.

Gustavo Gutiérrez grew up in Peru experiencing both poverty and physical illness, having been bedridden during his teenage years by osteomyelitis, a severe infection that causes swelling in bones. Initially interested in studying medicine, he later experienced a call from God, changed course, and entered into a Roman Catholic seminary. He was sent to Europe to complete his theological education but returned to Peru in 1959 to be ordained a priest. Back in his homeland, he began to name a theological tenet that would become central to his ministry, that "theology must be grounded in the concrete, lived faith of the Christian people—the vast majority of whom are poor, in Latin America and indeed throughout the world."[1]

Gutiérrez's Liberation Theology, as it would come to be called, is a vast and nuanced meditation on God's love for the poor and liberative action within history, and so I hesitate to reduce his writings to just a few insights. Nevertheless, the three insights I believe are key to keep in mind while reading Paul's letters are:

- First, that God has made a preferential option for the poor.[2] While scripture and tradition bear witness to a God who loves all people equally and gratuitously, a preponderance of texts bear witness to God's special concern for the poor, including orphans, widows, immigrants, refugees, prisoners, day laborers, slaves, as well as many other of society's most marginalized groups.

- Second, that this preferential option was expressed through God's entering human history in the poor person of Jesus. Embedded in Paul's Letter to the Philippians is an ancient hymn that captures the striking nature of God's act, for the Holy One, "though he was in the form of God, did not regard equality with God as something to be exploited, but emptied himself, taking the form of a slave, being born in human likeness" (Philippians 2:6-7). For both Paul and Gutiérrez, it matters that God did not enter history as a king, a military general, a philanthropist, a CEO in the corner office, or even a bishop or dean of a cathedral but rather as a poor person— indeed, "a slave"—whose entire life, from birth to horrific death by crucifixion, was lived in poverty and peril.

- Third, that insomuch as God chose to be incarnated and crucified in the person of Jesus, Christians are called to link up our lives with the crucified people of history.[3] Summarizing this aspect of Gutiérrez theology, Robert Goizueta writes, "Unless we place ourselves alongside the poor, unless we look at reality through their eyes, we are unable to see, recognize, or worship the God who walks with the poor. Conversely, if we lack such a practical solidarity with the poor, the 'god' in whom we believe and whom we worship will necessarily be a false god, an idol of our own making."[4]

Importantly, Gutiérrez argues that solidarity with the poor is expressed not only through political or ideological affiliation but also through friendship, celebration, liturgy, domestic life, and community belonging with the poor. Indeed, in his later writings, Gutiérrez emphasizes authentic friendships with poor communities as essential to the struggle for justice, for "the most fundamental form of solidarity is that friendship with individual, flesh-and-blood human persons without which 'the poor' too easily become reduced to a mere abstraction."[5] In friendship, the names, hopes and dreams, stories, and political challenges of people who are often rendered nameless and are frequently generalized as "the poor" become one's own.

I believe Gutiérrez's insights—God's preferential option for the poor, God's revealing of God's self in the form of a slave, and his belief that Christians are called into solidarity through friendship with the crucified people of the world—elucidate many of Paul's writings. This is especially so when exploring Paul's complicated discussion of compensation for ministry as there is evidence to suggest that Paul supported himself through manual labor as a means of drawing closer in solidarity and friendship to the very people he was organizing into early Christian assemblies.

Paul's frequent references to how he earns a living are one of the first times we hear about how the early Church wrestled with the sticky issue of compensation for ministry. Even as Paul elaborates on his unique position on the issue, he gives clues about where Jesus and the other apostles stood on the same matter. In 1 Corinthians 9, Paul names Jesus's teaching that those who proclaim the gospel should get their living by the gospel, only to then assert that he has decided to offer the gospel free of charge. Instead, Paul takes up manual labor in order to survive, a significant step down from his prior socioeconomic status. Pauline scholars view this decision to give the gospel free of charge while earning his living as a tentmaker as a way of becoming proximate to the people he was serving, an example of living into the kind of solidarity and friendship that Gutiérrez would later describe as central to what it means to become a follower of Jesus.

As is so often the case with Paul, the apostle's writing on compensation takes place within the tense atmosphere of conflict, in this case one created by the Corinthians' erroneous interpretation of their entitlements and new freedoms as followers of Christ.

In 1 Corinthians 8, Paul describes how some within the Corinthian community have begun boasting that their newfound faith in Christ allows them to transcend all the prior constraints of the law, including all dietary restrictions. Paul counters that while these individuals might be entitled to eat whatever they want with whomever they want, they should waive this entitlement out of respect for the members of the larger group who are still keeping dietary restrictions.[6] "Therefore, if food is a cause of their falling, I will never eat meat, so that I may not cause one of them to fall" (1 Corinthians 8:13).

From this particular disagreement around food, Paul then extrapolates a Christian understanding of freedom as a thing to be expressed or constrained depending on the wider needs of the community. For Paul, freedom and entitlements must be balanced with love of neighbor and the common good of the larger assembly. Indeed, the members of Christian communities must occasionally constrain their liberties when acting on them will impinge on their neighbors' well-being.[7]

To drive this point home, Paul illustrates this principle by discussing his personal compensation as an apostle (a title that was contested as Paul never saw Jesus while he was alive). This is the point at which my ears perk up as Paul begins bringing up examples and illustrations that depict how the early church thought about money.

Paul begins 1 Corinthians 9 with the question, "Am I not free? Am I not an apostle?" and argues that although he has many rights and entitlements as an apostle, including the right to be paid for his labor, he has foregone these out of respect for the well-being of the wider community. This decision to forgo payment creates discomfort within the Corinthian community, but he likens his decision to the dietary entitlements he just discussed in 1 Corinthians 8, insisting that not seeking compensation is simply a respectful refraining from what remains an apostolic freedom and entitlement.[8] "Nevertheless, we have not made use of this right, but we endure anything rather than put an obstacle in the way of the gospel of Christ."

Paul then elaborates on how the early church was thinking about the rights of the apostles as well as compensation generally. On the right of apostles to be married, Paul asks, "Do we not have the right to be accompanied by a believing wife, as do the other apostles and the brothers of the Lord and Cephas?"[9] (So much for clerical celibacy, by the way.) On the right to compensation, he asks, "Who at any time pays the expenses for doing military service?" Answer: the people, through imposed taxes. Paul also cites the example of priests employed in temple service receiving a share in the goods offered at the altar. Drawing on agricultural practices, Paul asks who plants a vineyard without getting to eat some of the fruit and who tends flocks without getting a share of the milk. Finally, Paul cites the law of Moses, quoting "you shall not muzzle an ox while it is treading out the grain." These illustrations culminate in Paul's insistence that it is perfectly reasonable to expect that the disciples, like the aforementioned ox or workers who are ploughing and threshing, would carry out the work of ministry and share in the crop. Paul asks, "If we have sown spiritual good among you, is it too much if we reap your material benefits?"[10] Paul then cinches his argument by invoking the words of Jesus himself: "In the same way, the Lord commanded that those who proclaim the gospel should get their living by the gospel."[11]

These examples of the disciples' rights and entitlements offer clues into how the early church was thinking about compensation. And yet, as is so often the case with Paul, these illustrations are actually just a set-up before he arrives at his counterpoint: namely, that while he and the other apostles are certainly *entitled* to compensation for their ministry, and while even Jesus supported this position, he (perhaps alone?) has chosen to give the gospel away free of charge.

On the whole, Paul references Jesus's earthly teachings and ministry only rarely, an awkward reality when one considers that Paul is often believed to be the second-most important figure in Christianity. The passage from 1 Corinthians 9:13-14 stands out, therefore, as one of the few instances in which Paul is clearly aware of Jesus's teaching that those who proclaim the gospel should get their living by such, a statement by Jesus that appears in both the gospels of Matthew and Luke.[12] Yet, Paul brings up Jesus's teaching in order to oppose it, at least for himself.

In *A History of Christianity: The First Three Thousand Years*, Diarmaid MacCulloch notes: "Characteristically, [Paul] takes a contrary line to the Lord. Jesus had said that those who 'proclaim the gospel should get their living by the gospel': that is, they deserve support from others. Paul emphasizes that he has not done this: he tells us that he has supported himself, although in what seems to be in an attempt to face down criticism, he proclaims his contradiction of Jesus's practice as a privilege renounced rather than an obligation spurned."[13]

Lest anyone believe that Jesus was expressing approval for a gospel of wealth and that he foresaw and endorsed ministers and priests, bishops, and pastors living in luxury, it's important to explore the broader context. Jesus's statement about compensation appears in both the gospels of Matthew and Luke—namely, the sending of the disciples two-by-two to proclaim the good news with nothing at all.

Jesus's statement that "laborers deserve to be paid" occurs in Matthew 10:10-11 and Luke 10:7-8 as part of his sending followers out to proclaim the gospel carrying nothing with them. Instead of telling the disciples to become wealthy, Jesus tells them to "Take no gold, or silver, or copper in your belts, no bag for your journey, or two tunics, or sandals, or a staff…" and "Carry no purse, no bag, no sandals; and greet no one on the road."[14] Jesus expects itinerancy and dependence on the hospitality of others for the disciples he is sending out, and it is within this context that Jesus says the disciples should be given at least some measure of payment and food.

Clearly, though, Jesus's expectation is that the disciples would carry out their itinerant work in an extremely vulnerable situation. The exposure and dependence Jesus expected of his disciples becomes even more clear when one considers that "laborers deserve to be paid" is itself a reference to the Deuteronomic laws regulating payment of the poor and oppressed found in Deuteronomy 24:10-22.

This powerful section of Deuteronomy connects treatment of the poor and the oppressed with the Jewish people's past as slaves in Egypt. "Remember that you were a slave in Egypt and the LORD your God redeemed you from there; therefore I command you to do this." It is with the experience of slavery in mind that Deuteronomy frames laws about payment for poor and needy workers: "You shall not withhold the wages of poor and needy laborers, whether other Israelites or aliens who reside in your land in one of your towns. You shall pay them their wages daily before sunset, because they are poor and their livelihood depends on them; otherwise they might cry to the LORD against you, and you would incur guilt."[15]

The fact that Jesus draws on Deuteronomic law about payment for the poor to describe why the disciples deserve some form of payment tells us a great deal about the level of wealth Jesus envisions for his followers. The disciples are expected to experience dependence, vulnerability, and exposure as they carry out their ministry. They deserve occasional payment because they are to be poor, and the poor should be treated fairly by the larger community.

As is oftentimes the case, Jesus's expectations are far more radical than Paul's (and hardly resemble the church's today, for that matter). Jesus sends disciples out with literally nothing to engage in the itinerant preaching of the good news. In Matthew and Luke, Jesus connects payment to the Deuteronomic laws regulating compensation for poor and needy laborers, and elsewhere in the Gospel of Matthew draws on the gleaning rights of the poor described in this same chapter (Deuteronomy 24:19-22) as justification for the disciples to get food now and then.[16] This suggests that when Paul cites and then rejects Jesus's specific teaching that laborers deserve to be paid, he is likely rejecting a teaching that is more than even he can bear, what I have jokingly come to refer to as Jesus's "try not to be anxious" health insurance and "you can always forage" compensation plan.

Paul, therefore, both cites Jesus's teaching but then rejects it, and he does so while sharing various other illustrations that describe how the early church is quickly moving away from Jesus's model toward a more institutional approach to compensation. Paul, however, decides to go an entirely different route by choosing to engage in manual labor to support himself as he spreads the gospel "free of charge." Paul's choice to do so comes with great hardship.

In his letters, Paul consistently speaks about his decision to support himself through manual labor as a kind of self-humiliation. This theme was enthusiastically picked up by monastics such as John Cassian and Benedict of Nursia, who spoke of monks' *abjection*—their being stripped of any titles and wealth and donning the common habit upon

entering a monastery. Paul's description of his self-humiliation has led
biblical scholars like Bruce Longenecker to conclude that Paul began
his life in very different socioeconomic circumstances. Longenecker
argues that "Paul's attitude toward manual labor betrays a man who
imagines it to be beneath his normal station in life."[17] Abraham
Malherbe notes, "Paul's attitude toward his labor is reflected by the
fact that he lists it in a series of hardships (1 Corinthians 4:12) and that
he regards it as service (1 Corinthians 9:19) and an act of abasement
(2 Corinthians 11:7)."[18] Placing Paul's descriptions of the hardship of
manual labor and his having "grown weary from the work of our own
hands" alongside his rhetorical skills and the likelihood that he was a
Roman citizen, has led such scholars to believe that Paul's life prior to
his becoming a follower of Christ was of a "middling economic profile."
This means that prior to his conversion, Paul occupied the category
of people in ancient Rome who enjoyed moderate surplus including
"some merchants, some traders, some freedpersons, some artisans
(especially those who employed others), and military veterans."[19]

After his conversion, however, Paul's socioeconomic profile drops
sharply, even to the point of experiencing life-threatening hardship.
Paul's comments cited above in 1 Corinthians 4:11-12 and then the
catalogue of difficulties described in 2 Corinthians 11:23-27—"in toil
and hardship, through many a sleepless night, hungry and thirsty,
often without food, cold and naked..."—suggest Paul's lowered
socioeconomic status resulted in danger for the apostle, including
periods of sustained hunger. Longenecker locates post-conversion
Paul on new and lower depths of the ancient Roman economic scale
in which he is much closer to being just at, if not oftentimes below, the
minimum subsistence level needed to sustain life.[20]

In other words, becoming a follower of Christ has made Paul poor.
I have a wonderful friend and colleague, the Rev. Anna Olson, who
points out that the trajectory of lives for those following Jesus in the
Bible isn't "from good to great" but "from great to much, much worse."
This is certainly the case for Jesus who is crucified by the very crowds
who adulated him just a week prior, and it also appears to be the case
for Paul whose conversion leads him into poverty, hunger, manual
labor, and torturous death. Concretely, Paul's conversion means the
lowering of his privilege and socioeconomic status to that of Jesus
and his disciples (Matthew 8:20), the Jerusalem Church (Romans

15:26; Galatians 2:10), and the people who make up the communities he founded (1 Corinthians 26-27; 2 Corinthians 8:1), all of whom belong to the "lower socioeconomic stratum and 'the poor' to varying degrees."[21] Longenecker writes,

> It should not be overlooked that, since Paul saw care for the needy as an integral component of the gospel he proclaimed, his self-imposed economic demotion was motivated, partially but nonetheless surely, by a concern to help alleviate the needs of the poor in the Greco-Roman world through the establishment of communities of Jesus-followers across the Mediterranean basin. Those communities that Paul "lowered himself" to serve were expected to "proclaim the Lord's death until he comes," a proclamation that included caring for the economically vulnerable as a central feature. In order to work toward the realization of that vision, Paul willingly compromised his own economic well-being. Making himself economically more vulnerable seems to have resulted from conviction that Israel's sovereign deity was at work in Jesus-groups, where the needs of economically vulnerable people were expected to be met as divine grace flowed through the lives of Jesus followers.[22]

Paul's decision, therefore, to give the gospel free of charge by earning his living as a tentmaker is a way of becoming proximate to the people he is serving, an example of living in the kind of solidarity and friendship that Gustavo Gutiérrez describes as central to what it means to be a follower of Jesus.

Of course, I suppose it's a bit rich for an ecclesiastical bureaucrat such as myself to be going on about Jesus sending out his disciples with the saying, "Take no gold, or silver, or copper in your belts, no bag for your journey, or two tunics, or sandals, or a staff…" and Paul's choice to give the gospel free of charge. After all, my entire professional career has been one in which I've been compensated for my work on behalf of the church. And yet, even hypocrites can occasionally bear sound witness to the radical challenge of scripture, and some of the best sermons are preached against one's self.

The truth is, I oftentimes feel that mainline Christianity—of which I am very much a part—is touching just the surface of this faith, and that membership in the church is to be swimming at just the surface waters of what it means to be a Christian. In her early life, the Roman Catholic radical Dorothy Day struggled, as so many others do, to reconcile the Jesus in the gospels with the "well-meaning, self-satisfied Episcopalians and Methodists she knew, people for whom, in her view, religion was largely a hymn-singing, tithe-paying Sunday-morning affair."[23] Her conversion to Roman Catholicism brought no solace in this area either, as she discovered that it tended to focus on revering custom and respectability and asked little of its members: her "idea of religion, from the first, was that its beauty had nothing to do with custom and respectability and everything to do with larger yearnings."[24]

In contrast, the radical example of Jesus in the gospels can feel like a dangerous undertow pulling the faithful toward a kind of death to one's self. Jesus's vision of discipleship (and to a certain extent, Paul's as well) requires followers to die to the security, comforts, and privileges that come with wealth. Drawing on the ancient language of baptism, early Christianity bore witness to the fact that there had to first be a drowning to such privileges and comforts before entering into this new life called Christianity.

What Jesus asks of his followers is no light thing. I truly believe that Jesus insisted on literal dispossession, non-ownership, and dependence on the hospitality and welfare of others for his disciples, right down to foraging in fields if needed. The fact that his statements on payment are rooted in Deuteronomy 24 shows that Jesus imagined the disciples' itinerant preaching as leaving them poor and incredibly exposed.

Not surprisingly, then, the early church's approach to compensation had already shifted considerably from Jesus's radical (and let's be honest, terrifying) statements even by the time Paul was writing 1 Corinthians in 53-54 CE. Paul's multiple illustrations speak to the other ways the early church had begun thinking about how to compensate apostles and community leaders for their labor. In his arguments,

Paul cites examples of compensation that are similar to the temple tax, the tax imposed for the services of mercenary soldiers, or the agricultural practice of allowing those who plant a vineyard to have a share of the fruit—illustrations that align more closely with current congregational practices of salaries being drawn from the offerings of the assembly. And yet, Paul cites these practices only to reject them as entitlements that he has chosen to refrain from out of respect for the needs of the wider community.

While Paul concedes that such compensation is an apostolic right and entitlement, he defends his choice to support himself through manual labor so as to give the gospel free of charge. Compensation, then, was an entitlement he had chosen to not take up. As the work of Longenecker highlights, this is a consequential decision, one through which Paul loses his relative economic stability and drops sharply on the economic scale. He becomes poor, in other words. Multiple references throughout his letters suggest that Paul experiences shock at the hardship of manual labor and the periods of hunger that are now his lot, though it is also clear these experiences are shared by most of the other members of the early church. And this must have been part of the larger point. Having experienced a life-changing vision of Christ, Paul chooses to live and proclaim the gospel in proximity, solidarity, and authentic friendship to the communities whom he is serving.

Discussion Questions

Paul develops an understanding of Christian freedom as a thing to
be expressed or constrained depending on the wider needs of the
community. For Paul, freedom and entitlements must be balanced
with love of neighbor and the common good of the larger assembly,
and therefore one must occasionally constrain their liberties when
acting on them will impinge on their neighbors' well-being. What
do you think of this notion of freedom? How does this align—or
contradict—with what most people mean by freedom in society?

Theologian Gustavo Gutiérrez describes solidarity as fundamentally
grounded in genuine friendships with the poor. Indeed, "the most
fundamental form of solidarity is that friendship with individual,
flesh-and-blood human persons without which 'the poor' too easily
become reduced to a mere abstraction."[25] Why do you think these
friendships come first? How do you see this playing out in Paul's life?

What do you make of Jesus's "try not to be anxious" health insurance
and "you can always forage" compensation plan? And what of
Paul's refusal of compensation as part of a larger strategy to lower
his socioeconomic status? Both Jesus and Paul's approaches to
compensation appear to have been radical for their times. Are Jesus
and Paul simply outliers in the Christian story, or do their teachings
on compensation have significance today?

A Next Step

Take a moment to reflect and journal about the people you call friends. Who are your friends? Whose homes do you visit for a fun and relaxed dinner? What are their lives like? If the Christian notion of solidarity with the poor is grounded in genuine friendships, how might this be reflected in your life? Imagine what would need to change (workplace, job, neighborhood, church) in order for this to become more so?

Dedicate time to learning more about what it is like to live on or below minimum wage in your community or state. This might include researching statistics and anecdotes but ideally will also include directly hearing people's (friend's) stories. There are also many excellent collections of stories including memoirs, podcasts, and interviews.

Endnotes

1 Robert Goizueta, "Gustavo Gutiérrez," in *Blackwell Companion to Political Theology*. (Hoboken, New Jersey: Blackwell Publishing, 2004), 290.

2 Goizueta, "Gustavo Gutiérrez," 288.

3 Goizueta, "Gustavo Gutiérrez," 296.

4 Goizueta, "Gustavo Gutiérrez," 296.

5 Goizueta, "Gustavo Gutiérrez," 294-295.

6 Malina and Pilch, *Social-Science Commentary on the Letters of Paul*.

7 I have wondered throughout the pandemic what Paul would say to people who refuse to wear a mask. I think his response is clear in these passages.

8 MacCulloch, *Christianity*, 113.

9 1 Corinthians 9:5.

10 1 Corinthians 9:8-11.

11 1 Corinthians 9:14.

12 Matthew 10:10-11, Luke 10:7-8.

13 MacCulloch, *Christianity*, 113.

14 Matthew 10:9-10 and Luke 10:4, respectively.

15 Deuteronomy 24:14-15.

16 Matthew 12:1-8.

17 Longenecker, *Remember the Poor*, 305.

18 Abraham J. Malherbe, *Paul and the Thessalonians: The Philosophic Tradition of Pastoral Care* (Philadelphia: Fortress Press, 1987), 56.

19 Longenecker, *Remember the Poor*, 45.

20 Longenecker, *Remember the Poor*, 307-308.

21 Rhee, *Loving the Poor, Saving the Rich*, 35.

22 Longenecker, *Remember the Poor*, 309.

23 Loughery and Randolph, *Dorothy Day*, 30.

24 Loughery and Randolph, *Dorothy Day*, 116.

25 Goizueta, "Gustavo Gutiérrez," 294-295.

6 Phoebe, Deacon and Benefactor of the Church

In late January 2021, I attended the diaconal ordinations of three seminarians I'd spent the past few years working with. The service was held at the Episcopal cathedral in Garden City, New Jersey, and I was there in my role as executive director of Episcopal Divinity School at Union Theological Seminary. During the service, a passage from Luke's Gospel long associated with deacons was read. This passage was Luke 22:24-27, one that speaks to how the spirit of reversal so evident in the *Magnificat* continues and illustrates how Jesus's followers are to approach power, wealth, and authority too.

The passage begins with the male disciples fighting again, arguing amongst themselves who is the greatest and who has the most authority. Jesus responds to their griping by first observing that "kings of the Gentiles lord it over them; and those in authority over them are called benefactors" (Luke 22:25). But greatness, power, and authority among Jesus's followers are to operate along entirely different lines: "But not so with you; rather the greatest among you must become like the youngest, and the leader like one who serves. For who is greater, the one who is at the table or the one who serves? Is it not the one at the table? But I am among you as one who serves" (Luke 22:26-27).

Part of the reason this passage is read at diaconal ordinations is because of that final sentence and, more particularly, that very last word. The English "to serve" is a translation of the Greek *diakonōn*. This notion that "deaconing" is serving—especially serving at tables—is echoed in Acts 6:1-6 in which seven are chosen "to serve." In Acts, the disciples are once again overly concerned with their roles and authority, and despite Jesus's earlier words that he himself comes as one who serves, they gripe that, "It is not right that we should neglect the word of God in order to wait on tables" (Acts 6:2). They therefore go about choosing seven— later considered to be the first deacons—to serve at the tables of the Jerusalem assembly's daily distribution of food to widows (Acts 6:1).

The passage from Luke 22:24-27 was read that January day because it depicts Jesus's view of how power and authority are to be wielded by his followers. Through this service, the diaconal ordinands were gaining greater authority within the Christian community, and so they were being reminded through the liturgy that power is expressed not by "lording it over others" or by wielding the clout of benefactors but rather by becoming like the often-unseen person serving at a table. Jesus insists that Christians are to express their power and authority in exactly the opposite way of kings and benefactors.

And yet, as Christianity grew, a number of wealthy benefactors began to be drawn to Christian assemblies. Although Christianity's relationship with such wealth would later become a full-blown love affair, these early stages were marked by moments of tension and awkward embraces. Such a tense moment has already been described in chapter four about how the wealthy had begun segregating themselves from the poor at the Lord's Supper in 1 Corinthians. A second example can be seen in the Letter of James wherein Paul warns assemblies against making distinctions in how they treat wealthy assembly members versus the poor: "For if a person with gold rings and in fine clothes comes into your assembly, and if a poor person in dirty clothes also comes in, and if you take notice of the one wearing the fine clothes and say, 'Have a seat here, please,' while to the one who is poor you say, 'Stand there,' or, 'Sit at my feet,' have you not made distinctions among yourselves, and become judges with evil thoughts?" (James 2:2-4). And yet still a third, more obscure example of both tension and awkward embrace comes from the Letter to the Romans, in which Paul uses two contradictory terms to introduce the person of Phoebe. The New Revised Standard Version renders Romans 16:1-2 as follows: "I commend to you our sister Phoebe, a deacon [*diakonos*] of the church at Cenchreae, so that you may welcome her in the Lord as is fitting for the saints, and help her in whatever she may require from you, for she has been a benefactor [*prostatis*] of many and of myself as well."

The curious case of Phoebe has to do with how she embodies the roles of both a *diakonos* (deacon) and *prostatis* (benefactor). As described above, being a deacon meant occupying a servant-like role whereas being a benefactor was decidedly about patronage and prestige. These are exactly the roles that Jesus pitted against each other in Luke 22:24-27. On Phoebe, the scholar Roman Garrison asks:

> How could this woman take on the role of *diakonos* (a term suggesting servant status) and *prostatis* (a term suggesting wealth and privilege)? The former term implies subservience, even social stigma, while the latter implies independence and status, perhaps even economic power. Even if these were not clearly defined as distinct positions (or offices such as that of bishops in the second century) in first-century Christianity, does the gospel tradition suggest that such combined ministry was encouraged?[1]

It would seem the answer to his question is a hesitant "yes," as Phoebe's two titles open a window into how Christians were wrestling with the arrival of wealthier patrons and benefactors into their ranks. Jesus's words on leadership through service may have led to early Christian assemblies thinking extensively about "the service of a patron" and about the role of wealthy benefactors in an assembly comprised of the mostly poor. There is intriguing evidence that women patrons like Phoebe in Romans 16:1-2 and Lydia of Thyatira mentioned in Acts 16:14-15 may have especially embodied this complex role through hospitality, for hospitality is a paradoxical act wherein patrons/benefactors become hosts and servers.

Paul's introduction of Phoebe in Romans 16:1-2 suggests that by the mid to late 50s CE, there were already moderately wealthy women who were serving as both deacons and as benefactors/patrons of the church, although Phoebe represents the only instance in which a woman is referred to using both terms. Paul describes Phoebe as a deacon (*diakonos*) of the church at Cenchreae, which was a village in Corinth, and as a patron/benefactor (*prostatis*) of "many and of myself as well."

A great deal of handwringing and conservative gnashing of teeth has resulted from Paul referring to Phoebe as *diakonos*, particularly from those quarters of Christianity that insist on the historicity of male-only ecclesiastical leadership. Despite their furrowed brows, there is abundant historical evidence of women occupying significant leadership roles in the early church, including as deacons. The Roman magistrate Pliny the Younger tells of how he put to torture two female deacons while investigating the Christian communities in Bithynia, who gave him information about the early eucharistic rite.[2] In Paul's letters, various women are named as office holders including Phoebe, Prisca, whom he calls a "fellow worker," Tryphaena and Tryphosa, whom he calls "workers in the Lord," and Junia, who is described as a female "apostle."[3]

In the case of Junia, some readers of Romans considered the notion of a woman apostle so galling that her name was frequently changed to a male form in later manuscripts—or they insistently believed it to be a man's name without justification.[4] Similarly, Phoebe's title of *diakonos* has frequently been translated as "servant" or simply as "helper" despite the fact that when referring to men, this same word is translated as "deacon." New Testament scholar Joan Cecilia Campbell points out that "the King James Version, the New King James Version, the New International Version, and the New American Standard Version all employ the word servant for *diakonos* in Romans 16:1 when applied to Phoebe."[5]

A subtler dampening of women's leadership has been to refer to Phoebe as a deaconess, yet here again there is no justification for this term. Historian Diarmaid MacCulloch writes, "While in English usage the title 'deaconess' designates female deacons, the Greek noun *diakonos* is masculine and has no feminine form in the New Testament."[6] He adds that using "deaconess" is inaccurate and is likely a "reading back from the third and fourth centuries, when female deacons were restricted to roles necessarily reserved for women, like looking after scantily clad female candidates in services of baptism."[7] First- and second-century Christians do not appear to have made such distinctions between male and female deacons; Phoebe should simply be referred to using the title of deacon.

As the focus of this book is on wealth and poverty, I won't go too far down this road. I'll end this digression by noting there needs to be a greater recognition—indeed, celebration—of the simple fact that, as Campbell puts it, "Phoebe is *diakonos* of an *ekklēsia* (a gathering of believers), a reference that seems to imply an official role for her among members of the Jesus group at [Cenchrae] (Romans 16:1)."[8]

Phoebe disrupts the hierarchical and gendered orders that the church has frequently presented as historical, and this disruption only intensifies when money is brought into the equation. In their social science commentary on Paul's letter to the Romans, Bruce Malina and John J. Pilch seem to strain against known definitions of what it meant to be a deacon and benefactor when they wonder aloud: "Perhaps a deacon such as Phoebe was a person in the service of the supervisor of the Jesus group in Cenchreae (the seaport of Corinth) or of the Jesus group in general (doing the service of patron, as noted in the next verse)."[9] It is delightfully challenging to place Phoebe into a comprehensible framework for what early Christian leadership was, and the use of these two terms for a woman leader raises the question of what the "service of a patron" could have possibly been.

When Paul speaks of Phoebe as a patron of himself and many others as well, what is the level of wealth and power that he is speaking of? Was she a member of the Roman aristocracy and imperial elite?

In *Remember the Poor*, Bruce Longenecker places Phoebe within the economic category of the 7-15 percent of the Roman population of "merchants, traders, freedpersons, artisans (especially those who employed others) and military veterans who primarily lived in urban areas and enjoyed some moderate surplus of wealth."[10] In this, she would have been in a similar economic category to Lydia of Thyatira of Acts 16:14-15, a woman who is described as "a dealer in purple cloth."

Insomuch as Phoebe and Lydia were among the category of those enjoying moderate surplus wealth, they were therefore *not* members of the 1-3 percent of the Roman population that constituted the imperial and aristocratic elite. This helps correct the notion that Roman aristocrats were hosting gatherings during a period in which the church was still very much a movement of the poor. While there were certainly people of moderate surplus wealth in the early Christian church, including women merchants and widows who served as benefactors/patrons of assemblies and house gatherings, it isn't until the mid-third century that decorative funerary evidence suggests the arrival of the Roman elite at church.[11]

But if Phoebe wasn't a member of the elite, neither was she a member of "the poor." Phoebe's moderate surplus wealth meant she was able to stand apart from the 75-90 percent of the Roman world that lived close to subsistence level—near, at, or below—who were struggling for survival and sustenance on a daily basis.[12] Significantly, historians like Helen Rhee hold that this latter category of "the poor" would have comprised the majority of the early Christian assemblies, and so even with moderate surplus wealth, Phoebe could have served as a patron to the church in Cenchreae and to Paul and many others as well.

Unlike the term for deacon, the word *prostatis* is a specific term for a female patron/benefactor, suggesting that Phoebe's patronage might best be understood through the lens of women's patronage as it was practiced in first-century Rome. Contrasting the feminine form *prostatis* with the masculine term *prostatēs,* Campbell writes that "*prostatis* refers to 'a woman in a supportive role, a patron, or benefactor.'"[13]

Campbell notes that, "During the first century, the women of [Cenchrae], one of the major Roman ports in Corinthia, likely enjoyed a relatively high degree of social freedom, particularly if they, like Phoebe, were women of means."[14] She continues, "Women, it seems, were able to act as patrons of individuals and to engage in civic benefactions. Their influence in public matters was strongest in areas such as Corinth, Philippi, and the Roman province of Asia where Roman influence heavily outweighed any other."[15]

An intriguing example of non-Christian women's patronage comes from the mid-first century in Corinth as well. This pertains to two decrees praising Junia Theodora of Corinth, a *prostatis* of the people of the Lycian cities of Telmessos and Patara, for her service of patronage through hospitality.[16] These decrees in praise of Junia align with descriptions of women's patronage focusing on "offering hospitality, hosting group meetings, and providing 'material and cash gifts, food and dinner invitations, lodging, favorable recommendations and appointments, help in matchmaking, and bequests and inheritances.'"[17]

With this in mind, it is possible that Phoebe was able to occupy both the role of *diakonos* (a term suggesting servant status) and *prostatis* (a term suggesting wealth and privilege) through extending hospitality, functioning as an intermediary, and offering financial gifts in support of a specific community.[18] Such "threading of the needle" of both service and patronage was happening more frequently in first-century Rome in general, as women were able to "present petitions to her husband about matters of public policy, to intercede with him on behalf of individuals, to lend money to people outside her own family, to make generous gifts of cash both to cities and individuals, to undertake building projects in her own name and at her own expense, and still to be presented in public as the embodiment of a wife's traditional virtues."[19] Much like the women who delicately balanced expressing power and authority within the traditional gender roles, Phoebe may have offered the diaconal service of a patron as a leader in the church of Corinth, a host of an assembly, an intermediary and/or host for Paul in Corinth, as well as being a financial patron of Paul and many others as well. The church, then, was discovering ways to embrace patrons with moderate wealth.

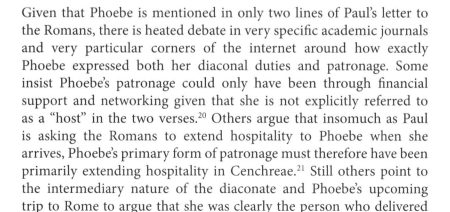

Given that Phoebe is mentioned in only two lines of Paul's letter to the Romans, there is heated debate in very specific academic journals and very particular corners of the internet around how exactly Phoebe expressed both her diaconal duties and patronage. Some insist Phoebe's patronage could only have been through financial support and networking given that she is not explicitly referred to as a "host" in the two verses.[20] Others argue that insomuch as Paul is asking the Romans to extend hospitality to Phoebe when she arrives, Phoebe's primary form of patronage must therefore have been primarily extending hospitality in Cenchreae.[21] Still others point to the intermediary nature of the diaconate and Phoebe's upcoming trip to Rome to argue that she was clearly the person who delivered

Paul's letter. It strikes me that we'll simply never know for sure, in part because we only have two short lines to consider.

And yet, there is a long-standing historical tradition of imagining Phoebe's "service as a patron" as that of hospitality. The fifth-century theologian Theodoret of Cyrus wrote, "And so large was the congregation of the assembly [ekklēsia] of Cenchreae that it even had a woman deacon [diakonos], one both famous and celebrated." In pondering her role as a benefactor, Theodoret takes a guess: "Now, by patronage I am inclined to think [Paul] refers to her hospitality and care, and he rewards her with multiple compliments. I mean, it is likely she received him into one house for a short time—namely, the period he spent in Corinth—whereas he introduced her to the world, and on all land and sea she became famous: not only the Romans and Hellenists knew of her but also all the barbarians."[22] Following Theodoret, then, I'd like to imagine what it would have meant for Phoebe to have expressed her diaconal service of patronage as the host of one of the house churches of Cenchreae.

In their essay, "The 'House Churches' in Corinth," Bruce Button and Fika J. Van Rensburg describe what some of the earliest forms of gatherings of Christianity might have looked like in the area where Phoebe was serving. They argue that when Paul spoke of "the church" he was actually speaking of a single body that gathered in two ways: in both larger, public assemblies as well as in smaller, more private meetings at patrons' homes.[23] Acts 2:46-47a describes this relationship between the public assemblies and house gatherings, where it states, "Day by day, as they spent much time together in the temple, they broke bread at home and ate their food with glad and generous hearts, praising God and having the goodwill of all the people."[24] These scholars argue that unlike the larger, public assembly at the temple, the home gatherings would likely have been of more specific groups of people ranging between five and twenty, depending on the size of the home of the patron.[25]

This confirms that patrons like Phoebe and Lydia would not have needed to be extremely wealthy, and it is more likely they were of the moderate wealth of merchants. Button and Rensburg write:

> The general assumption in the literature is that "house church patrons" were well-to-do, and this leads to an attempt to identify wealthy Christians in Corinth and to attach "house

churches" to them. It is obvious that a potential host for a home-gathering had to have accommodation at his or her disposal, but the above discussion on the meaning of *oikos* shows that this requirement does not imply the need for as much wealth as is often supposed.[26]

Phoebe therefore may have been the moderately wealthy patron of a regular gathering of Christians in her home in Cenchreae. The church was still an assembly of the mostly poor in which only a few moderately wealthy patrons, perhaps especially women, offered their homes for smaller group meetings alongside larger public assemblies. These house gatherings may have even been primarily made up of the members of the household themselves, though this would have included "people from all stations in life—household heads, women, children, slaves and other dependents."[27] Recalling the equality between rich and poor that Paul envisioned for the Lord's Supper, Button and Van Rensburg argue that even in this smaller setting, "since Paul insisted repeatedly on the gospel's obliteration of social distinctions (1 Corinthians 12:13; Galatians 3:28), it is inconceivable that he would have allowed the home-based gatherings to distinguish between different classes of people."[28]

In this lengthy journey to try to wrap our minds around Phoebe, deacon and patron of the early church, I began with the ordination of three students to the diaconate, an order of ministry long associated with Jesus's emphasis on service as Christianity's most profound expression of authority. In Luke 22:24-27, Jesus pointedly contrasts such service with the way kings and benefactors tend to lord their power over others.

Intriguingly, however, Phoebe is described by Paul in Romans 16:1-2 as somehow integrating the roles of both deacon and benefactor. She opens a window into what might be called "the diaconal service of a patron," an idea filled with both tensions and promise for transforming how some larger donors might see themselves in relationship to their communities. What would it mean to practice the diaconal service of a patron today?

Of course, with only two verses to work with (Romans 16:1-2), it is impossible to know exactly how Phoebe expressed her leadership and patronage, nor can we be sure that Paul himself knew fully what Phoebe may have been up to. Was Phoebe preaching regularly? Did Phoebe also preside over the Lord's Supper during gatherings at her home? Would Paul have ever known this? Every study I've cited tends to assume Paul had a clear sense of what was taking place in the church in Corinth, though elsewhere Paul himself writes the Corinthians were scandalized by what he had just learned through "Chloe's people," (1 Corinthians 1:11). My own gut sense—or is it simply a hope?—is that Phoebe was skilled at wielding her power and authority the way many marginalized people do, that is, on a slant—creatively, perhaps indirectly and intentionally confusingly, like a person walking on snow carefully brushing away their tracks.

Discussion Questions

In Luke 22:26-27, Jesus states that "the greatest among you must become like the youngest, and the leader like one who serves. For who is greater, the one who is at the table or the one who serves? Is it not the one at the table? But I am among you as one who serves." This is a profoundly challenging statement, especially to the powerful and wealthy who are accustomed to occupying positions of authority. What do you think this statement means for someone who is accustomed to sitting at the head of a table?

Phoebe represents a curious case insomuch as she is somehow both a deacon and patron of the early church. The first title suggests a servant-like status, yet the second title is one of power, wealth, and authority. Is it possible to embody both at the same time? How do you think Phoebe might have lived these two titles out?

Hospitality is a way in which the contradictions of diaconal service and patronage are resolved. Perhaps for this reason, Phoebe has regularly been imagined as expressing her "service as a patron" through hospitality, specifically as a host of a house church in Corinth. How can hospitality still be an aspect of congregational life and particularly the work of the patrons of your community?

Does your congregation or community have its own twenty-first century version of patrons? How might today's wealthier donors come to embody the "diaconal service of a patron" that Phoebe appears to have embodied in the first century?

A Next Step

The example of Phoebe's "service of a patron" suggests that there is important, internal ego-work that has to take place among the wealthiest and most powerful members of Christian congregations. Sometimes such members will assume they should be seated at the heads of the table, will guide the direction of the congregation through gifts (or through the threatened removal of gifts), and have a direct line to the priest and vestry as one of the most important patrons of the community. Unfortunately, they may be right—for many churches wrestle with "the tail wagging the dog" rather than funding appropriately following mission and vision.

Yet Jesus's critique of "kings of the Gentiles" and "benefactors" in Luke 22:25 calls all members of the church to embody a very different type of relationship to wealth and power. The example of Phoebe calls the wealthiest patrons and benefactors to begin the internal labor of figuring out how to be in a healthier and more service-oriented relationship to the wider community, unlearning the ingrained habits of wielding wealth and power by lording it over others but rather by practicing the diaconal service of a patron for the greater good of the whole. Take some moments to reflect on what this internal shift would look like in your own life and among the communities that you help to financially support.

Endnotes

1   Roman Garrison, "Phoebe, the Servant-Benefactor and Gospel Traditions," in *Text and Artifact in the Religions of Mediterranean Antiquity : Essays in Honour of Peter Richardson*, ed. Stephen G. Wilson and Michel Desjardins (Waterloo, Ontario: Wilfrid Laurier University Press, 2006), 63.

2   McGuckin. *The Path of Christianity*, 991.

3   MacCulloch, *Christianity*, 117.

4   MacCulloch, *Christianity*, 117.

5   Joan Cecelia Campbell, *Phoebe: Patron and Emissary* (Collegeville, Minnesota: Liturgical Press, 2009), 59.

6   Campbell, *Phoebe*, 59.

7   MacCulloch, *Christianity*, 117.

8   Campbell, *Phoebe*, 77.

9   Malina and Pilch, *Social-Science Commentary on the Letters of Paul*, 292.

10 Longenecker, *Remember the Poor*. See pages 241-242 and then pages 45 and 51 for an explanation of income categories.

11 MacCulloch, *Christianity*, 160.

12 Rhee, *Loving the Poor, Saving the Rich*, 5, 11.

13 Campbell, *Phoebe*, 91.

14 Campbell, *Phoebe*, 101-102.

15 Campbell, *Phoebe*, 101-102.

16 Esther Yue L. Ng, "Phoebe as Prostatis," *Trinity Journal*, NS 25, No. 1 (2004): 9-10.

17 Campbell, *Phoebe*, 103-104.

18 Garrison, "Phoebe, the Servant-Benefactor and Gospel Traditions," 63.

19 Bruce W. Winter, *Roman Wives, Roman Widows: The Appearance of New Women and the Pauline Communities* (Grand Rapids, Michigan: Wm. B. Eerdmans Publishing, 2003), 34-35.

20 M. Bruce Button and Fika J. Van Rensburg, "The 'House Churches' in Corinth," *Neotestamentica* , Vol. 37, No. 1 (2003): 1-28.

21 Ng, "Phoebe as Prostatis," 3-13.

22 Robert Charles Hill, tr.., *Theodoret of Cyrus: Commentary on the Letters of Saint Paul* (Brookline, MA: Holy Cross Orthodox Press, 2001), 135.

23 Button and Rensburg, "The 'House Churches' in Corinth," 1-28.

24 Button and Rensburg, "The 'House Churches' in Corinth," 8-9.

25 Button and Rensburg, "The 'House Churches' in Corinth," 16.

26 Button and Rensburg, "The 'House Churches' in Corinth," 13.

27 Button and Rensburg, "The 'House Churches' in Corinth," 15.

28 Button and Rensburg, "The 'House Churches' in Corinth," 15.

7 The Jerusalem Collection

This book was begun just a few weeks into the COVID-19 pandemic and was concluded during yet another ten-day isolation period at the beginning of January 2022 as my husband and I recovered from the virus. The chaos of this pandemic and the vast poverty and inequality that it exacerbated and exposed suffused the writing of this book in many ways. Some of the most striking images I will retain from this period are of the long lines of people waiting for food as well as the many news stories of pantries and soup kitchens being in short supply of both staples and volunteers. Hunger, already a pervasive problem in the city I live in, descended with a force I never thought I'd see in my lifetime.

As I watched hunger and desperation grow, I found myself recalling the earliest historical reference to Christian communities taking up a collection in response to famine, an event described in Paul's First Letter to the Corinthians, written around 50 CE. Frequently called "the Jerusalem Collection," it represents the first record of a concerted effort among Christian assemblies to respond to a natural disaster.

Paul's instructions in 1 and 2 Corinthians about this collection are terse and pragmatic; he tells the Corinthians to follow the same instructions he had already given to the Christians in Galatia: "On the first day of every week, each of you is to put aside and save whatever extra you earn, so that collections need not be taken when I come. And when I arrive, I will send any whom you approve with letters to take your gift to Jerusalem. If it seems advisable that I should go also, they will accompany me."[1]

Paul's instructions give insight on the economic network that the international movement of Jesus followers had already become by 50 CE.[2] He writes about the logistics of this collection in 1 Corinthians 16:1-4, its underlying theology in 2 Corinthians 8-9, and describes his plans to deliver the collection in Romans 15:25-29. There is considerable debate about what prompted this collection (Was it the Jerusalem apostles' instruction to "remember the poor" as recorded in Galatians 2:10?) and even more speculation as to the nature of this collection (Was this a freewill offering instead of a tithe as suggested by the language of 2 Corinthians 8-9?). Nevertheless, the fact that Paul's thoughts on the collection are spread across the four major Pauline letters (1 and 2 Corinthians, Romans, and possibly Galatians) attest to its importance for the apostle and early church.[3]

Studies of the Jerusalem Collection often focus on how it was an expression of church unity among the early assemblies, the way the collection reflected a spiritual connection and fellowship from the smaller assemblies to the mother church in Jerusalem.[4] The unity between churches is certainly important, but it's also worth noting the practical dimensions too. As early as 50 CE, we find the energetic Paul giving instructions to the Corinthian community for a collection of monies to be sent to Jerusalem that Paul sincerely hopes will be accepted (Romans 15:30-31). Monies would be taken up in Galatia, Corinth, and eventually Rome and would be physically brought to the Jerusalem assembly. Logistics were arranged (1 Corinthians 16:1-4), accusations of impropriety made, transparency ensured by having multiple people handling the funds (2 Corinthians 12:14-18), and protection against theft/robbery secured as the funds were brought to Jerusalem (Romans 15:25-29).

These practical details speak to something so essential about Christianity that many Christians fail to fully appreciate it: Christian churches have been taking up collections and sending monies to one another since our origins. Further, this collection was one in which slightly wealthier churches in urban areas sent resources to the mother church in Jerusalem as its members were experiencing famine.

This first instance of Christian churches taking up a relief collection to "remember the poor" has profound implications for the way the church should think about money today. The language Paul uses to describe this Jerusalem Collection in 2 Corinthians 8-9—including his avoidance of terms such as "stewardship" and "tithes"—is surer ground for thinking about how and why the church raises money in our own time.

The belief that the Jerusalem Collection was in response to a time of famine comes from both the Book of Acts as well as external historical evidence that Jerusalem underwent a period of famine around 45-47 CE. In the Book of Acts, we hear that Agabus the prophet "predicted by the Spirit that there would be a severe famine over all the world; and this took place during the reign of Claudius."[5] This famine prompted an international collection wherein "the disciples determined that according to their ability, each would send relief to the believers living in Judea" by "sending it to the elders by Barnabas and Saul."[6] This relief operation described in Acts closely resembles the arrangements in Paul's letters around this collection.[7]

Beyond the Book of Acts, Jewish historian Josephus (37-c.100 CE) describes a famine taking place in Jerusalem during this same period. These references to a famine around 45-47 by Acts and Josephus are further supported by studies that confirm famines occurred in Roman Palestine as regularly as every twentieth year, including in 25/24 BCE, 38/39 CE, 45/46 CE, as well as a local famine in Jerusalem in 69 CE.[8] The famine of 45-47 CE should therefore shape how we read Paul's writings on this collection for the saints in Jerusalem, for it helps us understand the urgency in his voice about this undertaking.

Even in the best of times, it is estimated that 75-90 percent of the Roman world lived close to subsistence level—near, at, or below—and struggled for survival and sustenance on a daily basis.[9] Life expectancy was somewhere between twenty and thirty years old, and nutritional deficiencies were widespread.[10] In times of natural disaster and political calamity, to be poor meant (and still means) being among the first victims.

To say, then, that Jerusalem experienced a famine around 45-47 is to speak of a period of severe hunger and desperation. Both the Old and New Testaments place famine alongside pestilence and sword as a "negative triad" that frequently occur together; famine was often the result of bad harvests compounded with political instability caused by warfare and disease.[11] As I describe in a later chapter, Basil of Caesarea spoke of famine in the fourth century as the principle human calamity, the "most miserable of deaths" being that of starvation.[12] As famine tightened its grip on his city of Caesarea, he described parents agonizing over the question of whether to sell their children into slavery so that the rest of the family might have a chance at survival.[13]

Paul's instructions to the Corinthians to "put aside and save whatever extra you earn" should be read with this sense of urgency and tragedy in mind, with an awareness of the desperation that famine had brought to Jerusalem. Although the Jerusalem Collection may very well have been an expression of unity between Paul and his Jerusalem counterparts and ecclesiastical unity between the Gentile assemblies and the Jerusalem mother church, it was also a relief collection taken up by churches who were not experiencing famine to give to a community in a desperate situation. We can look to much more recent history for an understanding of how a collection in a time of need can serve all those purposes.

In 2020, pestilence (COVID-19), political instability, a leadership vacuum, and unemployment gave rise to a shocking rise in hunger and desperation across the United States. This resulted in examples of collections being taken up among churches that resemble the Jerusalem effort in many ways. In May 2020, for example, the Episcopal Diocese of Northern Michigan built on its long-standing relationship with the bishop and people of Navajoland to create an online fundraiser called Indigi-aid to address growing hunger. In the end, the $40,000 that was raised went specifically to feeding ministries, and "a diverse group of church leaders and businesses nationwide offered logistical and delivery assistance, and volunteers...have traveled village to village to distribute the food."[14]

The Jerusalem Collection of 50 CE, like the Navajoland collection of 2020 CE, leveraged long-standing relationships, strengthened a sense of unity among churches experiencing different levels of hardship, and served as a concrete gift that helped to feed hungry people. This redistribution of wealth through relationships is, at its best, what the church has always done.

Having looked at the practical implications of the Jerusalem Collection, I want to turn to the theological language Paul employs in 2 Corinthians 8-9 to describe this effort.

First, it's important to name what Paul *doesn't* say. Nowhere in 2 Corinthians 8-9 does Paul refer to the collection as an act of stewardship or as a tithe. As I've written earlier, it is odd that one of the main money messages of mainline Christianity is that of prudent stewardship, particularly in light of the character of the unjust steward in Luke 16:1-13. So many money passages within the gospels see prudent stewardship as part of the problem and celebrate returning money to poor communities, holding big feasts, and practicing seemingly irresponsible generosity. Further, Paul does not refer to this collection as a tithe. While Paul certainly would have been aware of the tradition of the biblical tithe, he doesn't use the term to describe this early collection.

This aligns with the view of MacCulloch who describes the Christian tithe as a tenth-century development, one that came about with the emergence of the parish system. He argues it was only then that the biblical tithe was dusted off as a rationale for a new ecclesiastical tax on the laity:

> As parishes were organized, it became apparent that there were new sources of wealth for churchmen as well as for secular landlords. The parish system covering the countryside gave the church the chance to tax the new farming resources of Europe by demanding from its farmer-parishioners a scriptural tenth of agricultural produce, the tithe.[15]

In contrast, in 2 Corinthians 8-9, Paul speaks about money in ways that are subtler and more intriguing: he meditates on Christ's poverty, the grace of giving, the economic bondedness communities have for one another, and the question of fair balance between those who have abundance and those who are in desperate need.

This passage from 2 Corinthians 8-9 includes many references to grace—*charis*—including the grace of Jesus's becoming poor so that we might become richly blessed. Paul also speaks of *koinonia* to describe Christians' bondedness and financial fellowship with one another. Whereas *charis* is frequently translated as both "grace" and "privilege," *koinonia* has a wider range of meanings, from "fellowship"

to "collection" to a "collective" and "a sharing." Both terms appear in
the verses 2 Corinthians 8:2-4 where Paul describes how the churches
of Macedonia "overflowed in a wealth of generosity" and "voluntarily
gave according to their means, and even beyond their means" for
the "privilege [charis] of sharing [koinonia] in this ministry to the
saints."[16] Paul understands this "generous undertaking" as grounded
in the "generous act [charis] of our Lord Jesus Christ, that though he
was rich, yet for your sakes he became poor, so that by his poverty you
might become rich."[17] Paul implies that the Corinthian community
can follow in Jesus's generous act (charis) by becoming poorer for the
sake of the Jerusalem community experiencing famine.

Paul is characteristically blunt in urging the Corinthians to consider
their abundance, and he speaks of "fair balance" as the rationale for
this collection: "I do not mean that there should be relief for others
and pressure on you, but it is a question of a fair balance between
your present abundance and their need, so that their abundance may
be for your need, in order that there may be a fair balance."[18] And
though he tells the Corinthians that this is to be a "voluntary gift" and
"not an extortion," he also states that "the one who sows sparingly
will also reap sparingly, and the one who sows bountifully will also
reap bountifully."[19] It is within this context that we hear the (cloying)
phrase that so often appears as part of congregational fundraising
campaigns: "God loves a cheerful giver."[20]

Unfortunately, churches have often lifted lines from 2 Corinthians
8-9 with little regard to its original intention: a relief collection for
a community experiencing famine. This strikes me as an example
of how the church often conflates giving for relief with fundraising
for institutional growth. Paul, in contrast, is clearly referring to
the righteousness and generosity of those who give to people in a
desperate situation. In 2 Corinthians 9:9, Paul cites Psalm 112:9 when
he celebrates such generosity: "As it is written, 'He scatters abroad, he
gives to the poor; his righteousness endures forever.'" In the following
verses, he speaks explicitly about supplying "bread for food" to fulfill
"the needs of the saints."[21]

A more accurate interpretation of these chapters comes from
the middle of the fifth century, when Pope Leo the Great drew on
2 Corinthians 8-9 to urge wealthy Christians to donate to the poor
of Rome.[22] This series of five sermons, called De Collectis, was for an
annual collection taken up for the poor and sick in Rome.[23] In the

sermons, Pope Leo interweaves Paul's language on the grace of Jesus's becoming poor for our sake with the judgment language of Matthew 25:31-46:

> Rightly indeed do we see the person of our Lord Jesus Christ in the poor and needy. "Although he was rich," as the blessed Apostle said, "he became poor so that he might make us rich by his own poverty." So that his presence would not seem removed from us, he ordained the mystery of his glory and humility in such a way that we might nourish in his poor the very same one whom we worship as King and Lord in the majesty of the Father. Thereby are we "to be freed" from eternal condemnation "on that terrible day." "It is in return for our care of the poor so regarded" that we are to be admitted into fellowship with the kingdom of heaven.[24]

Beyond the language of grace, generosity, fair balance, and the powerful imagery of Jesus becoming poor for our sake, Paul also emphasizes what it means for Christians to be in *koinonia* with one another—a word frequently translated as fellowship. But "fellowship" is a watery translation of a much richer word meant to convey bondedness, community, and sharing.

Julien Ogereau of the University of Vienna has looked closely at 2 Corinthians 8-9 and notes that "fellowship" for *koinonia* is "often all too vague a word to capture fully what Paul is trying to convey." As a term drawn from the language of Roman administration and law, Ogereau contends that *koinonia* actually refers to "the idea of commonality, and by extension, of community on the basis of a common bond."[25] Elsewhere in Paul's letters, *koinonia* is used to describe "the sharing" in the body and blood of Christ at eucharist (1 Corinthians 10:16) and in Paul's desire "to share" in Christ's suffering (Philippians 3:10). *Koinonia* brims with complex meaning, and Ogereau argues that the term "evokes a certain sense of political unity and socioeconomic equality within the (global) Christ followers to an extent that is observed nowhere else in the New Testament except perhaps in Luke's summary description of the original Jerusalem community."[26]

That original Jerusalem community that Ogereu refers to is described in Acts 2:44 and 4:32-37. These passages have often been downplayed in American Christianity because of the way they mention holding all things in common, selling possessions and goods and distributing the proceeds to all, with no one claiming private ownership of any possessions.[27]

That the term *koinonia* springs forth from this frothy Christian collectivism has led more recent translators to reevaluate the nature of the material sharing that took place among early Christian communities. In 2017, in the provocatively titled Op-Ed for *The New York Times* "Are Christians Supposed to be Communists?", American philosopher David Bentley Hart wrote about the difficulties of translating *koinonia* in his new translation of the New Testament:

> I came to the conclusion that *koinonia* often refers to a precise set of practices within the early Christian communities, a special social arrangement—the very one described in Acts—that was integral to the new life in Christ. When, for instance, the Letter to the Hebrews instructs believers not to neglect *koinonia,* or the First Letter to Timothy exhorts them to become *koinonikoi,* this is no mere recommendation of personal generosity, but an invocation of a very specific form of communal life.

> As best we can tell, local churches in the Roman world of the apostolic age were essentially small communes, self-sustaining but also able to share resources with one another when need dictated. This delicate web of communes constituted a kind of counter-empire within the empire, one founded upon charity rather than force—or, better, a kingdom not of this world but present within the world nonetheless, encompassing a radically different understanding of society and property.[28]

An attempt to summarize Paul's theological rationale for the Jerusalem Collection might therefore sound like this: the joy and privilege of an assembly's generosity is ultimately rooted in God's grace of becoming poor for our sake. Yet, clearly, a need for fair balance between those with great wealth and those in poverty, hunger, and destitution remains. It is from a deeply rooted sense of bondedness and economic fellowship with one another (*koinonia*) that we have the grace and privilege (*charis*) of sharing our resources as a single community, particularly to alleviate the poverty and hunger of the most vulnerable members of the body of Christ. This spirit of grace and economic fellowship ground the striking examples of the wealthiest assembly members voluntarily selling their property and offering the proceeds to the wider collective. Through our generosity, we join Jesus in becoming poor for the sake of our siblings in Christ who are suffering.

Frankly, this understanding strikes me as a much more interesting—and faithful—starting point as we think about how voluntary collections of money are taken up in congregations. Further, recentering giving practices in this Jerusalem Collection/relief fund model raises important questions about the goal of these collections. It matters, for instance, that the first collection was not aimed at an organ restoration or the purchasing of vestments or for Tiffany stained-glass windows but rather on getting food to the desperately hungry—an urgent need that is still very much a part of our world today.

This model should help us reflect on the collections and annual fundraisers we hold in our congregations. Does the money we are raising benefit people in need? In many congregations, a gift to the annual fund will indeed do so, especially in congregations where a spirit of advocacy, charity, and service to "the least of these" is deeply engrained into the DNA of the assembly.

In contrast to the richness of the language of *charis* and *koinonia* and the overall framework laid out in 2 Corinthians 8-9, the language of prudent "stewardship" and "tithes" continues to strike me as painfully thin. Paul offers a rich chocolate cake in such language to the people of Corinth, yet we have replaced it with the milquetoast mindset of prudently stewarding institutional wealth. In 2 Corinthians, Paul talks about Christ entering into poverty, fair balance and sharing, and an interconnectedness among communities that includes financial responsibilities for caring for the poor. This is a far better basis for describing what the church is doing (or should be) when the congregation takes up collections and redistributes money from those with abundance to those in need.

Discussion Questions

Written around 50 CE, Paul's descriptions of the Jerusalem Collection are among the earliest historical references to Christian assemblies taking up a relief collection in the New Testament. This suggests that the practice of collecting and sending monies to other Christian assemblies who are experiencing hunger or other disasters is part of what it means to be in a network of Christian assemblies. How might your church take up a collection to send to communities in greater need during times of natural disaster? How might organizations such as Episcopal Relief & Development be a resource in this?

The language of 2 Corinthians 8-9 holds profound significance for how individuals and faith communities think about money. Paul urges the Corinthians to give to the collection by pointing to how Christ became poor for our sake so that we might have the grace and privilege (*charis*) of sharing our resources. He appeals to a sense of economic fellowship and financial bondedness (*koinonia*) with one another to collect and send resources to those in need. As members of a Christian community, what do you think of Paul's description of being in economic fellowship with one another?

This first collection reveals something that remains true today: namely, that many of the church structures that we might take for granted (dioceses, church buildings, clergy) can become essential parts of a distribution network in times of desperation and need. A prime example is the Indigi-Aid collection between the Diocese of Northern Michigan and Navajoland. How might church structures be improved so as to become better partners in times of disaster?

A Next Step

One of the "crown jewels" of the Episcopal Church is Episcopal Relief & Development, originally called the Presiding Bishop's Fund for World Relief when it was founded in the 1940s to support refugees fleeing war-torn Europe. In some respects, Episcopal Relief & Development's work is akin to the Jerusalem Collection on a global scale insomuch as it leverages long-standing and authentic relationships with partners both in the United States and across the Anglican Communion to direct resources to areas that are in the most need, including during times of natural disaster. To employ Paul's language, churches have before them the grace and privilege (*charis*) of giving to an organization that thoughtfully leverages our interconnectedness as a communion (*koinonia*) to help address need. One practical way of living out Paul's Jerusalem Collection today is by making regular contributions.

Another approach is to follow the example of the middle of the fifth century, when Pope Leo the Great drew on 2 Corinthians 8-9 to establish an annual collection taken up for the poor and sick in the city of Rome.[29] Dioceses and individual congregations can create a focused annual fundraising campaign, one aimed at supporting the most vulnerable populations in one's community. Following Paul's language, this can be an invitation for congregants to consider questions of "fair balance" and to live into the sense of *koinonia*—the financial interconnectedness to one another.

Endnotes

1 1 Corinthians 16:2-4.

2 1 Corinthians 16:1-4.

3 Ze'ev Safrai and Peter J. Tomson, "Paul's 'Collection for the Saints' (2 Cor 8–9) and Financial Support of Leaders in Early Christianity and Judaism," in *Second Corinthians in the Perspective of Late Second Temple Judaism*, ed. Reimund Bieringer, Emmanuel Nathan, Didier Pollefeyt, and Peter J Tomson (Netherlands: Koninklijke Brill, 2014).

4 Julien M. Ogereau, "The Jerusalem Collection as Κοινωνία: Paul's Global Politics of Socio-Economic Equality and Solidarity," in *New Testament Studies*, ed. Simon Gathercole, Vol. 58, No. 3 (2012): 362.

5 Acts 11:28.

6 Acts 11:29-30.

7 Acts 11:27-30, New Oxford Annotated Bible, Third Edition.

8 Jensen, "Climate, Droughts, Wars, and Famines in Galilee as a Background for Understanding the Historical Jesus," 323.

9 Rhee, *Loving the Poor, Saving the Rich*, 5, 11.

10 Atkins and Osborne, *Poverty in the Roman World*, 4.

11 Jensen, "Climate, Droughts, Wars, and Famines in Galilee as a Background for Understanding the Historical Jesus," 319-320.

12 "Homily 8: In Time of Famine and Drought," *Wealth and Poverty in Early Christianity*, ed. Helen Rhee, (Minneapolis, Minnesota: Fortress Press, 2017), 66.

13 "Homily 6: I Will Pull Down My Barns," 59.

14 David Paulsen, "Church's Grassroots Efforts Help Navajoland Feed Families Impacted by COVID-19 Outbreak," Episcopal News Service, May 14, 2020.

15 MacCulloch, *Christianity*, 369.

16 Commentary on 2 Corinthians Chapters 8-9, New Oxford Annotated Bible, Third Edition.

17 2 Corinthians 8:9.

18 2 Corinthians 8:13-15.

19 2 Corinthians 9:5-6.

20 2 Corinthians 9:7.

21 2 Corinthians 9:10, 12.

22 Safrai and Tomson, "Paul's 'Collection for the Saints' (2 Cor 8–9) and Financial Support of Leaders in Early Christianity and Judaism."

23 "Saint Leo the Great," in *Sermons: The Fathers of the Church*, ed. Jane Patricia Freeland and Agnes Josephine Conway (Washington, D.C.: Catholic University of America Press, 1995), 34.

24 "Saint Leo the Great," *Sermons: The Fathers of the Church*, ed. Freeland and Conway.

25 Ogereau, "The Jerusalem Collection as Κοινωνία", 371-372.

26 Ogereau, "The Jerusalem Collection as Κοινωνία", 372.

27 A more recent example of how *koinonia* is countercultural to American Christianity can be seen in Koinonia Farm, an interracial farming community founded in 1957 in southern Georgia. Such *koinonia* was threatened by the Klu Klux Klan and was left unprotected on account of being considered "race mixers" and Communists in that period of American history. (Loughery and Randolph, *Dorothy Day*, 270).

28 David Bentley Hart, "Are Christians Supposed to be Communists?" *The New York Times*, November 4, 2017.

29 "Saint Leo the Great," *Sermons: The Fathers of the Church*, ed. Freeland and Conway, 34.

8 Justin Martyr's Liturgy of Word, Table, and Koinonia

As I hope has become clear by now, I believe the Lord's Supper has profound socioeconomic implications. After all, the first historical record of the words of institution in 1 Corinthians 11 occur as part of Paul's broader chastising of the Corinthian community for separating themselves out by class when it came time for the Lord's Supper. Paul's fury suggests that no matter how widely accepted status-specific gatherings were nor how forceful the lure of caste divisions remain in our own time, the Lord's Supper is supposed to be a time of coming together across socioeconomic divisions. Indeed, part of what it means to "discern the body" in Paul's language is to see the full body, including its most vulnerable members, gathered together at the table.

This vision of the Lord's Supper as a meal in which caste divisions are broken down and both the poor and rich, the hungry and full, gather for a shared meal, continued to challenge the emerging church. Justin Martyr, an early Christian apologist and philosopher, followed upon Paul's vision with his second-century description of a Sunday evening eucharist.

Justin Martyr's *First Apology*, written about one hundred years after Paul's letter to the Corinthians, in approximately 155 CE, was addressed to the Roman Emperor Antoninus Pius and was composed with the threat of violent persecution against Christians flickering in the background. Justin included in this apology a general outline of how Christians assembled for worship in the second century. While not exactly a worship bulletin preserved in amber, Justin's description is a detailed and fascinating account of how second-century Christians gathered and worshipped.

Justin's description of this gathering has been extensively studied for the way it reveals how some early Christians sequenced their worship along a word and meal pattern. His description also reveals how attuned these assemblies were to distinctions between the rich and poor and the ways in which the early church emphasized the socioeconomic dimension of the eucharist. In a chapter that begins with "Those who have the means help all those who are in want, and we continually meet together," Justin describes how the Christians assembled on a Sunday, then heard a reading from "the writings of the prophets," followed by exhortation from the presider. After a period of prayer, the service proceeded to a meal of bread, wine, and water with the remaining portions taken by deacons to those who could not be present. Finally, the community took up a collection given to the presider specifically for aid to the poor among the assembly. Justin concludes his description on the role of the presider as one who "aids orphans and widows, those who are in want through disease or through another cause, those who are in prison, and foreigners who are sojourning here. In short, the presider is a guardian to all those who are in need."[1]

Justin emphasizes the presider as guardian and describes how food was sent to those who could not be present. Together with the emphasis he places on the assembly as a space where those with means and those in want came together, Justin articulates the understanding that the Lord's Supper was intended to cross socioeconomic divides and serve the needs of the most vulnerable. Indeed, the meal was not just religiously symbolic; it generated food and money to aid to the poor.

Working as I do in a seminary setting, with people who are being formed for the priesthood, this ancient vision of the priest as an exhorter, as one who presides at the Lord's Supper and who serves as a guardian to those in need, strikes me as a profound understanding of priestly vocational identity worth resurfacing. Justin's description of the role of the presider as "guardian to all those who are in need"— including to "orphans and widows, those who are in want through disease or through another cause, those who are in prison, and foreigners who are sojourning here"—shows not only the extent to which such groups made up an integral part of the community but also an early understanding of the presider's vocational identity as outward-facing. The presider offers a sacramental presence in the liturgy as well as a prophetic and service-oriented one, a guardian for those on the margins of society.

In addition, one liturgical scholar, Gordon Lathrop, has suggested that this early liturgy actually has three, not just two, focal points: 1. word and exhortation, 2. the meal at table, 3. a collection for the poor.[2] This is in contrast to contemporary Christianity's customary pattern of just two focal points of word and table. Whatever happened to that third? Lathrop's observation offers many possibilities for liturgical renewal and suggests an opportunity to make a collection for the poor a permanent part of the eucharistic liturgy. Doing so would reconnect our contemporary Lord's Supper service with the threefold focus we see in Justin Martyr's description of a Sunday worship service attuned to the needs of the most vulnerable members of the community.

To understand Justin's description of the Lord's Supper, it's helpful to explore his journey of faith. Justin Martyr (100-165) was born in Flavia Neapolis, Samaria, in a Greek-speaking town in Judea of the Roman Empire. Along his path to Christianity, Justin journeyed from Stoicism to Aristotelianism to Platonism, eventually encountering an old man near the Ephesus seashore who told him of the Hebrew prophets who had foretold Christ.[3] His past explorations of Greek philosophy and conversion to Christianity led Justin to create a synthesis of these many schools of thought, an effort neatly symbolized by his continuing to wear the philosopher's cloak even after his conversion.

A layman, Justin is considered the most important Christian apologist of the second century and the first of whose written works significant parts are extant. These include his two *Apologies* and the *Dialogue*.[4] Justin is especially remembered for his synthesis of Platonism and John's Gospel's use of the term *Logos*, arguing that it was through the divine *Logos* that God prepared the way for his final revelation in Christ: "For all writers were able to see the truth darkly, on account of the implanted seed of the *Logos* which was grafted into them."[5]

Justin's theology of the *logos spermatikos* sought to fuse Platonist philosophy and Christian claims about Jesus's divinity. He did this work at a time when violence against Christians, while sporadic rather than systematized, was compelling leaders to demonstrate how Christianity represented continuity with—rather than opposition to—the Roman Empire.[6] In the end, however, Justin was not successful in convincing the Roman authorities. Approximately a decade after he wrote the *First Apology*, Justin was accused of being a Christian before the Roman prefect Junius Rusticus, and he and several students met a grisly end in 165 CE.[7]

The beheading of Justin and his students by Roman imperial authorities reflects how the empire viewed Christianity as a growing nuisance. While there were a variety of reasons for this, including secrecy and a refusal to worship the emperor, Roman historian Mary Beard notes that, fundamentally, Christianity represented a challenge to Roman values on wealth and poverty.

Although Christians represented a relatively small percentage of the population—approximately 200,000 in an empire-wide population of 50-60 million—they provoked the ire and frustration of many Romans. According to Beard, the Romans regularly incorporated the gods of their subjugated peoples into a diverse pantheon, and they understood gods to be rooted in a specific region (Isis from Egypt, the Jewish god from Judea, Mithras from Persia). Conversely, Christians were regarded as secretive, stubbornly monotheistic, and exclusive. Worse still, Christians claimed their faith was universal as opposed to geographically bound, and they were constantly seeking new adherents. Christians also provocatively appropriated terms from Rome's imperial theology, such as the "Good News" of Augustus's birth, to the annoyance of traditional-minded Romans. Further, their preaching "threatened to overturn the most fundamental Greco-Roman assumptions about the nature of the world and of the people within it: that poverty, for example, was good; or that the body was to be tamed or rejected rather than cared for."[8]

On issues of wealth and poverty, Beard describes a wide gulf between traditional Roman values and the great reversal that Jesus of Nazareth preached in both words and through his interactions with the rich and poor:

What all would have agreed, both rich and poor, was that to be rich was a desirable state, that poverty was to be avoided if you possibly could. Just as the ambition of Roman slaves was usually to gain freedom for themselves, not to abolish slavery as an institution, so the ambitions of the poor were not radically to reconfigure the social order but to find a place for themselves nearer the top of the hierarchy of wealth.... The idea that the rich man might have a problem entering the kingdom of heaven would have seemed as preposterous to those hanging out in our Ostian bar as to the plutocrat in his mansion.[9]

Jesus's vision of reversal, his critique of wealth and the rich, and the understanding of the eucharist as a time that erased caste divisions represented a major challenge to Roman values. Amid this broader clash in practices and values, Justin took up writing, perhaps nervously, to the Roman Emperor Antoninus Pius. Justin employed a standard Roman legal petition to address the main criticisms of Christianity. In his petition, Justin expounded on Christianity's compatibility with Greek philosophy and described the worship practices of the Christian assembly. In the course of his letter, Justin offered one of the earliest descriptions of how Christians assembled on Sundays.

Beginning with the observation that in the Christian assembly, "those who have the means help all those who are in want," Justin describes how the community gathered "on the day named after the sun" wherein "records of the apostles or the writings of the prophets are read for as long as there is time" followed by a discourse from the presider who "admonishes and invites us into the pattern of these good things." After a period of prayer which followed the presider's exhortation, the assembly proceeded to the simple meal. Justin writes:

And, as we said before, when we have concluded the prayer, bread is set out to eat, together with wine and water. The presider likewise offers up prayer and thanksgiving, as much as he can, and the people sing out their assent saying the amen. There is a distribution of the things over which thanks have been said and each person participates, and these things are sent by the deacons to those who are not present.[10]

Just a few sentences into this chapter, then, Justin already emphasizes that those with means and those in want come together to share a meal and that deacons are charged with bringing a remaining portion to those who are not able to be present. Who were those members of the community who were not able to make it? Were they ill? Were they in prison? This goes left unsaid. What follows the focal points of word and table is the taking up of a collection to aid the poor:

> Those who are prosperous and who desire to do so, give what they wish, according to each one's own choice, and the collection is deposited with the presider. He aids orphans and widows, those who are in want through disease or through another cause, those who are in prison, and foreigners who are sojourning here. In short, the presider is a guardian to all those who are in need.[11]

One of the many reasons this is such a profoundly moving—even beautiful—text is that it's immediately recognizable as similar to what many churches do today. Even 2,000 years later, one can witness Justin's "pattern of these good things." It is exciting, then, to consider how this could be more so, perhaps by bringing back a third focal point explicitly meant as aid to the most vulnerable members of the community.

Justin Martyr's *First Apology* offers clues to how the eucharistic liturgy developed in the early church, especially with the evolution of what day and time worship took place as well as the sequencing of the liturgy. In *Word and Table: The Origins of a Liturgical Sequence*, early Christian liturgical scholar Charles Cosgrove notes that second-century Christians organized their community meals along the same lines as established patterns in Greco-Roman dining, although they adapted these patterns to their own needs.

After comparing various examples of early Christian literature that describe a variety of different sequences, Cosgrove concludes that "(1) an evening meal was the primary church gathering in the early period, eventually being replaced by a morning service as the main eucharistic meeting; and (2) a predominantly table-word pattern was at some point eclipsed by a predominantly word-table sequence."[12]

Surprisingly enough, this later move toward word followed by table may have been meant to ensure people were still sober during the preaching/exhortation part of the service, something that reflects the fact that these Lord's Suppers were full meals with wine.[13] The pattern described in the *First Apology*, then, is an early example of the word-table sequencing that would ultimately prevail, although it is also likely that the service Justin described occurred in the evening.

As important as this discussion on sequencing is, however, Cosgrove's assessment left out the service's remarkably close connection to the poor, including a focus on the ritualized collection following the meal for the most vulnerable members of the community. Liturgical scholar Gordon Lathrop notes that, "Among the many remarkable features of this text is the presentation of the Sunday assembly as the most focused instance of the Christian community's devotion both to thanksgiving at meals and to care for the poor. Indeed, the two seem to be closely related."[14] Unlike Cosgrove, Lathrop observes a threefold pattern that proceeds from word and exhortation to a shared meal to a collection for the poor. "Instead of ignoring the poor while religiously eating to the full (1 Corinthians 11:21-22), the community now, at least according to its ideals, receives the ritual part of the meal and gives most of the food away."[15] The Lord's Supper quite literally generated monies and food, which were redistributed to the most vulnerable members of the assembly.

Further, in contrast to some contemporary practices primarily aimed at the poor outside church's walls—as suggested by the term "outreach"—Justin describes a collection and distribution aimed at the most vulnerable members who were part of the worshiping assembly. As I will discuss in the next chapter, one of the most remarkable aspects of these early assemblies is how they established a safety net for members, one that seems to have extended to assisting with the cost of burials when members died. In the case of Justin's community, he writes that the collection took place after the shared meal and possibly constituted the final liturgical action, a third focal point, before he launches into an explanation about why the assembly took place on the day of the sun.

Justin's description urges Christian communities to ask questions about how they gather today. Given the significant attention that Justin paid to diminishing distinctions between "those with means" and "those in want," I wonder how and if this same spirit is reflected in our worshiping assemblies. As I noted in an earlier chapter, I'm struck by how many mainline congregations were built and have remained in wealthy enclaves, reflecting a preferential option for wealth and an intentional separation from the marginalized. Amidst this separation, the eucharist offers an opportunity to embody the coming together of rich and poor for a common meal.

Justin's description of the early church gatherings sets my imagination afire. What would it be like to return to a threefold ordo of worship, one that proceeds from word to table to collection for the poor? Within the Episcopal tradition, the Book of Common Prayer's *Order for Celebrating the Holy Eucharist* offers creative license for congregations to immediately develop a weekday eucharist that reflects the threefold order found in Justin Martyr's *First Apology*.[16] And, to be clear, I'm not suggesting that the collection for the poor replace the current offering of monies embedded in the table portion of the service. The theological underpinning of that collection is very different—so much so, in fact, that the Book of Common Prayer's various offertory sentences make no reference to the poor whatsoever.[17]

This represents an opportunity because offertory sentences can urge reflection on the sources of wealth offered to God. One particularly significant passage comes from Ecclesiasticus: "If one sacrifices ill-gotten goods, the offering is blemished; the gifts of the lawless are not acceptable," and "Like one who kills a son before his father's eyes is the person who offers a sacrifice from the property of the poor" (Ecclesiasticus 34:21 and 24).

These passages from Ecclesiasticus are especially important to those of us who live in the Americas, as they are the scriptural lines that resulted in the repentance and transformation of the priest Bartolomé de las Casas. Robert Goizueta writes of this moment,

> As he read [these passages], las Casas saw himself mirrored in and challenged by those words: he was preparing to offer to God bread and wine produced by his own Indian slaves. What was thus ostensibly an act of Christian worship was, in fact, an act of idolatry; he was purporting to worship the God

of Jesus Christ while, in reality, worshiping a god of violence and destruction, a god who accepted the fruit of exploited human labor.[18]

Bartolomé de Las Casas would go on to become a chronicler of the atrocities committed against the indigenous and would be given the title of "Defender of the Indians." His conversion is all the more significant when one considers that he began his journey as an *encomendero*, a slaveholder, and that it was a meditation on the exploitative sources of gifts offered to God that led to his transformation. What would it sound like for an offertory sentence or hymn that references these passages that are so important to the story of Christianity on this continent?

Returning to Justin's description of the service, I also want to point out that whereas the collection during the table portion of our eucharist services typically goes toward the general needs of the church (which may include monies for the poor), Justin's collection is far more focused and explicit in that it is intended solely for addressing the hunger and wider needs of the community's most vulnerable members. Rewriting the offertory sentences would help connect this moment in the liturgy to the scriptural teaching on the sources of wealth offered to God. In addition, restoring the collection described by Justin would be faithful to one of the earliest outlines of how Christian assemblies gathered, fulfilling the ancient role of Christians providing direct aid to the poor and helping communities focus on the needs of the most vulnerable members of its community on a more regular basis.

Discussion Questions

Justin Martyr describes the presider's role as one who "aids orphans and widows, those who are in want through disease or through another cause, those who are in prison, and foreigners who are sojourning here. In short, the presider is a guardian to all those who are in need."[19] What do you think of this description of what it means to be a priest and presider at the Lord's Supper? What would it mean for an entire assembly to understand itself as guardians of all in need?

Liturgical scholar Gordon Lathrop makes the provocative claim that this earliest extant description of the liturgy of the Lord's Supper contains a threefold ordo of worship, one that proceeds from word to table to collection for the poor. Can you imagine being a part of a community whose eucharistic liturgy includes such a threefold focus?

The collection that Justin Martyr describes isn't for "outreach." It doesn't appear to be a collection for a group outside the church but rather for the most vulnerable members within the assembly itself. What does this tell you about who made up the first assemblies? How does this change your understanding of the purpose of this collection? How might this apply to your own community?

Many eucharistic liturgies contain a collection of money as part of the table portion of the service. In the Episcopal tradition, the offertory sentences within the Book of Common Prayer employ the language of sacrifice to describe what is taking place at this moment in the liturgy. There is no mention of the poor. Should the poor be mentioned in light of the biblical passage that transformed the life of Bartolomé de las Casas (Ecclesiasticus 34:21 and 24)? How is this collection similar to and different from what Justin Martyr describes?

A Next Step

Identify a set period of time or perhaps a liturgical season—Advent or Lent, for example—to test out instituting a second collection that is exclusively for helping the most vulnerable members of the community. After the period is completed, reflect on what happened as a result of this collection. What did people think and say about it? Did overall giving increase or decrease? Could you imagine making a second collection a permanent part of your regular Sunday service?

Draw on language from Justin Martyr's *First Apology* to write a prayer that explains what the community is doing in this second collection. For example, "Called to be 'guardians of all in need', we make this offering to you, O Christ, who meets us in the hungry, the thirsty, the refugee, those needing clothes, the sick, and the imprisoned."[20]

Endnotes

1 "1 Apology 67," *Holy Things: A Liturgical Theology*, ed. Gordon W. Lathrop (Minneapolis, Minnesota: Fortress Press, 1998), 45.

2 "1 Apology 67," 45.

3 MacCullough, *Christianity*, 142.

4 Attwater and John, "Justin, Martyr," in *The Penguin Dictionary of Saints* (New York: Penguin, 1996), 204-205.

5 Alister E. McGrath, *Christian Theology: An Introduction* (Hoboken, New Jersey: Wiley-Blackwell, 2016) 16.

6 Mary Beard, *SPQR: A History of Ancient Rome* (New York City: Liveright, 2016), 518.

7 Tobias Georges, "Justin Martyr," in *Brill Encyclopedia of Early Christianity Online*, ed. David G. Hunter, Paul J.J. van Geest, and Bert Jan Lietaert Peerbolte.

8 Beard, *SPQR*, 516.

9 Beard, *SPQR* 472.

10 "1 Apology 67," *Holy Things*, ed. Lathrop, 45.

11 "1 Apology 67," *Holy Things*, ed. Lathrop, 45.

12 Charles Cosgrove, "Word and Table: The Origins of a Liturgical Sequence," *Vigiliae Christianae*, Vol. 74 (2020): 372.

13 Cosgrove, "Word and Table," 365.

14 "1 Apology 67," *Holy Things*, ed. Lathrop, 45.

15 "1 Apology 67," *Holy Things*, ed. Lathrop, 45.

16 The Book of Common Prayer, 400.

17 The Book of Common Prayer, 343. General Convention recently authorized Rite III for Sunday use as long as the diocesan bishop permits it.

18 *The Wiley Blackwell Companion to Political Theology*, Second Edition, ed. William T. Cavanaugh and Peter Manley Scott (Hoboken, New Jersey: John Wiley & Sons Ltd, 2019), 287.

19 "1 Apology 67," *Holy Things*, Lathrop, 45.

20 Drawn from both "1 Apology" and the categories of vulnerable groups depicted in Matthew 25:40-45.

9 Christianity as a Burial and Mutual Aid Society

On December 31, 2019, the government in Wuhan, China, alerted the world that health authorities were treating dozens of cases of pneumonia of an unknown cause. By January 21, a man in Washington state along with people in Japan, South Korea, and Thailand, were among the first confirmed cases of this new virus outside mainland China. The first US death was reported in late February, and by March 26, 2020, the United States was leading the world in both confirmed cases and deaths. By May 27, just four months after the first confirmed case in the US, COVID-19-related US deaths surpassed the grim milestone of its first 100,000.[1]

Safely sheltered and able to work from home, I and many others were struck by the profound differences in experiences between those who were inconvenienced and those who were completely devastated by this pandemic. My husband and I were able to begin social isolating in our one-bedroom apartment in March and watched with dread as New York City's death toll approached and then surpassed 10,000 in mid-April.[2] We stayed inside, wore masks, washed our hands, and wiped down surfaces. We read and listened to too much news. We drank too much wine. I kept my outings limited to long walks.

One evening in May, I leashed up my dog and put in my earbuds to listen to a podcast. For the past few weeks, my daily route had involved walking past the refrigerated morgue trucks parked just outside Brooklyn Hospital on my way to Fort Greene Park, a disturbing reminder of this time of overflowing death. The podcast episode I was listening to was entitled "Why Is the

Pandemic Killing So Many Black Americans?" In it, journalist Linda Villarosa refuted the notion of COVID-19 as the great equalizer.

Villarosa's reporting confirmed what had been painfully obvious for a while now. By May in New York, it was clear that infection and mortality rates were much higher for those who could not socially isolate and that the pandemic exacerbated the divides of race and poverty. The majority of people who were becoming infected and dying were essential workers, people living in crowded apartments, and those living in homeless shelters—that is, anyone who couldn't afford to isolate, stay at home, or flee the city.

On my walks, I reflected on how COVID-19 exposed New York City's caste system in ways similar to what happened amidst natural disasters in Ancient Rome. Contrary to how Pompeii is often presented, for example, archeological evidence reveals that the wealthy had already fled the city by the time the volcano erupted, and so it was the poor and enslaved who were left behind to take care of properties. It is their bodies who are cast in ash, including a disproportionate number of people wearing the broad belt of the enslaved.[3] Similarly, we now know that 420,000-plus people from the wealthiest zip codes fled New York City during the pandemic to (oftentimes newly purchased) second homes even as the "coronavirus tore through low-income neighborhoods, infected immigrants and essential workers unable to stay home, and disproportionately killed Black and Latino people, especially those with underlying health conditions."[4]

The resulting disparities in outcomes are startling. By July 2021, *The New York Times* reported that while national life expectancy experienced the steepest decline since World War II, these declines differed greatly along the lines of race and ethnicity: "From 2019 to 2020, Hispanic people experienced the greatest drop in life expectancy—three years—and Black Americans saw a decrease of 2.9 years."[5] Such declines can largely be attributed to the way race and poverty are intertwined in this country. Even as the wealthy escaped the city, "Black and Hispanic Americans were more likely to be employed in risky, public-facing jobs during the pandemic—bus drivers, restaurant cooks, sanitation workers—rather than working on laptops from the relative safety of their homes," with far more Black and Hispanic Americans relying on public transportation and living in intergenerational homes.[6]

The pandemic was especially deadly for those with no place to lay their head. Over the course of that first year of the pandemic, my colleague, the Rev. Dr. Kelly Brown Douglas, and I attended virtual memorial services for homeless New Yorkers who died of COVID-19, including many who died before their names were known. At one service, the calling out of real names was separated by approximately ten or so Jane and John Does. These deaths were largely the result of the inability of homeless people to self-isolate in New York's overcrowded shelter systems, places where more than 60,000 people, including 20,000 children, faced the early months of the pandemic. Between May and August 2020, the mortality rate from COVID-19 for homeless New Yorkers was 78 percent higher than for the average New Yorker.[7]

A July 2020 investigation by *The New York Times* also highlighted how the lack of access to private health insurance made COVID-19 especially dangerous for the poor. Disparities in mortality rates frequently reflected the vast difference in care received at private medical centers in Manhattan versus the under-resourced public hospitals in outer boroughs like Queens, the borough that had the most coronavirus cases and the fewest hospitals to care for patients. The difference in ICU mortality rates—1 in 10 in some prestigious medical centers versus 1 in 3 at community hospitals outside of Manhattan—frequently came down to differences in levels of staffing. People with private insurance were cared for in hospitals that had more nurses and medical care; in contrast, hospitals serving low-income areas had so many people in intensive care, with so few staff and inadequate sedatives, that some low-income patients did not receive even the most basic of treatments, like being turned onto their stomach. "The technique, called proning, has helped many patients breathe, but because it requires several workers to keep IV lines untangled, some safety-net hospitals have been unable to provide it."[8]

Amidst the anxiety of rising infection rates and death count, it was easy, at times, to get lost in the trends and numbers and forget that each of these figures represented a person with dignity and loved ones. These were not simply Jane and John Does but people with real names, lives, and personal histories—each made in the image of God.

This is partly why Villarosa's voice on the podcast stood out to me at the time. The interview began with Villarosa telling the story of one man, Cornell Charles, who went by Dickey with his friends and family. Charles was a member of the New Orleans's Zulu Club and one of several members who contracted COVID-19 after attending the Zulu Club's annual Governor's Ball in late February. In telling this tragic story, Villarosa comments on the origins of the Zulu Club as one of New Orleans's oldest burial societies and noted the tragic irony of how the self-isolation guidelines meant this burial society wasn't able to honor the death of its multiple members who had died in the pandemic. The entire episode on the racial disparities in mortality rates for COVID-19 is incredibly powerful, and Villarosa's reporting movingly conveys the tragedy of Charles's death and the loss his passing represented to the New Orleans's community.

Villarosa's story stayed with me for a long time, disquieting in its portrayal of how the pandemic was playing out along the lines of race and poverty. Further, her mentioning of the Zulu Club's origins as a burial club eventually reminded me of one of the strangest details about Christianity's origins: namely, that the early Christian assemblies were understood by non-Christians to be burial clubs. Diarmaid MacCulloch puts this succinctly in *Christianity: The First Three Thousand Years*. He writes that in the first and second century, "the first official status for a Christian Church community was registration as a burial club" and that one of the most frequent and normal interactions between a Christian and a Roman official involved bureaucratic transactions around cemeteries.[9]

This may strike some as a bizarre but ultimately frivolous detail about Christianity's origin story. And yet, as a church comprised mainly of the poor in the first and second centuries, death was all around the women, immigrants, and slaves who filled the ranks of early Christians. Among these were the so-called "essential workers" of their time—slaves, immigrants, and day laborers whose work was so essential that their lives were deemed expendable.

In these burial clubs, the practices of *koinonia*—economic bondedness and sharing—were very much alive. Second-century descriptions of Christian assemblies called them local clubs or associations that had a common chest, offered some basic aid for members in need, and were closely involved in offering burials for their members. They served as bulwarks, then, against the vicissitudes and dangers of a life of poverty.

This brings us to a point that merits deeper reflection from faith leaders today—namely, in the early days of the church, there were concrete, practical benefits for the vulnerable people who belonged to such assemblies. The notion of material benefits for members occasionally makes some faith leaders uneasy, including those who see such practical benefits as parroting gym memberships, for example— or worse, yet another example of entitlements. They argue that the only "benefit" the church should offer is the opportunity to draw nearer to a transcendent God through worship in community. Yet these burial societies suggest an ancient, practical aspect to Christian assembly membership, for these early assemblies offered a limited safety net and possibly even a rudimentary form of life insurance, where membership and dues helped to defray costs associated with burial and offered some protection for one's family in case of injury or death. This speaks to the way *koinonia*—economic bondedness and sharing—characterized these early assemblies for whom "salvation" was as much about the kingdom of God on earth as it was in heaven.

Interestingly, there have been other moments in history when Christian burial societies and their material benefits have flourished, including in nineteenth- and twentieth-century America. This is where this exploration of Christianity's origin story intersects with Charles's membership in the Zulu Club in New Orleans. This Zulu Club had its beginnings in the rise of Black benevolent aid and burial societies that flourished from the end of slavery through the Jim Crow era, clubs that frankly sound a lot like what early Christians were up to in those first and second centuries. In 1909, during the Second Slavery of Jim Crow in which Black communities were stripped of the wealth they had accumulated since the end of slavery, members of the Black community in New Orleans pooled resources together to be able to offer members some measure of assurance (insurance?) that their family members would be taken care of if they died, pledging to bury members in a dignified manner.[10] These clubs—many of which grew out of Black churches—expanded rapidly amidst extreme poverty, exploitation, and vicious persecution, factors that call to mind some of the circumstances of those early Christians.

Indeed, the similarities between these ancient burial clubs and the benevolent aid and burial societies of the late nineteenth and twentieth century were so striking that in writing this chapter, I frequently had to check and recheck my notes to be sure that I was referring to the right millennium. As we consider how COVID-19 has devastated Black and Latino communities, we would do well to revisit the history of Christian assemblies as burial and mutual aid societies as inspiration for what it means to be church among some of the most vulnerable communities today.

Telling the story of Christian burial societies requires returning to the fraught relationship between early Christians and the Roman empire. Around 112 CE, the Roman governor Pliny the Younger wrote what is considered to be the first known pagan reference to Christians who were gathering in his region of Bithynia and Pontus, in what is now modern-day Turkey. In a letter addressed to the Roman Emperor Trajan, the governor Pliny described how he was conducting trials of suspected Christians and sought counsel from the emperor on how they should be treated.[11] Pliny writes that he had banned Christians from gathering in *hetaeria*, a pejorative word for associations.[12] In Trajan's reply to Pliny the Younger, the emperor used the same term of *hetaeria* to convey broader imperial anxiety about how such associations had a tendency to become political clubs and factions, "a natural breeding ground for grumbling about political affairs."[13]

The term *hetaeria* had similarly negative connotations to words like political faction or sect. The fact that Christians in this region were prohibited from gathering in this way and that both a governor and emperor saw these Christian gatherings as troublesome to the smooth administrative functioning of the Roman empire speaks volumes about the church's early, oppositional relationship to imperial power. Christians were a suspect minority group, a standoffish and secretive sect making disturbing claims about the body, wealth, and poverty. They prohibited members from serving in the Roman army and were generally seen as up to no good.

Even so, some Christians were already making strenuous efforts to smooth over the relationship between Christians and imperial leadership. In his *Apologeticum* from the late second century, the North African theologian Tertullian denied the notion that Christians were *hetaeria* and argued that they should instead be treated like other harmless, legal associations and benefits societies that were found across the Roman Empire.[14]

Tertullian described Christian gatherings in terms that would have been familiar and nonthreatening to imperial authorities. Christian assemblies were like other clubs and associations across the Roman empire, he argued. Christians met for a common meal, had an initiation rite, and elected members to serve as officers and administrators. Importantly, such Christian associations "also had a common chest drawn from the contributions of members, looked out for the needs of its members, provided for a decent burial, and in some cities had its own burial grounds."[15] They were, then, hardly the threatening factions or sects they were purported to be but more like the *collegia funeratica* and other forms of clubs that were prevalent in second-century Rome.[16]

Amid all the murkiness around how Christians in this period were organizing themselves, it appears, then, that "the first official status for a Christian church community was registration as a burial club."[17] This is important as the association between Christianity and all-things-death-and-burial would become a refrain through the fourth century. For instance, the Roman Emperor Constantine's interest in the new faith had to do with both the religion's connection to military victory as well as to Christianity's long association with burials and death.[18] As Diarmaid McCullough wrote, "The Emperor's generosity showed a lively awareness that the Christian religion (and therefore presumably its God) had long paid particular attention to providing properly for burial."[19] Subsequently, Constantine would fund the building of six funeral churches in Rome as gifts to his Christian subjects, sites that accommodated Christians in both life and death.

The Roman catacombs of the late second century are further evidence of this strong connection between early Christians and their close association with death and burial practices. While the catacombs have often been presented as refuges for Christians amidst Roman persecution, the actual history of the catacombs is both less romantic and yet more intriguing, particularly as it offers visual clues into the early church's evolving relationship to wealth, status, and power.

The earliest of the burial sites in the Christian catacombs were simply the fruit of Christians operating like *collegia funeratica*, purchasing and creating burial sites for their members in Rome's soft tufa soil.[20] As

Diarmaid MacCulloch noted, one of the most striking features of the earliest burials sites is "the relative lack of social or status differentiation in them: bishops had no more distinguished graves than others, apart from a simple marble plaque to record basic details such as a name. This was a sign of a sense of commonality, where poor and powerful might be all one in the sight of the Saviour."[21]

Over just a few centuries, however, Christianity transformed from being a church of the poor and the enslaved to a church that drew its leadership from the highest ranks of Roman society, with wealthy members and bishops who owned extensive property as well as slaves. This transition is reflected by increasingly intricate artwork adorning the tombs of the wealthy and powerful. A marked visual change emerged among the graves of the mid-third century and beyond when wealthy Christians began to pay for more elaborate wall paintings and expensive stone coffins. Also during this same period, elaborate artwork adorned the resting places of important and wealthy bishops. "The upper classes were beginning to arrive at church," and decoration signaled wealth, power, and bishops.[22]

In addition to Christianity's emphasis on Jesus's death by crucifixion as well as an intense focus on martyrdom of persecuted Christians, there were also some very pragmatic reasons why Christians may have first organized themselves as burial associations. The challenge of having a dignified burial was (and remains) very important for marginalized members of society, communities for whom death was an omnipresent reality. These burial societies offered members mutual aid in times of difficulty. They buried members or helped offset payment for burial in the event of death and promised some basic support for one's family in the case of injury and death. In *The Christians as the Romans Saw Them*, Robert Wilken makes the stunning claim that if all of this sounds like rudimentary life insurance, it is, in part, because incipient forms of insurance may have been an outgrowth of such burial associations, with membership functioning as a type of agreements and dues functioning as premiums.[23] It appears, then, that there were concrete benefits that came with assembly membership, especially for the poor, and this is one of those many factors that likely contributed to the church's early growth among some of the Roman Empire's most vulnerable populations.

The history of New Orleans's Zulu Club offers an opportunity to look at much more recent examples of how burial societies served and functioned among another persecuted group in society. The Zulu Club originated as one of the many benevolent aid and burial societies that "were the first forms of insurance in the Black community where, for a small amount of dues, members received financial help when sick or financial aid when burying deceased members."[24]

Black benevolent aid and burial societies were one of the most important organizations for Black communities after the Civil War, even occasionally outstripping the churches they were connected to as the predominant organizational structure among free Blacks.[25] These societies were a practical response to the economic insecurity of newly freed Blacks who had migrated to cities and the high mortality rate among Black workers, and they served to offer a measure of security for families' well-being.[26]

In "Black Benevolent Societies and the Development of Black Insurance Companies in Nineteenth Century Alabama," C.A. Spencer noted that in Alabama, during the period after the Civil War, the state was flooded with vast numbers of destitute people, both Black and white, in which there was almost no form of a social safety net to aid them. "The antebellum welfare system, which had financed aid to the poor by means of county tax monies, ceased to function for several years...Widows and orphans, the old and the sick, had nowhere to turn except to friends and relatives whose resources were equally meager."[27] As was likely the case in second-century Rome, these associations whereby members pooled resources together emerged out of both a sense of economic bondedness and desperation.

Also like the *collegia funeratica* of the second century, these benevolent aid and burial societies were social clubs. "That these voluntary associations were evidence of early insurance against illness, accident, and death is beyond dispute, but that was not their principal reason for being."[28] The Zulu Club is a good example of how a later burial society also offered regular social gatherings, had many different forms of charity, and held major annual celebrations— indeed, very much like a church. Such societies offered "support, comfort, and status to people adjusting to a strange environment, and were a key element in the transition from slavery to freedom."[29]

Robert L. Harris's work, "Early Black Benevolent Societies, 1780-1830," offers further insight into the history and character of these societies, including on the practical *koinonia* that characterized them. He notes that "the major features of Black benevolent societies were sickness and disability benefits, pensions for deceased members' families, burial insurance, funeral direction, cemetery plots, credit unions, charity, education, moral guidance, and discussion forums. Although each organization did not encompass all of these activities, they in large measure characterize most of the voluntary associations."[30]

Nursing services were also often supplied by the rotation of watching members, and in some instances, societies had physicians on retainer.[31] Further, "the benevolent societies did not simply provide monetary assistance for disabled members but also supplied companionship in time of need. Baltimore's Free African Civilization Society, for instance, insisted that its elected stewards visit all shut-in members within twenty-four hours of written application."[32]

Particularly in the south, these societies walked a fine line in relationship to legality in a way that recalls the early Christian *collegia funeratica* of the second century. In Charleston, South Carolina, the Brown Fellowship Society was begun at St. Philip's Episcopal Church when its rector, the Rev. Alexander Garden, urged free Blacks to form a benevolent society. This suggestion reflected the discriminatory practices of St. Philip's in that free Blacks could attend services, be baptized, and be married at the church, but they could not participate in governance or be buried in the church cemetery.[33] Harris notes: "On October 12, 1794, the organization purchased a burial plot, to serve Charleston's entire Black population, slave or free, mulatto or not."

Most likely, because of the restrictions placed on their activities, southern free Black benevolent societies made burial arrangements one of their most prominent features. This responsibility relieved white officials from having to tend to Black corpses, prevented a health hazard, and provided for burial in specific places rather than randomly in fields. For these reasons, no doubt, southern states tolerated the voluntary associations even though they breached the law. Free Blacks in the South took advantage of this opportunity to serve the additional needs of their people.[34]

One fascinating aspect of these Black benevolent societies is how many of these evolved into for-profit Black-owned insurance companies while retaining many aspects of their past as mutual aid societies with strong connections to the church. The Union Central Relief Association of Birmingham, Alabama, is a good example of how a benevolent society became the first Black-owned industrial insurance company.

Founded as an eleemosynary association of Sixth Avenue and Shiloh Baptist Church, the Union Central Relief Association's benefits that they provided to Black workers led the Alabama commissioner of insurance to reclassify the benevolent society as an industrial insurance company. "Premiums ranged from 5 cents per week with a ten-dollar death benefit and a one dollar per week sick benefit to a premium of 40 cents per week with an eighty-dollar death benefit and an eight-dollar per week sick benefit."[35] In some instances, this represented an only slightly more formalized version of the benefits provided by benevolent societies, and many of these insurance companies were never intended to be profitable. "These societies still referred to their policy-owners as members and premiums as dues because they were still in the process of evolving from benevolent societies or fraternal benefit orders into full-fledged industrial insurance companies. In addition, many members still considered the commercial connotation of insurance as being repugnant."[36]

Generally speaking, these societies were still aiming to be about more than profits, something more along the lines of *koinonia*.

The early description of church as a burial society for the poor has remained with me throughout the pandemic. I was reminded of all this once again in mid-December 2020 as news organizations began running celebratory stories of healthcare workers finally being able to receive the vaccine, a day of relief and jubilation. It just so happened that on that very same day, Washington National Cathedral tolled its bell 300 times for the 300,000 who had died by that point in the United States.[37]

The contrast of where the church could be found was striking. I'll always recall listening to the joyful stories of nurses and healthcare workers finally being able to receive their vaccines and then tuning in to listen to a bell toll for a loss that no statistic can ever fully convey. The pain of this ritual—the tolling of the bell 100 times for every 100,000 dead—would necessarily continue despite all the initial hopefulness of that day, even as the death toll now tops more than 1 million American lives lost. This has served for me as a reminder of what I first observed that day at my grandparents' kitchen table: the solemn presence and proximity of the church amidst death and mourning and its unique role in helping the hardest hit communities to name what has taken place, understand the inequities, and to mourn.

In doing so, Christians can draw upon its ancient as well as its more recent history of being a burial and mutual aid society. For across millennia, the most vulnerable populations have always had to pool resources together to offer some minimal support to one another in extreme situations, even if that has simply been scrounging together enough money for a dignified burial. The historical evidence on how early Christians of the second century and the Black churches did this in nineteenth- and twentieth-century churches can inspire the church today as it wrestles with what it means to serve communities where death is always proximate. What might this ancient and recurring linkage between the church and burial societies have to teach us about the role of faith communities in the twenty-first century?

The history of burial societies suggests that there are also material aspects to what it means to be church—literal benefits, in some cases—that may not be as well-known or emphasized today. As this pandemic has shown so starkly, death is hardly the great equalizer it is oftentimes portrayed to be, and faith leaders need new (or in this case, very ancient) organizational models for thinking about the role and purpose of the church amidst so much inequality and death. In other words, our society still needs Christian *collegia funeratica*, and the models developed in the second century and nineteenth and twentieth ones represent intriguing examples of Christian assemblies serving this purpose by offering practical benefits, companionship, and burial services in marginalized and persecuted communities.

Discussion Questions

Second-century descriptions of Christian assemblies are of local clubs or associations that had a common chest, offered some basic aid for members in need, and were closely involved in offering burials for their members. These early assemblies were oftentimes bulwarks against the vicissitudes of the dangers of a life of poverty. How might congregations and dioceses build upon this legacy?

Early Christian assemblies offered a limited safety net and possibly even an early and informal type of life insurance, where membership dues helped defray the costs associated with burial and offered some protection for one's family in case of injury or death. What do you think about this focus on material assistance and even benefits?

What might this ancient and recurring linkage between the church and burial societies have to teach us about the role of faith communities in the twenty-first century?

A Next Step

Some Christian denominations offer discounted or sliding scale premiums for members of congregations. The Episcopal Federal Credit Union (efcula.org), based in the Diocese of Los Angeles, offers all members basic banking services and lower interest loans for both individuals and churches. Another example is Thrivent Financial (Lutheran), which cites Martin Luther's 1523 document "Fraternal Agreement on the Common Chest of the Entire Assembly at Leisnig" as their inspiration for pooling resources to help people in need.[38] Interestingly, in 2014, Thrivent Financial expanded their offerings to non-Lutherans, and so members of other denominations now have a variety of economic tools and benefits (banking, life insurance, loans) at their disposal, presumably at discounted rates. For church leaders who wish to explore what concrete benefits they can offer their most vulnerable congregation members, researching the details of denominational plans like those of Thrivent and the Episcopal Federal Credit Union is a good first step.

Endnotes

1   Derrick Bryson Taylor, "A Timeline of the Coronavirus Pandemic," *The New York Times*, March 17, 2021.

2   J. David Goodman and William K. Rashbaum. "N.Y.C. Death Toll Soars Past 10,000 in Revised Virus Count," *The New York Times*, April 4, 2020.

3   McGuckin, *The Path of Christianity*, 1061.

4   Kevin Quealy, "The Richest Neighborhoods Emptied Out Most as Coronavirus Hit New York City," *The New York Times*, May 15, 2020, and Brian M. Rosenthal, Joseph Goldstein, Sharon Otterman, and Sheri Fink, "Why Surviving the Virus Might Come Down to Which Hospital Admits You," *The New York Times*, July 1, 2020.

5   Julie Bosman, Sophie Kasakove, and Daniel Victor, "U.S. Life Expectancy Plunged in 2020, Especially for Black and Hispanic Americans," *The New York Times*, July 21, 2021.

6   Bosman, Kasakove, and Victor, "U.S. Life Expectancy Plunged in 2020," July 21, 2021.

7   Zoe Christian Jones, "COVID-19 Is Driving New York City's Record Homelessness Figures, advocates say," CBS News, December 11, 2020.

8   Rosenthal, Goldstein, Otterman, and Fink, "Why Surviving the Virus Might Come Down to Which Hospital Admits You," July 1, 2020.

9   MacCulloch, *Christianity*, 190.

10   Lee, Trymaine. "How America's Vast Racial Wealth Gap Grew: By Plunder," *The New York Times Magazine/The 1619 Project*, August 14, 2019.

11   Benko, Stephen, "Letter X.96," *Pagan Rome and the Early Christians* (Bloomington: Indiana University Press, 1986), 4-7.

12   Robert L. Wilken, "Toward a Social Interpretation of Early Christian Apologetics," *Church History*, Vol. 39, No. 4 (1970): 451.

13   Wilken, "Toward a Social Interpretation of Early Christian Apologetics," 452.

14   Wilken, "Toward a Social Interpretation of Early Christian Apologetics," 452.

15   Robert L. Wilken, *The Christians as the Romans Saw Them*, Second Edition (New Haven, Connecticut: Yale University Press, 2003), 31-47.

16   Wilken, "Toward a Social Interpretation of Early Christian Apologetics," 454.

17   MacCulloch, *Christianity*, 190.

18   MacCulloch, *Christianity*, 292.

19   MacCulloch, *Christianity*, 292.

20   MacCulloch, *Christianity*, 190.

21   MacCulloch, *Christianity*, 190.

22   MacCulloch, *Christianity*, 190.

23   Wilken, *The Christians as the Romans Saw Them*, 31-47.

24   Clarence A. Becknell, Thomas Price, and Don Short, "History of Zulu Club," kreweofzulu.com/history.

25   Robert L. Harris, "Early Black Benevolent Societies, 1780-1830," *The Massachusetts Review*, Vol. 20, No. 3 (1979): 603–625.

26 Harris, "Early Black Benevolent Societies," 615.

27 C. A. Spencer, "Black Benevolent Societies and the Development of Black Insurance Companies in Nineteenth-Century Alabama," *Phylon* Vol. 46, No. 3 (1985): 251.

28 Harris, "Early Black Benevolent Societies," 611.

29 Harris, "Early Black Benevolent Societies," 611.

30 Harris, "Early Black Benevolent Societies," 614.

31 Spencer, "Black Benevolent Societies and the Development of Black Insurance Companies in Nineteenth-Century Alabama," 255.

32 Harris, "Early Black Benevolent Societies," 616.

33 Harris, "Early Black Benevolent Societies," 619.

34 Harris, "Early Black Benevolent Societies," 619.

35 Spencer, "Black Benevolent Societies and the Development of Black Insurance Companies in Nineteenth-Century Alabama," 260.

36 Spencer, "Black Benevolent Societies and the Development of Black Insurance Companies in Nineteenth-Century Alabama," 260.

37 David Paulsen, "National Cathedral Tolls Bell 300 times as United States Passes 300,000 COVID-19 deaths," Episcopal News Service, December 15, 2020.

38 David Yonke, "Thrivent Financial Is No Longer for Lutherans Only," Religion News Service, March 28, 2014.

10 The Shepherd of Hermas and the Elm and the Vine

In January 2020, I traveled with a group of seminarians from Episcopal Divinity School at Union to the sister cities of El Paso, Texas, and Ciudad Juárez, Mexico, to participate in a week-long border pilgrimage organized by Annunciation House, a Roman Catholic sanctuary for immigrants and refugees. One day early in the trip, the group loaded into a van and headed up to a scenic mountain bluff on the United States side of the border. High on that bluff, it was difficult to see the snaking border wall that separated El Paso and Ciudad Juárez. The two cities—one American, one Mexican—spread before us as one single, teeming organism. I learned that this teeming organism has been described as "The Borderplex," a term for the largest bi-national community in the world: two cities connected by four international bridges that make up the single busiest crossing of people and cargo on earth.[1]

Despite the apparent interconnectedness of the two cities in both geography and history, there are remarkable differences between the two places. From my position on the El Paso, Texas, side, I was standing in one of the safest cities in the United States.[2] Yet with my naked eye, I could look down and see the movement of cars and streets in Ciudad Juárez, the glint of tall office buildings, and the *colonias* of what is one of the most violent places on earth, a city where in 2008 a civilian had a greater likelihood of being kidnapped and murdered than in Baghdad.[3]

On the El Paso side, on the very mountain where we were gathered, stood a ring of mansions with spectacular views looking out toward the desert mountains. Our guide pointed out that many of these mansions were owned by the upper management of the more than seventy Fortune 500 companies that did their manufacturing in Ciudad Juárez. Despite their physical proximity, the owners of these mansions inhabited a world light years away from the people who worked in the 300 factories, or *maquiladoras*, located in Ciudad Juárez. These *maquiladoras* are notoriously exploitative operations, sites where in 2016 manufacturing wages were 40 percent cheaper than factory wages in China.[4] Referred euphemistically to as a "low-cost geography," Ciudad Juárez is where many of the components of the cheap goods that we Americans purchase every day are produced.[5]

I looked out at two cities with one border between them, one relatively wealthy and safe and the other remarkable for its poverty and violence, seemingly living and breathing as one. There are many ways to describe the peculiar relationship between these two cities. In 2008, Bob Cook, US president of the economic development corporation for the Borderplex region, stated that "the two cities function symbiotically," citing how the then-recent rise in manufacturing had brought more than 260,000 factory jobs to Ciudad Juárez.[6] Yet the contrast between the mansions and the *maquiladoras* reminded me of one of those facts from biology class that Cook had likely forgotten, which is that parasitism is a form of symbiosis.

Parasitism—whereby one organism draws its strength and nourishment by exploiting its host—is a more accurate way of describing the symbiotic relationship between the two cities of El Paso and Ciudad Juárez. In a 2016 Fronteras article on attempts by *maquiladora* employees to unionize for fairer wages, Dr. Kathy Staudt, professor of political science at the University of Texas, noted that the global competitiveness of this "low-cost region" is exercised entirely on the backs of workers. Further, when we descended the mountain and met with justice advocates on both sides of the border wall, they named the causal links between those exploitative factory jobs and the desperate poverty, rise in corruption, and the extreme violence for which Juárez has become so known.

Whether discussing two cities, two nations, or two economic classes of people, an ancient way of making sense of how wealth and poverty function together is to observe that the wealthy and the poor are locked in some type of symbiotic relationship. Whether one understands this symbiosis to be mutually beneficial, as Cook argued regarding the many jobs the US factories had brought to Ciudad Juárez, or parasitic oftentimes has a great deal to do with whether one's people have been at the top or on the underside of this arrangement. As for me, I know in my bones that this scenario is the latest chapter in America's long history of settlers making extraordinary wealth off of stolen lands and by exploiting the labor of Brown and Black people. Just consider that "the richest 1 percent of Americans own 40 percent of the country's wealth, while a larger share of working-age people (18-65) lives in poverty than in any other nation belonging to the Organization for Economic Cooperation and Development."[7]

Further, as a Christian, I am reminded that throughout the gospels—and particularly in Luke—Jesus speaks and teaches about this arrangement from the bottom up. As discussed in earlier chapters, the gospels include a distinctly negative view of the rich and elaborate on "pious poor, oppressive rich" traditions that long for God's apocalyptic reversal of society. We hear Mary in the *Magnificat* celebrating how God casts the mighty down from their thrones, lifts up the lowly, fills the hungry with good things, and sends the rich away empty. In Luke's Beatitudes, Jesus states that it is the poor who are blessed and goes on to pronounce woes on the rich and those whose stomachs are currently full. Then there is that troubling exchange between Jesus and the rich young man/rich young ruler recorded in Matthew, Mark, and Luke, a story that has caused consternation among wealthy Christians and their apologists ever since. After the rich young ruler refuses to sell his possessions and give his money to the poor, Jesus stuns the disciples by telling them it is easier for a camel to pass through the eye of a needle than for the wealthy to enter the kingdom of God.

And yet, by the second century, as more and more wealthy people were becoming part of the Christian assemblies, some creative theology focused on reversing this reversal and diluting the forceful power of these passages. The arrival of wealthy Christians resulted in explorations of whether the relationship of the wealthy to the poor was a bit more complicated, and the widening of the eye of the needle was begun in earnest. A second-century text, *The Shepherd of Hermas*, addressed these questions and ultimately argued that the church can bring the rich and poor into a reconciled and mutually beneficial, symbiotic relationship through a particular form of Christian philanthropy now termed "redemptive almsgiving."

The Shepherd of Hermas and its vision of redemptive almsgiving met a need among those seeking to build a church that was inclusive of rich and poor alike. The text became highly popular among wealthier second- and third-century Christians and was even considered holy scripture by some later Church Fathers. It represents one of the earliest examples of Christian thinkers wrestling with the question of how the rich could fit into this growing movement that was still primarily comprised of and led by those living at, near, or below subsistence-level poverty, and it offers a new interpretation of philanthropy as a way for the wealthy to expiate their sins and attain salvation.

The Shepherd of Hermas was written during the first half of the second century and over the next 500 years became one of the most popular and widely read Christian books outside our present biblical canon. To wit: more copies of *The Shepherd of Hermas* have been discovered in Egypt before the fourth century than any New Testament book. The fourth-century Codex Sinaiticus included it among the books of the New Testament, and it is referred to as scripture by Irenaeus, Clement of Alexandria, Origen, and Tertullian.[8]

The popular text was composed in Rome over the span of about forty years and is comprised of five visions, twelve moral mandates, and ten similitudes (or parables) given to a Christian man named Hermas.[9] Today, *The Shepherd* is placed in a collection of writings called The Apostolic Fathers, which together give insight into the development of the Christian church in the immediate years after the New Testament was written. These writings "belong to the world of the house church or the incipient rise of the monarchical bishops, and their overall focus on moral encouragement in a markedly eschatological context or outlook gives us a sense of what most of the earliest episcopal preachers must have sounded like in their own time." [10] Although the book was not ultimately included in what is today considered the New Testament, *The Shepherd* remained very popular and was used extensively in catechesis, and later leaders like Athanasius of Alexandria in the fourth century urged it upon his literate—and therefore wealthier—Christians for private study.

Part of the text's popularity likely came from the fact that the writer of the text, Hermas, traversed many socioeconomic boundaries in his own life. Born a slave, sold to a Christian named Rhoda, manumitted by his owner, Hermas became wealthy through some form of commerce but then lost it all when he was denounced as a Christian. In *The Shepherd*, Hermas looks back on his worldly success with a sense of shame and regret.[11] He reflects on the fact that his children are terrible—they denounced him to the Roman imperial authorities as being a Christian—and there are repeated insinuations that his wife committed adultery.[12] An old woman who symbolizes the church places the full blame for Hermas's ruinous familial life on the distractions of his prior wealth: "And you, Hermas, have endured great personal tribulations on account of the transgressions of your house, because you did not attend to them, but were careless and engaged in your wicked transactions."[13]

Having once been wealthy but now returned to relative poverty, Hermas writes about the emptiness of his prior luxurious life and how it resulted in fretting over trivialities. He urges the wealthy to distance themselves from "the desire after another's wife or husband, and after extravagance, and many useless dainties and drinks, and many other foolish luxuries; for all luxury is foolish and empty in the servants of God."[14] We meet Hermas, then, as a formerly wealthy man who realizes that for all his prior external success, he had been frittering his life away on the trivialities and frivolities of a wealthy lifestyle.

Hermas's strange visions began well before he made this wealth. His first vision occurred while he was still a slave and was caught spying on his master taking a bath. In this vision, the church comes to Hermas as a salty and sarcastic old woman who calls him out for his luring.[15] Greeting Hermas with a hearty "Hail Hermas!", this moment represents one of the first times the church is imagined as a woman—indeed, she is "an old woman, arrayed in a splendid robe, and with a book in her hand" who concludes her first revelation two chapters later with the blunt admonition to "Behave like a man, Hermas."[16]

In addition to chastising Hermas for spying on his slave master, the old woman points to a tower that represents the church. The tower is being built of square white stones, and the old woman tells Hermas that "those square white stones which fitted exactly into each other are apostles, bishops, teachers, and deacons, who have lived in godly purity, and have acted as bishops and teachers and deacons chastely and reverently to the elect of God. Some of them have fallen asleep, and some still remain alive. And they have always agreed with each other, and been at peace among themselves, and listened to each other. On account of this, they join exactly into the building of the tower."[17] Other square stones represent those who suffered martyrdom and those who faithfully followed God's commandments. These too fit perfectly into the building up of the tower.

The text then shifts to a description of those stones that do not fit in or are being cast away by workers as useless. "These are they who have sinned, and wish to repent. On this account they have not been thrown far from the tower, because they will yet be useful in the building, if they repent."[18] In addition, there are rough stones representing "those who have known the truth yet not remained in it," stones with cracks in them representing church members who are forever fighting with one another, as well as stones who are truly beyond saving who represent "the sons of iniquity" who believed "in hypocrisy, and wickedness did not depart from them."[19] These stones are cast far away from the tower.

The old woman then spends a considerable amount of time discussing a set of round white stones that symbolize the rich, an indication of how vexing the issue of wealth was during this period in the life of the church. She tells Hermas that these round white stones must have their wealth cut away from them to be useful to God and to fit into the overall building up of the church. It is only in doing so that the rich—perpetually distracted as they are by their wealth and all that it brings them—would ever be able to find their place in the Church and possibly be redeemed:

> "But who are these, Lady, that are white and round, and yet do not fit into the building of the tower?" She answered and said, "How long will you be foolish and stupid, and continue to put every kind of question and understand nothing? These are those who have faith indeed, but they have also the riches of this world. When, therefore, tribulation comes, on account of

their riches and business they deny the Lord." I answered and said to her, "When, then, will they be useful for the building, Lady?" "When the riches that now seduce them have been circumscribed, then will they be of use to God. For as a round stone cannot become square unless portions be cut off and cast away, so also those who are rich in this world cannot be useful to the Lord unless their riches be cut down. Learn this first from your own case. When you were rich, you were useless; but now you are useful and fit for life. Be ye useful to God; for you also will be used as one of these stones."[20]

In contrast to the way some congregations and organizations organize their identities around the round white stones of a few wealthy members, this second-century depiction of the church insists the rich must first cut away their wealth before they can enter the life of the church. Hermas's visions are those of a formerly wealthy person who personally knows how wealth and privilege are barriers to life in Christian community, an ancient message about the ways that riches, power, and privilege must first be "cut away" in order to become a follower of Christ.

In contrast to the severity of this first vision of the round white stones, what becomes *The Shepherd's* most well-known and beloved image is a considerably softer approach to the wealthy. This image is that of an elm tree and a fruiting vine. Not surprisingly, especially in light of later Christians' desire to build a church inclusive of the wealthy, this image became the more popular of the two. This is undoubtedly because it depicts a hopeful vision of how the wealthy and the poor can be brought into a seemingly reconciled and symbiotic relationship.

Just prior to *The Shepherd's* discussion of the elm and the vine in the second similitude, the first similitude frames a vision of two distinct homelands and their associated expenditures. A particular type of transaction takes place in the heavenly homeland, one in which the wealthy are told to make right use of their wealth: "Instead of lands, therefore, buy afflicted souls, according as each one is able, and visit widows and orphans, and do not overlook them; and spend your wealth and all your preparations, which ye received from the Lord, upon such lands and houses."[21]

This advice to "buy afflicted souls" then sets up the second similitude, one in which a divine shepherd (the one for whom the text is named) guides Hermas and directs his attention to a fruitless elm tree and a fruiting vine. The shepherd says the elm and the vine have been placed on earth by God to symbolize a reconciled relationship between the rich and the poor and to show how the rich and poor can be brought into right relationship through the church: "As I was walking in the field, and observing an elm and vine, and determining in my own mind respecting them and their fruits, the Shepherd appears to me, and says, 'What is it that you are thinking about the elm and vine?' 'I am considering,' I reply, 'that they become each other exceedingly well.' 'These two trees,' he continues, 'are intended as an example for the servants of God.'"[22]

The wealthy are described as the fruitless elm tree who, on account of the many distractions that riches bring, are unable to bear good fruit for God: "The rich man has much wealth, but is poor in matters relating to the Lord, because he is distracted about his riches; and he offers very few confessions and intercessions to the Lord, and those which he does offer are small and weak, and have no power above." In contrast, "the intercession of the poor man is acceptable and influential with God."[23] Despite their proximity to God, however, the lives of the poor on earth are like the unsupported grapevine whose fruits are small due to the absence of shade and protection from wild predators. They are exposed and vulnerable to persecution and attack.

It is only when the two are brought together, therefore, with the fruitless elm tree serving as a source of shade, protection, and support for the fruiting vine, that rich and poor can become as one organism working together for the glory of God:

> Among men, however, the elm appears not to produce fruit, and they do not know nor understand that if a drought comes, the elm, which contains water, nourishes the vine; and the vine, having an unfailing supply of water, yields double fruit both for itself and for the elm. So also poor men interceding with the Lord on behalf of the rich, increase their riches; and the rich, again, aiding the poor in their necessities, satisfy their souls. Both, therefore, are partners in the righteous work.[24]

What *The Shepherd of Hermas* represents, then, is the rise of "redemptive almsgiving," a particular version of Christian philanthropy that came out of Rome wherein the wealthy offered financial support and protection to the poor in exchange for the poor's prayers to God for the redemption of their new, wealthy patrons. These poor are the afflicted souls Hermas urges wealthy Christians to purchase. Roman Garrison writes, "Hermas insists that wealthy Christians are obligated to help the needy. Riches are a danger to faith, even where repentance is possible (Vision 1.1.8-9). Repentance by the rich must be 'speedy' if they are to enter the kingdom of God, and that repentance must be shown in 'doing good.'" In this way, he continues, "almsgiving has the potential to be redemptive because of the prayers of the poor who intercede for the rich."[25]

Such symbiosis between the rich and the poor, wherein one contributes material goods in exchange for the prayers of the poor, will become a recurring theme in later Christian literature on almsgiving.[26] Because the prayers of the poor were considered to be more effective, it was thought that the eye of the needle could be successfully widened, and the wealthy would have a chance at salvation if they gave generously. Of course, the fact that the "the poor" do not necessarily agree to this transaction speaks to the issue of agency that lurks behind so much of philanthropy, including almsgiving for the expiation of sins. The historian Justo González notes of *The Shepherd of Hermas*, "The primary question is not, How can the poor be helped? It is rather, How can the rich be saved? Naturally, this requires helping the poor, and the rich are given some guidelines for doing it. But in general the book addresses the rich. The poor are spoken *about* in the third person."[27]

In redemptive almsgiving, the gospel's dream of reversal—one in which the first shall be last, and the last shall be first—is reinterpreted in such a way wherein the first remain the first, the last remain the last, but through the church these first and last can live in harmony with one another in reconciled symbiosis.[28] It is always worth asking of such philanthropy models: who is really being served by this arrangement?

A few days after we ascended the mountaintop during our pilgrimage, our group journeyed from Annunciation House across one of the four international bridges that lead from El Paso into Ciudad Juárez. We traveled five miles into Ciudad Juárez and finally stopped at a large garbage dump where women and children could be found foraging for food, clothing, and other basic necessities. This dumpsite is where, more than two decades ago, Roman Catholic nun Sister Donna Kustusch founded Centro Catalina, a center for the women and children she saw picking through the garbage. In 2009, *The New York Times* published a six-minute film about how Centro Catalina became a safe haven amidst the spike in poverty and violence created by the desperation of the *maquiladoras*.[29]

We had traveled to Centro Catalina to visit *Las mujeres de esperanza y fe*, a women's cooperative housed at the Centro comprised of 16 members who sew and sell scarves, handbags, coin purses, and tortilla warmers, among many other items. They sold some items at the Centro Catalina to visitors but primarily through a volunteer-run store in El Paso. Many of the women were former *maquiladora* workers who described to us how this collective had helped them to escape that miserable life. During a presentation, one woman mentioned that their goal for annual income for the entire collective of 16 women was $7,000, a total I have since confirmed that I heard correctly. Even split among the members, this still represented a significant improvement in their overall quality of life over their time as factory workers because of the childcare, schooling, and health services offered through the Centro.

Hearing that figure made me pause and do a little math. An annual goal of $7,000, split among 16 members, means that each member could receive $437 per year. I found myself comparing this number to figures I'm much more familiar with and would invite you to do the same. I thought about how many times the $437 could go into my annual income, not to mention my household's annual income. I thought about that $437 in relation to the income made from investments—monies made by doing nothing at all. I thought about how much I had recently spent on my wedding and on how much I spend on vacations, and I was struck, once again, by the way that just a few people—including a great many of us who may not necessarily consider ourselves to be rich—hold a disproportionate amount of wealth even as half the globe lives on less than $5.50 a day.[30]

The trip to Ciudad Juárez and El Paso was disturbing in the very best sense. For weeks after returning from the border, I would awaken from dreams in which I would see the faces of the women and children I met both at Centro Catalina and at Annunciation House's shelter for refugees. But even as these images faded from memory, this exceptionally cruel math remained with me. Question: How can a family survive on the amounts described? Answer: In Ciudad Juárez, many don't. And what are we, the consumers of all the cheap goods that are manufactured in Juárez, to make of the fact that even this small amount still represents a significant improvement over the women's lives as *maquiladora* workers?

In the most generous reading of *The Shepherd of Hermas*, the wealthy are urged to cut away their wealth and privilege and to finally make use of their wealth as a source of support, protection, and shade to the poor and destitute. An example of this philanthropic relationship can be found at Centro Catalina itself, in that many of the services provided to the women and children are funded by donations. This is to say that checks are written in homes like yours and mine as well as, perhaps, in some of the homes I saw atop the mountain bluff. To be clear: these funds are absolutely necessary. The support and protection offered by the elm tree is real and much-needed, and it's hard to argue with *The Shepherd's* description of the lives of the poor as vulnerable and exposed to attack. And yet I'm struck by the way redemptive almsgiving glosses over the structural causes of poverty and subsequently ignores the gospels' broader critique of wealth and its vision of reversal. *Who is ultimately served by this arrangement?*

Unfortunately, of the various images that *The Shepherd of Hermas* offers regarding wealth and poverty, the pastoral image of the elm and vine has maintained its currency. I've personally never heard a preacher suggest that the rich are like round white stones who must first have their wealth cut away from them in order to become useful to God. Quite the opposite. Rather, the church ultimately embraces the second image in *The Shepherd of Hermas*, that of the elm and the vine, offering a vision of hope in the expiating power of redemptive almsgiving to bring the wealthy and the poor into a reconciled, albeit highly transactional, symbiotic relationship.

Discussion Questions

One ancient way of describing how wealth and poverty function together is to argue that the wealthy and the poor are locked in some kind of symbiotic relationship. Whether one understands this symbiosis to be mutually beneficial or parasitic oftentimes has a great deal to do with whether one's people have been at the top or on the underside of this arrangement. Reflect on your own and your family's economic journey. Where do you see yourself in this symbiotic relationship?

The boldest claim in *The Shepherd of Hermas* is that the rich must first cut away their wealth before they can enter the life of the church. Hermas's visions are those of a formerly wealthy person who personally knows how wealth and privilege are distractions and barriers to life in Christian community, an ancient message about the ways that riches, power, and privilege must first be "cut away" in order to become a follower of Christ. What do you make of this vision?

The vision of the elm and the vine became a symbol for "redemptive almsgiving," a particular version of Christian philanthropy wherein the wealthy offer financial support and protection to the poor in exchange for the poor's prayers to God for the redemption of their wealthy patrons. What happens to the agency of the poor in this scenario? Who do you think this philanthropy is really for? Do you see examples of "redemptive almsgiving" operating in the church and wider society still today?

A Next Step

In 2020, as the COVID-19 pandemic exacerbated shocking economic inequality, the South Korean film *Parasite* became the first non-English language film to win the Academy Award for Best Picture. Take a moment to watch (or rewatch) this powerful film and journal or discuss the following questions. What does the film say about the relationship between the rich and the poor in South Korean society? Why do you think it captured global imagination in 2020? Who is the parasite in this film? Finally, how does this compare with the image of the elm and the vine in *The Shepherd of Hermas*? Please note that this film includes sex and violence.

Endnotes

1 "The Ciudad-Juárez Borderplex: The U.S. Mexico Border Done Right" and Lisa Chamberlain, "2 Cities and 4 Bridges Where Commerce Flows," *The New York Times*, March 28, 2007.

2 This sense of safety had been recently shaken by a mass shooting in August 2019 in which a white nationalist and anti-immigrant gunman opened fire at a Walmart, killing 23 people and injuring 23 others.

3 Brent Renaud and Craig Renaud, "Return to Juárez," *The New York Times*, October 16, 2009.

4 Mónica Ortiz Uribe, "Factory Workers in Juárez Unionize for Higher Pay, Better Working Conditions," *Fronteras*, February 10, 2016.

5 Chamberlain, "2 Cities and 4 Bridges Where Commerce Flows."

6 Chamberlain, "2 Cities and 4 Bridges Where Commerce Flows."

7 Matthew Desmond, "In Order to Understand the Brutality of American Capitalism, You Have to Start on the Plantation," *The New York Times Magazine/The 1619 Project,* August 14, 2019.

8 Philip F. Esler, ed., *Early Christian World: Volume 1* (England: Routledge Worlds, 2000), 469.

9 Carolyn Osiek, "The Apostolic Fathers," in *The Early Christian World: Volume 1*, 533-535.

10 McGuckin, *The Path of Christianity*, 54.

11 Osiek, "The Apostolic Fathers."

12 McGuckin, *The Path of Christianity*, 61.

13 Shepherd of Hermas, (Aeterna Press, 2016), Second Vision, Chapter 3.

14 Hermas, Twelfth Commandment, Chapter 2.

15 McGuckin, *The Path of Christianity*, 61.

16 Hermas, First Vision, Chapters 2 and 4.

17 Hermas, Third Vision, Chapter 5.

18 Hermas, Third Vision, Chapter 5.

19 Hermas, Third Vision, Chapter 6.

20 Hermas, Third Vision, Chapter 6.

21 Hermas, First Similitude.

22 Hermas, Second Similitude.

23 Hermas, Second Similitude.

24 Hermas, Second Similitude.

25 Roman Garrison, "Redemptive Almsgiving in Early Christianity," Available from ProQuest Dissertations & Theses Global.

26 Justo L. González, *Faith and Wealth: A History of Early Christian Ideas on the Origin, Significance, and Use of Money* (New York City: HarperCollins, 1990), 99.

27 González, *Faith and Wealth*, 96.

28 Matthew 20:16.

29 Brent Renaud and Craig Renaud, "Juárez: Amid Violence, a Haven," *The New York Times*, April 15, 2009.

30 "Nearly Half the World Lives on Less Than $5.50 a Day," World Bank Group, October 17, 2018.

11 Spiritualized Wealth and Poverty in the Hymn of the Pearl

In December 2011, I had one of those money conversations that are hard to forget. It was during a holiday party at a friend's home at a moment in American society when issues of inequality, wealth, and poverty were very much in the air. At this party, I struck up a conversation with a successful finance type. Let's call him David.

On most days, the Davids of the world and I tend to run in different circles, so this represented a unique opportunity for me to ask a wealthy person many awkward questions. As I knew from others, David had recently left a hedge fund to develop his own investment firm. At the tender age of 29, he had also just purchased a three-story, multi-million-dollar brownstone home in the Cobble Hill area of Brooklyn.

Our conversation drifted from one topic to another until we landed on the Occupy Wall Street protests that had just begun in Zuccotti Park. I had been there just a few days prior and wanted to talk about what I had seen—namely, a group of peaceful people hanging out, living in tents, and protesting the growing inequality in US society. As I recall, David was open to the idea that something was profoundly amiss about the growing wealth inequality in our country and across the globe, but the conversation took a turn when I suggested there were ethical obligations that came with wealth. "I'm not wealthy," he shot back. "I'm middle class. I don't think you know what wealth really is…"

David and I kept talking. Eventually it became clear that we were each using the terms "wealth" and "poverty" with very different reference points in mind. David was comparing himself to the wealth of his former colleagues and supervisors, people who perhaps owned not just one but likely several million-dollar homes around the globe and whose vast wealth made his own three-story Brooklyn brownstone seem like simple living. In contrast, I often feel embarrassingly well off in a hurting world. In the story of Jesus's encounter with the rich man, I've always seen myself as the one grasping at riches, unwilling to part with wealth even as so many others struggle to survive.

My brief conversation with David has stayed with me for these several years, in part, because it speaks to the elasticity of what is meant by wealth and poverty in the first place, as well as the peculiar psychology of money. I believe my own interpretation of these words is more grounded in reality—an understanding that bears in mind the fact that 10 percent of the world lives in extreme poverty (less than $2 per day) and approximately half the world lives on the only somewhat less extreme $5.50 per day. But this elasticity means that even the rich can spend their days feeling "poor" in relation to their more well-off neighbors.

New York City is a kind of petri dish in this regard, a city whose shocking inequalities in wealth and poverty can induce a form of spiritual madness around these issues. In just a one-block radius from my apartment, for example, there are both 548-square-feet studio apartments selling for $900,000 as well as hotels that have been recently converted into housing for homeless families amidst the COVID-19 pandemic.[1] [2] I'm convinced that if a survey was conducted on this one block alone, you might be surprised to discover who considers themselves to be poor and rich, who sees themselves as having less than their neighbors, and who describes themselves as finally having enough.

Such elasticity of terms and psychology end up being key in the early church as Christians continued to wrestle with whether there was any space for the materially wealthy in the church. Even as some Christians were being persecuted for their faith and were losing their wealth in the process (Hermas from the previous chapter, for example), others retained their wealth, property, and slaves and hoped to hear fewer depressing sermons from their local clergy, an increasing number of whom were now themselves wealthy slaveowners. Christians in the late second and third centuries began to develop sophisticated techniques for softening Jesus's statements on wealth. These include the development of redemptive almsgiving discussed in the prior chapter as well as a refining of what was meant by wealth and poverty, and who was rich and who was poor, in the first place.

One place where historians see this latter strategy at work is in the evocative poem, *Hymn of the Pearl*, a second-century spiritual epic that is embedded in the third-century text, The Acts of Thomas.[3] *Hymn of the Pearl* helped to spiritualize Jesus's teachings on wealth and poverty and reframed these terms as part of the lost soul's journey toward salvific wisdom and self-knowledge. In this poem, "wealth" is defined as living in a state of transcendent wonder and having attained full self-knowledge, whereas "poverty" is the absence of this self-knowledge, the darkness of ignorance. The physical reality of "hunger" is spoken of as the spiritual longing for God, and "slavery" becomes a symbol for over-attachment to the passing material world. Ironically, by generally distancing itself from materiality and physical world, the *Hymn of the Pearl* helped lay the groundwork for a broader spiritualization of terms like wealth and poverty.

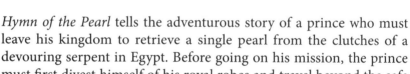

Hymn of the Pearl tells the adventurous story of a prince who must leave his kingdom to retrieve a single pearl from the clutches of a devouring serpent in Egypt. Before going on his mission, the prince must first divest himself of his royal robes and travel beyond the safe confines of his parents' kingdom. When he enters Egypt—the "land of the yoke of slavery"—he vests in the dirty rags of the Egyptians to conceal his true identity. He is then tricked into eating the food of the locals and falls into such a deep sleep that he forgets his identity as a prince and the purpose of his mission. Upon hearing of their son's confusion, his parents, the king and queen, send him a magical letter to remind him of who he actually is and what he is there for. The adventure continues as he retrieves the pearl from the dragon and subsequently returns to his kingdom.

Vivid images of wealth and poverty are interwoven throughout the poem. After snatching the pearl from the dragon, the prince "took off the dirty clothing and left it behind in their land" and returned to his parents' kingdom where "they had my money and wealth in their hands and gave me my reward: The fine garment of glorious colors, which was embroidered with gold, precious stones, and pearls to give a good appearance."[4] In contrast to the "dirty clothing" of the land of slavery, this fine garment stirred with the "movement of knowledge" and served as a mirror of his true self.

In *Lost Scriptures: Books That Did Not Make It Into the New Testament,* Bart D. Ehrman summarizes the traditional understanding of the meaning of this hymn. For Ehrman, *Hymn of the Pearl* "represents a Gnostic allegory of the incarnation of the soul, which enjoys a glorious heavenly existence ('my father's palace') from which it descends (to 'Egypt') to become entrapped in matter ('clothed myself in garments like theirs'). Forgetting whence it came, the soul eventually relearns its true nature from a divine emissary. When it awakens to its true identity ('son of kings'), it returns to its heavenly home where it receives the full knowledge of itself."[5]

Hymn of the Pearl is an evocative and complicated text, and I've enjoyed reading scholarly debates about whether the hymn is, in fact, an example of Gnosticism and whether this poem was originally composed as a Christian text or was simply popularly interpreted as such for centuries afterward due to its having been embedded in the Acts of Thomas.[6] As fascinating as these debates are, my main concern is how it represents a milestone along Christianity's journey toward speaking of wealth and poverty as inner spiritual realities. For in this hymn, wealth becomes about living in wisdom, wonder, and self-knowledge, and poverty is equated with spiritual ignorance.[7]

The Acts of Thomas, in which the *Hymn of the Pearl* is embedded, was likely written in Syria during the first half of the third century and "hovered on the borders of acceptability in Christian sacred literature until the sixteenth century" until the Council of Trent ultimately dismissed it as heretical.[8] *Hymn of the Pearl* is likely a much earlier text inserted into the Acts of Thomas, included in the same way the New Testament interweaves poems and teachings from the Old Testament. The hymn itself is "perhaps originally a narrative text of Babylonian Syria, since its language attests to a non-Edessan and preclassical

Syriac" and is therefore likely a non-Christian text, insomuch as Jesus or other specifically Christian language is not mentioned.[9] Nevertheless, due to its inclusion in the Acts of Thomas, the hymn was popularly reinterpreted in Christian settings for generations and significantly shaped Christian understandings of spiritual wealth and poverty.

Hymn of the Pearl may have been included in the Acts of Thomas because it serves as "a summary (perhaps a popular one) of the Thomasine theological framework and model."[10] Thomasine literature is described as reacting to the persecution of Christians through an intense focus on the need for Christians to renounce material wealth and sex and turn inward. The hymn encapsulated the theme of ascetic renunciation by depicting the taking off the robe of material wealth to go and retrieve a single pearl, which then opens the door to salvific self-knowledge. In his article "The Search for the True Self in the Gospel of Thomas, the Book of Thomas, and the Hymn of the Pearl," Patrick Hartin writes that the Thomasine Christians' detachment from the world is the result of persecution "both from outside as well as from within." He continues, "Without doubt, the world has the power to affect them and to persecute them. But, only through a process of separation from the world do the Thomas Christians come to know the Father."[11]

Perhaps, then, a charitable reading of the hymn's spiritualization of wealth and poverty is to say that it has its origins in the trauma of persecution. Such texts would become popular among later generations of Christians, including those no longer experiencing persecution, who were eager for a less rigorous approach to material wealth and poverty. In a spiritualized reinterpretation of Jesus's Beatitudes, for instance, "the hungry are those Thomas Christians for whom the search for the Father is an all-consuming desire and struggle" and "the hungry will ultimately be filled with a knowledge of the Father."[12] As beautiful as such language can be, much gets lost when Jesus's teachings about societal poverty and hunger are made to refer exclusively to the spiritual realm.

The story of the *Hymn of the Pearl* includes many of the elements of a form of Christian spirituality that is alive and well today. There is a retreat from the dangers and complications of the outer world in favor of an intense focus on the inner journey toward knowledge of the true self. Many of Jesus's statements about external injustices such as poverty are reread as referring to inward realities; the thirst and hunger of the "least of these" that Jesus speaks of satisfying in Matthew 25:31-46 becomes the spiritual thirst and hunger of Christians seeking salvific self-knowledge and a closer relationship with the transcendent Lord God. Jesus's Beatitudes and his descriptions of the kingdom of God—on earth as it is heaven—become reframed within the terms of Christian's interior journey. On the one hand, this can be read as a remarkable contribution to the richness of Christianity, and yet, I've often experienced the exact opposite. Often (though not always), advocates of inwardly focused spirituality argue that critical engagement on issues of societal wealth and poverty are a distraction from the deeper meaning of the gospels, a confusion of real Christian spirituality with what they dismiss as social work and political activism.

Having said all this, it is hard not to fall under the spell of the *Hymn of the Pearl*. The text opens with a king and queen divesting their son of a royal robe—a garment "set with gems and spangled with gold which they had made out of love for me"—and setting a covenant with their son.[13] The covenant states: "If you go down to Egypt and bring the one pearl which is in the land of the devouring serpent, you shall put on again that garment set with stones and the robe which lies over it, and with your brother, our next in command, you shall be a herald for our kingdom."[14]

Having been stripped of this gem-and-gold-studded robe, the prince journeys to Egypt in search of the pearl, and in doing so, he travels to a land long associated with the memory of slavery. There he takes on the garments of the Egyptians to avoid detection: "Being exhorted to guard against the Egyptians and against partaking of unclean things, I clothed myself in garments like theirs, so that I would not be seen as a stranger, and as one who had come from abroad to take the pearl."

Despite the prince's best efforts at slumming it, the local Egyptians realize that he is not their countryman. The Egyptians trick him into eating food that makes him forget both his true identity and why he went there in the first place. This is the nadir of the poem, a time of profound interior confusion, lack of self-knowledge, and enslavement.

"They dealt with me treacherously, and I tasted their food. I no longer recognized that I was a king's son, and I served their king. I forgot the pearl for which my parents had sent me. And I fell into a deep sleep because of the heaviness of their food."

It is only through a magical letter then sent by his parents that he is able to recall his true identity and purpose. "Awake, and rise from your sleep. Listen to the words in this letter, Remember you are the son of kings, you have fallen beneath the yoke of slavery. Remember your gold-spangled garment, recall the pearl for which you were sent to Egypt." Critically, this moment is marked by another divestment of robes—specifically, of the rags he had put on as a disguise in Egypt: "And I snatched the pearl and turned about to go to my parents. And I took off the dirty clothing and left it behind in their land."

The prince then successfully retrieves the pearl and is able to return to his home kingdom as well as to his beloved robe. Having just removed the dirty rags of the land of the Egyptians, we hear his joy at returning to his wealth: "And they had my money and wealth in their hands and gave me my reward: The fine garment of glorious colors, which was embroidered with gold, precious stones, and pearls to give a good appearance." And yet, during his time away, the royal robe had transformed into something even greater: "Stones of lapis lazuli had been skillfully fixed to the collar, And I saw in turn that motions of knowledge were stirring through it." The robe now somehow held the saving knowledge of his true self: "But, when suddenly I saw my garment reflected as in a mirror, I perceived in it my whole self as well, and through it I knew and saw myself."

Putting on the robe of salvific self-knowledge, the prince is able to enter even further into the kingdom by the poem's end: "When I had put it on, I ascended to the land of peace and homage. And I lowered my head and prostrated myself before the splendor of the father who had sent it to me. For it was I who had obeyed his commands and it was I who had also kept the promise, And I mingled at the doors of his ancient royal building. He took delight in me and received me in his palace."

In his essay on the depictions of wealth and poverty in the *Hymn of the Pearl*, Edward Moore reflects on the way that "Poverty, the 'servile yoke', here denotes not lack of material wealth but the ontological status of a soul that has lost and forgotten its true wealth. The wealth in question, of course, is not temporal or worldly wealth but the promised eschatological wealth of a soul embroiled in history and seeking repose."[15]

This marks an important milestone in the development of the Christian spiritual tradition. It speaks of a moment when "Poverty became defined as ignorance, that is, as a lack of knowledge of one's homeland," whereas "Wealth became defined as knowledge of one's homeland." In sum, Moore writes, "Poverty is lack of this transformative vision of God. Wealth is living in wonder, knowing that God's love pervades all things and that we, like the prince in the *Hymn of the Pearl*, are on a journey to our Father's kingdom."[16]

Wait. What?

John Anthony McGuckin names what must be said regarding this spiritualized interpretation of wealth, poverty, and slavery. Zeroing in on this second- and third-century tendency to spiritualize these terms, McGuckin writes, "This overall position became very widespread in the Christian consciousness. But even so, is it not dangerous to transmute poverty into a 'spiritual' symbol? Poverty is actually profoundly noxious to health and human life. It is not 'spiritual detachment' we mean when we normally speak of poverty, but bad health, bad education, bad housing, social oppressions, injustice, and often violent lives. And the endemic 'spiritualizing approach' to poverty (glossing it in a bourgeois manner as long as the bitter effects of impoverishment have passed the commentator by) has often masked what is nothing other than the wealthy's tolerance of inequity under a cloak of pious romance."[17]

McGuckin sees Christianity's moves in the second and third centuries to both internalize and spiritualize wealth and poverty as rooted in a broader clash of cultures. He states that the spiritualizing of these terms—often through allegorical interpretation—came about as the result of a conflict between the message of Jesus in the gospels and Hellenistic culture's valuing of self-knowledge over any practical concern for the destitute.[18] If the *Magnificat* contains a startling vision of God's dream of reversal, the rise of this spiritualized approach in the second and third centuries helped generations of wealthier Christians return things to their proper place.

In later centuries, amidst church tussles over fundraising, Jerome and Augustine would take this redefining to new heights. Each in their respective way argued that when Christ urged the rich man to dispossess himself of his wealth and give to "the poor," what he really meant was the "holy poor" of ascetic communities (Jerome's argument while fundraising for monasteries) or "the empty coffers of the bishop" (Augustine's amidst a church-building campaign). The realities of poverty as referring to the destitute and slavery as referring to the widespread institution of enslavement get lost in the fog of metaphor.

Like the rich man Jesus encountered, the church has a long tradition of turning away from Jesus's teaching that we must sell all that we possess and give all to the poor in order to follow him, for "he was very rich." Later generations of Christians offered creative strategies for circumventing Jesus's statement, thinking up new ways of insisting that Jesus was not being literal on this point and that we need to understand the deeper, more spiritual meaning of the words "wealth" and "poverty" themselves. This led many Christians to embrace a spirituality in which "poverty is lack of this transformative vision of God. Wealth is living in wonder, knowing that God's love pervades all things and that we, like the prince in the *Hymn of the Pearl*, are on a journey to our Father's kingdom."[19]

This form of spirituality is alive and well in the church. Strange creature that I am, I've made it a point over the past couple of years to visit particular parishes when the story of Jesus's encounter with the rich young man comes up in the lectionary. I've heard it preached from a very wealthy pulpit that Jesus wasn't being literal when he told the rich man to give up all his wealth and that ultimately all God wants is for us to follow our joy.[20] In contrast, I recently heard a sermon that somehow managed to bring many of these disparate strands together, including both the spiritual and material meaning of what it means to be rich.

In October 2021, I took the subway to San Andres Episcopal Church in Sunset Park, Brooklyn, a Spanish-speaking congregation made up of mostly Latino immigrants. The priest, Fr. Francisco Rodriguez, preached about how the wealth of the congregation was primarily its people. "If someone came into the sanctuary to rob us, and no one was here, let's be honest in that there wouldn't be anything for them to steal!" he said. He then spoke about how the community was actually very wealthy but not only in the spiritual sense. As it was Hispanic Heritage month at the time, he pointed to the flags hanging in the sanctuary depicting each of the nations and places congregants had emigrated from: El Salvador, Ecuador, Puerto Rico, Cuba, Mexico, Guatemala. He then asked his congregants to reflect not on how wealthy they were in relation to people in the United States but also in relation to the places they had come from. He said that despite the way many people might perceive the members of the congregation, San Andres was rich in people, love, and yes, even material wealth, and Christ was calling the congregants to give their abundance away for the benefit of those who had less. "Para la humanidad," he said.

This reflects what I have found to be a deep truth within the church: if you wish to hear a sermon where the story of Jesus's encounter with the rich man is taken seriously, it is best to avoid the wealthy, powerful congregations. The sermons offered there tend to add so many caveats, asterisks, and qualifiers to a story recorded in Matthew, Mark, and Luke that one ends up being able to squeeze an entire bishop's manse through that eye of the needle. Such churches tend to be more deeply invested in offering pastoral comfort to their wealthiest members than in faithfully conveying the challenge of the gospels, a bracing call that very few of us truly live into. And, in fairness to those preachers and assemblies, they can readily draw on an ancient historical tradition for doing so. The *Hymn of the Pearl* is representative of what became a richly developed trend in the second and third centuries of internalizing and spiritualizing the very meaning of the terms of wealth and poverty, a redefining that we still have to come to terms with today.

Discussion Questions

Throughout the Bible and subsequent Christian literature, images of wealth and poverty, thirst and hunger are used to depict the soul's longing for God. In Psalm 63, for instance, we hear the psalmist crying out "my soul thirsts for you; my flesh faints for you; as in a barren and dry land where there is no water" (Psalm 63:1). Later the psalmist declares, "My soul is content, as with marrow and fatness, and my mouth praises you with joyful lips" (Psalm 63:5). As someone who loves reading the psalms on a daily basis as part of Morning Prayer, I recognize the value in such evocative language, and I certainly identify times in which my own soul as seemed to be thirsting in a dry and weary land. So what is the issue with treating poverty and wealth, thirst and hunger primarily as metaphor? What is gained and what is lost in the process of doing so?

A spiritualizing approach to wealth and poverty began to emerge in second- and third-century Christianity, wherein Jesus's statements about material poverty became reinterpreted as referring primarily to inward states. Historian John Anthony McGuckin notes that "the endemic 'spiritualizing approach' to poverty (glossing it in a bourgeois manner as long as the bitter effects of impoverishment have passed the commentator by) has often masked what is nothing other than the wealthy's tolerance of inequity under a cloak of pious romance."[21] Do you see spiritual piety fostering or tolerating social inequity through a romantic vision of poverty and holy simplicity?

There is, at times, a tendency to lapse into binaries of politics versus religion and polarized thinking regarding spirituality and the material realities of poverty and inequality. Engagement around the realities of material poverty, injustice, and social inequities is dismissed as a non-spiritual endeavor, relegated to the realm of outreach and perceived as over-involvement in the political affairs of the world. How can this be overcome? How might one's spiritual practices instead nourish social justice engagement and social justice engagement serve to strengthen one's spiritual life? What does a "both/and" approach look like here?

A Next Step

Reflecting on the *Hymn of the Pearl* and the tendency to
spiritualize wealth and poverty more generally offers us the
opportunity to engage in self-critique of our spirituality and day-
to-day Christian practices. In our spiritual lives, have wealth and
poverty become primarily metaphors? Has "hungering for God"
become disconnected from the day-to-day hunger that is in one's
neighborhood and wider city? Has Jesus's forceful critique of wealth
become so abstracted that one has never seriously considered
Jesus's emphasis on dispossession, his warnings on the dangers and
distractions of money, and his embrace of radical simplicity in life?
Has spiritual life become primarily about living in the abundance
of wonder and joy? These are all questions and critiques I have of
my own spiritual practice, and I believe they are worth raising for
individuals and congregations.

Endnotes

1 brooklynpointnyc.com/availability, price of studio apartment as of November 3, 2021.

2 Jones, "COVID-19 Is Driving New York City's Record Homelessness Figures, Advocates Say," CBS News. These hotel rooms finally afforded a measure of safety for families, including children, who had previously been living in New York's crowded homeless shelter system. The inability to self-isolate in homeless shelters was one of the factors that led to a 78 percent higher mortality rate for homeless people from COVID-19 than the average New Yorker.

3 Bart D. Ehrman, *Lost Scriptures: Books That Did Not Make It Into the New Testament* (Oxford: Oxford University Press, 2003), 324.

4 Ehrman, *Lost Scriptures*, 324.

5 Ehrman, *Lost Scriptures*, 324.

6 Robin Darling Young, "Notes on Divesting and Vesting in the Hymn of the Pearl," in *Reading Religions in the Ancient World : Essays Presented to Robert McQueen Grant on His 90th Birthday*, ed. David Edward Aune and Robin Darling Young (The Netherlands: Brill, 2007), 204.

7 Edward Moore, "Wealth, Poverty, and the Value of the Person: Some Notes on the Hymn of the Pearl and Its Early Christian Context," in *Wealth and Poverty in Early Church and Society*, ed. Susan Holman (Ada, Michigan: Baker Academic, 2008), 59.

8 MacCulloch, *Christianity*, 202.

9 K. den Biesen, "Hymn of the Pearl," *Encyclopedia of Ancient Christianity*, ed. Angelo Di Berardino (Westmont, Illinois: InterVarsity Press, 2014).

10 Patrick Hartin, "The Search for the True Self in the Gospel of Thomas, the Book of Thomas, and the Hymn of the Pearl," *HTS Teologiese Studies/Theological Studies*, Vol. 55, No. 4 (1999): loc. 1015 (Kindle).

11 Hartin, "The Search for the True Self," loc. 1002 (Kindle).

12 Hartin, "The Search for the True Self," loc. 1002 (Kindle).

13 Ehrman, *Lost Scriptures,* Verses 9-11.

14 Ehrman, *Lost Scriptures,* 324.

15 Moore, "Wealth, Poverty, and the Value of the Person," 58.

16 Moore, "Wealth, Poverty, and the Value of the Person," 63.

17 McGuckin, *The Path of Christianity*, 1042.

18 John A. McGuckin, *The Westminster Handbook to Patristic Theology* (Louisville, Kentucky: Westminster John Knox Press, 2004), 360.

19 Moore, "Wealth, Poverty, and the Value of the Person," 63.

20 I believe this may have been a reference to Augustine's understanding of God's riches as something to be both enjoyed and used, although Augustine urged the wealthy to strictly avoid enjoying those things that were meant to be used, such as money, and to avoid confusion of the two. The boiled-down version that came through in the sermon focused on God's longing for all of us to follow our joy and the usefulness of wealth in this pursuit. This memorable homily was preached at St. Paul's Chapel, Trinity Wall Street.

21 McGuckin, *The Path of Christianity*, 1042.

12 Clement of Alexandria on the Usefulness of Staying Wealthy

In *SPQR: A History of Ancient Rome*, historian Mary Beard describes a scene of rare interaction between the very rich and very poor in ancient Roman society. This scene is part of a faded illustration from the House of Julia Felix from first-century Pompeii depicting life in the Forum. In this illustration, a wealthy woman is handing a hunched beggar a coin.

While this might at first seem to be a touching scene, one that celebrates the woman's compassionate generosity, this illustration more likely depicts what one is not supposed to do, akin to New York City signs advising subway passengers to not give money to people who are begging for help. Beard writes, "Roman moralists make numerous references to beggars— often to the effect that they are better ignored—and a series of paintings in Pompeii depicting life in the local Forum includes a cameo scene of a hunched beggar, with dog, being handed some small change by a posh lady and her maid, who are not obeying the moralists' advice."[1]

In her discussion of how poverty was generally viewed in ancient Rome, Beard notes that "Elite Roman writers were mostly disdainful of those less fortunate, and less rich, than themselves. Apart from their nostalgic admiration of a simple peasant way of life—a fantasy of country picnics, and lazy afternoons under shady trees—they found little virtue in poverty or in the poor or even in earning an honest day's wages."[2] In this, Romans were drawing on prior Hellenistic traditions that understood the disparities between rich and poor as foreordained by the gods. The inequalities in life were as the gods would have it, and it was not worth spending time worrying about the poor.[3] Such fatalism was compounded by the insulated existence of the wealthy. Scholar Annaliese Parkin notes, "Probably the rich did not in fact often give to the destitute: they will have been largely protected from the attentions of beggars in public by their servants, clients or lictors, and many, entrenched in the doctrine of *euergetism* or *beneficentia*, may genuinely have held that it was money not well used."[4]

Although good deeds in the form of generous gifts were considered virtues among the Roman wealthy, these were generally extended only toward those who could be useful on down the road: that is, worthy and respectable citizens, with a special relationship to the giver, who were able to offer something in return.[5] Indeed, when "the poor" are mentioned by elite Roman writers, they are most often referring to formerly wealthy people who have fallen into some misfortune, including formerly elite families who were still quite wealthy in relative terms but who were now less wealthy and thus saw themselves as poor. Like today, such situations were frequently the sources of dark humor in Roman dramas, with the first-century Roman poet Juvenal quipping, "There is nothing in the calamity of poverty that is harder to bear than the fact that it makes men ridiculous."[6][7]

It's helpful to keep these attitudes toward the poor by the Roman elite in mind when looking at Clement of Alexandria (c.150-c.215 CE). Author of a treatise, "Who Is the Rich Man That Shall Be Saved," Clement is one of the earliest Christian apologists for the wealthy and one of the main architects of Christianity's current teachings around wealth stewardship. When set beside the writings of other Christian writers, several of Clement's pro-wealth and anti-poor ideas may appear to come out of nowhere. Yet Clement represents a continuation—a baptism of sorts—of the Roman elite's comfortability with wealth disparities and their unabashed disdain for the destitute. Clement's baptism of a pro-wealth stance ultimately served the institutional church well, for his views on the utility of wealth, the holiness of the pious wealthy, and his belief in "the unholy poor," are expanded upon by Augustine of Hippo in the fifth century and remain foundational for mainline Christianity's current views on the usefulness of building up wealth and power.[8]

In the second and third centuries, as Christianity advanced into the higher ranks of society, the wealth of newer members became a theological problem that had to be addressed. As discussed in prior chapters, these communities wrestled with Jesus's exchange with the rich young ruler wherein Jesus concluded that it was easier for a camel to go through the eye of a needle than for the rich to be saved.[9] As the wealthy became members of Christian communities, new questions emerged: could these rich also be saved? Did the rich have to give away their possessions before they became members in the Christian assemblies? What was happening when the rich gave alms to the poor in exchange for the prayers of the poor? Clement of Alexandria was the first theologian to systematically address faith and wealth, offering a comprehensive meditation on the usefulness of wealth, the respective roles of the wealthy and the poor, and redemptive almsgiving.[10]

Both Clement's social and educational upbringing and audience for his ministry are key when reading his treatise on wealth and poverty. Clement was a member of elite Alexandrian society, was deeply rooted in both Platonism and Stoicism, and became the head of the catechetical school in Alexandria c. 200. His ministry, teachings, and writings primarily reflect a pastoral concern for the wealthy Christian families of Alexandria, which leads him to argue, as Justo González summarizes, "that the way of salvation is not entirely closed to the rich, and that what really counts is one's love of God above anything else."[11]

Controversial in his own time, Clement represents one of the most intimate relationships to Greek philosophy within early Christianity, and his insistence, derived from Plato, that knowledge increases one's moral worth was critiqued as elitist and unhealthy even by his contemporaries.[12] Further, his desire to find a passionless middle way resulted in some of the most bizarre conclusions that Christianity has come to, particularly in the area of sexuality. While he argued that both abstinence and promiscuity were unnatural, Clement was among the first Christian writers to say that sex between married couples should be intended for procreation rather than mutual pleasure. This position still undergirds much of Roman Catholic sexual ethics and remains a cherished theological framework for making many Christian heterosexual couples' sexual lives miserable and for the categorization of homosexuality as unnatural.

So thanks, Clement.

Though less well-known, Clement's views about wealth and poverty have been even more impactful on the shape of mainline Christianity than his views on sexuality. According to Diarmaid McCulloch, "In defending a Christian's responsible stewardship of riches, he provided an extended framework for Christian views of money and possessions for centuries to come."[13]

At the outset of his treatise, Clement sounds a lot like his Christian predecessors, describing wealth and luxury as "a dangerous and deadly disease," one that endangers the salvation of the wealthy. He also enjoins the wealthy to practice discipline around their wealth, to find a spiritual mentor if needed, to avoid all luxury and to instead find satisfaction with having "enough," an idea that will get picked up and elaborated on by many later writers.

Yet by the end of this same treatise, Clement has made one of the most vigorous defenses yet for the usefulness of holding onto wealth. He howls against the "eye of the needle" and the first two centuries of Christianity's critiques of wealth when he asks,

> What harm has been done by one who builds economic security and frugality prior to becoming a Christian? What is to be condemned if God, who gives life, places a child in a powerful family and a home full of wealth and possessions? If one is to be condemned for having been born into a wealthy family through no personal choice, that person would be wronged by God who would offer a worldly life of comfort but deny eternal life. Why would wealth ever have been found within creation if it causes only death?[14]

This full-throated defense of wealth as well as the God-given nature of (his) inheritance—one that conveniently eschews any discussion of how such wealth was made—rounds out a treatise full of surprising theological moves.

The first and perhaps most striking thing Clement does is insist on an allegorical interpretation of the parable of the rich young ruler. Clement argues: "'Sell all that you possess': what does that mean? It does not mean as some superficially suppose, that he should throw away all that he owns and abandon his property. Rather he is to banish those attitudes toward wealth that permeate his whole life, his desires, interests, and anxiety."[15] I would like to point out here that Jesus did not suggest "throwing away" or "abandoning" wealth but rather giving it to the poor. Clement, nevertheless, argues that it was the rich young ruler's failure to understand that Jesus was speaking about spiritual attachment to wealth, rather than his actual refusal to give his money to the poor, that led to his condemnation.

Therefore, instead of requiring the rich to dispossess themselves of their wealth, Clement believes the new and unique message of Christianity is that Jesus asks both the wealthy and the poor to rid themselves of their inner passion and desire for wealth.[16] Clement draws heavily on Stoicism when he argues that Jesus's statement to the rich man is best understood as a command to eliminate inner passions: "If an affluent person can control the power that wealth brings and remains modest and self-controlled, seeking God and placing God above all else, that person can follow the commandments as a poor individual, one who is free and unencumbered by the wounds of wealth."[17] By translating "dispossession" as referring to one's inner passions, Clement took a Stoic's crowbar to Jesus's eye of the needle so that he and his fellow wealthy could pass through far more easily.

In discussing this parable, Clement also engages in a biblical sleight of hand that ultimately helps relegate the dispossession of material wealth to ascetics, an understanding of this encounter that still prevails today. Although Clement is using Mark's Gospel for his treatise, he inserts the Gospel of Matthew's qualification of "if you wish to be perfect" at the corresponding point in the Marcan passage. This is significant for, as Joost Hengstmengel writes, "In the patristic era, the parable of the rich young man—a parable which appears in all three synoptics—was invariably quoted in the version of Matthew, who, unlike the other evangelists, added the qualification 'if you wish to be perfect' to Christ's challenge to the rich man..."[18] "Thus, the command to sell everything and to live a life of voluntary poverty literally became a counsel of perfection to Christians, rather than a precept. The *vita perfecta*, with complete renunciation of wealth, was only required of ascetics and monks."[19]

This history of interpretation raises a serious question for Christianity today as to whether dispossession of wealth and property should be a normative precept for all Christians and not just relegated to the realm of ascetics. Perhaps this literalist interpretation is an ideal that many of us (including myself) do not live up to, but precepts we fail at can nonetheless serve the deeper spiritual purpose of helping us to grow in humility, aiding us in seeing our fallibility and dependence on God's grace. Better to reside in the bracing awareness of Christ's expectations than to be content in the delusion that Christ's call to material dispossession is only for the few and the strange.

Having made wealth a matter of inner disposition and having relegated the requirement of dispossession solely to those "who wish to be perfect," Clement then argues that wealth should be considered as morally neutral as a tool. "An instrument, used with skill, produces a work of art, but it is not the instrument's fault if it is used wrongly. Wealth is such an instrument. It can be used rightly to produce righteousness. If it is used wrongly, it is not the fault of wealth itself but of the user. Wealth is the tool, not the craftsman."[20]

Distinctly absent from this depiction of wealth are prior Christians' critiques of the brutal sources of wealth, particularly of accumulated riches as the result of stealing from the poor and the exploitation of both lands and peoples. Missing too is the long history of thought around the unacceptability of offerings to God made from exploitation and of wealth as the sinful accumulation for one's self and one's children of that which God intended for the common good. For Clement, these are secondary considerations to how such wealth ends up being used. Like a hammer, wealth can be used to build up or destroy, and he holds that Christians are uniquely able to offer wealth for the building up of righteousness. Therefore, wealthy Christians should not be asked to give up their wealth but rather to use it for the glory of God, particularly through contributions to the church.

Clement arrives at this point through an intricate bit of circular logic. He turns to several examples in the gospels wherein Jesus assumes the wealthy have wealth to give away (Luke 16:9; Matthew 6:20; Matthew 25:41-43) and asks, "If we are to give to any who ask, as the Lord commanded, how can we do this if nothing is our own?"[21] Clement reasons that one cannot give what one does not have, so Jesus must have expected the rich to retain their wealth so as to later have something to give away. This interpretation strikes me as far more clever than wise, a reading that evades the spirit and meaning of these passages.

Significantly, the primary biblical example Clement uses for this argument is Jesus's parable on the unjust steward in the Gospel of Luke. It is telling that he doesn't focus on the steward's release of his master's wealth to the debtors. Rather, Clement zeroes in on Jesus's instruction to the disciples to be like the unjust steward and make use of dishonest wealth to gain friends for themselves, "so that when it is gone, they may welcome you into the eternal homes."[22] Clement reasons that since the wealthy are to be like the steward in using dishonest wealth to gain such friends, this means that they must first retain their dishonest wealth for making friends along the way. Clement concludes that the wealthy should therefore not dispossess themselves of all their wealth but keep it for the building up of these friendships.

Augustine would later expand on this view of wealth's usefulness, making a breathtaking theological argument that would serve the church well as the Roman Empire crumbled and the church's institutions came to replace the prior systems and structures in late antiquity. The question of "right use" led Augustine to broader reflections on who rightfully owned the wealth and property that was "misused" and "abused." Augustine would ultimately argue that insomuch as the moral value of wealth and property was determined by use, and since right use required right faith and since the Catholic Church alone represented the true faith, "the Catholic Church was the rightful owner of all property, including the property of [heretical] sects" who were misusing their wealth and properties.[23] As we will see in the final chapter of this book, Augustine employed this argument about right use and right ownership of property to call down state violence upon the heretical Christian sect of the Donatists, whose wealth and property he seized.

Finally, and perhaps most disturbingly, Clement's narrow focus on the interior attitude toward wealth opened the door for that long-established, ancient Roman view of "the unworthy poor" that I described at the beginning of this chapter. How this occurs calls to mind the so-called "equality" of city laws that ban both the rich and poor from sleeping on the streets, both rich and poor from living under bridges, both rich and poor from loitering. Such "equality" is pointedly about making life a great deal harder for the most vulnerable, and I think it is important to linger on this point as Clement's introduction of notions of "the unworthy poor" still shape most Christians' views of the poor in the twenty-first century.

With the sin of wealth now transformed into a matter of inner attachment, Clement makes the case for the rich who practice inner personal poverty—that is, those who live with humility and detachment from their wealth and use it rightly for the glory of God. He then contrasts the "poor rich" with those "unworthy poor" who he characterizes as rich in vice and avarice. Much like the Roman moralists who would have clucked their tongues at the sight of a wealthy woman giving to a beggar, Clement argues,

> Again, in the same way there is a genuinely poor person and also a counterfeit and falsely named: the former is the one poor in spirit with inner personal poverty, and the latter, the one poor in a worldly sense with outward poverty. To the one poor in worldly goods but rich in vices, who is not poor in spirit and not rich toward God, God says: 'Detach yourself from the alien possessions that are in your soul, so that you may become pure in heart and see God.[24]

Clement's description of "the unworthy poor" leads to his remarkable conclusion that the poor are not blessed by God on the grounds of material poverty alone. He writes,

> It is not a great thing or desirable to be without any wealth, unless it be we are seeking eternal life. If it were, those who possess nothing—the destitute, the beggars seeking food, and the poor living in the streets—would become the blessed and loved of God, even though they did not know God or God's righteousness. They would be granted eternal life on the basis of this extreme poverty and their lack of even the basic necessities of life![25]

Jesus's simple statement that "Blessed are the poor"—by which Jesus most certainly meant the destitute, the beggars seeking food, and the poor living in the streets—made no sense to the elitist Clement. Instead, Clement argues that what Jesus must have really meant to say (but seemingly failed to mention) is "blessed are the holy poor," including the rich who could answer Christ's call by practicing spiritual detachment from avarice.

In reflecting on Clement of Alexandria, I keep coming back to the fact that he was himself a member of the Alexandrian elite and wrote this treatise from a place of pastoral concern for the wealthy families who were joining the church. He must have seen the way that a simple reading of many of Jesus's statements was problematic for his people, and so he offers a reinterpretation of those statements with an eye toward building a more inclusive church. Clement's conclusions sound like most Christians' views on wealth today, "that the way of salvation is not entirely closed to the rich, and that what really counts is one's love of God above anything else."[26]

This pastoral concern is evident throughout his treatise. Instead of discussing how wealth is made, for example, Clement refocuses the conversation to how this wealth, including inheritances, might be used. Instead of preaching that the materially poor are preferentially blessed, he argues that both the rich and poor are equal in needing to practice spiritual detachment from the sin of avarice. Finally, Clement renders a reading of the parable of the unjust steward that must have become a source of solace for those with a great deal of "dishonest wealth" at their disposal. He argues that the meaning of this parable is to retain and use "dishonest wealth" to make holy friendships in this life, particularly through contributions to the church.

A generous reading of Clement of Alexandria, then, will celebrate how he employs a non-literal reading to not only widen the eye of the needle but also to widen the tent to help build a church that embraces rich and poor alike. Through his defense of wealthy Christian's responsible stewardship of riches, "he provided an extended framework for Christian views of money and possessions for centuries to come."[27]

But in the end, I don't think his arguments for wealth stewardship hold up to scrutiny. I've stated this from a variety of angles but wish to conclude this section by bringing in the father of Latin American liberation theology, Gustavo Gutiérrez, who strongly critiqued this rather abstract approach to wealth and poverty.

Gutiérrez writes extensively about how this widespread misinterpretation of "spiritual poverty" ultimately serves the material and economic interests of primarily first-world, wealthy Christians. By separating spiritual and material poverty, first-world Christians have been able to rationalize their wealth: the rich are allowed to be wealthy so long as they remain emotionally detached from their possessions.[28]

Yet Gutiérrez holds that even this proclaimed spiritual detachment is false, for how detached can the rich truly be when they consistently retain their wealth in the face of so much desperation and poverty?[29]

It is a comforting thought that a person can be both wealthy and spiritually detached from one's wealth at the same time. Gutiérrez's piercing questions, however, lead me to believe this spiritual detachment is ultimately disingenuous, a philosophical rendering of this difficult passage that reflects "too much the devices and desires of our own hearts."[30] I confess that I am a literalist on this question of material dispossession even if, in the end, I find I lack the courage to follow this teaching. Better, I think, to simply be bracingly honest about one's capacity and willingness to live into this aspect of what it means to follow Christ and to pray and strive for transformation.

The second half of this book can be read as an all-out battle over clashing ideas over the usefulness of wealth and power in the public square. Clement's understanding of wealth is solidified with the rise of the first Christian emperor, Constantine, and as Christianity becomes the church of the Roman Empire. In many respects, this was a point of no return for Christianity, one in which the new religion became inseparable from imperial wealth and power.

At the same time, however, I am inspired and strengthened by the many voices of critique and resistance that emerge in response to this turn. These voices seek to remind the church of the old notions of *koinonia*, to redirect Clement's "stewardship of wealth" toward something along the lines of "stewardship of humanity," and aim to reconnect a religion obsessed with "golden cups" and "bespangled cloths" and "silver chains" to the people needing a cup of water, a winter coat, and those who were held in chains in prison. There is also, at last, a full-throated Christian critique of the economic institution of slavery—something embarrassingly absent from the earliest Christian literature even though Jesus identified himself and is repeatedly described as a slave. These forthcoming counterpoints and prophetic voices murmuring off to the side can still be a source of hope and inspiration for the church today.

Discussion Questions

The historian Mary Beard notes that "Elite Roman writers were mostly disdainful of those less fortunate, and less rich, than themselves. Apart from their nostalgic admiration of a simple peasant way of life—a fantasy of country picnics, and lazy afternoons under shady trees—they found little virtue in poverty or in the poor or even in earning an honest day's wages."[31] They largely understood the disparities between rich and poor as foreordained by the gods and, as such, believed it wasn't worth spending time worrying about the poor.[32] How do you see these attitudes reflected in society today? Are there differences in how the urban poor are depicted versus depictions of poverty in rural life? Do popular fantasies about rural poverty (country picnics, lazy afternoons under shady trees) still shape political and economic life?

Clement argues that Jesus's statement to the rich man is best understood as a command to eliminate inner passions: "If an affluent person can control the power that wealth brings and remains modest and self-controlled, seeking God and placing God above all else, that person can follow the commandments as a poor individual, one who is free and unencumbered by the wounds of wealth."[33] What do you make of this argument? Do you think this is faithful to Jesus's message in the gospels?

Clement was member of the Alexandrian elite and wrote this treatise from a place of pastoral concern for the wealthy families who were joining the church. In many respects, his arguments helped to build a more inclusive church, one that was able to embrace both the rich and the poor (albeit in that order). This leads me to a series of challenging questions: What constitutes faithful pastoral care for the wealthy? What is lost when a church is no longer primarily made up of the poor? How can the values of pastoral care and inclusivity toward the wealthy be honored while still remaining true to the bracing message of the gospels?

A Next Step

Clement ushers into Christianity notions of the "worthy" and
"unworthy" poor, a distinction that has become deeply ingrained
in contemporary Christianity. Clement is among the first Christian
voices to conclude the poor are not blessed by God on the grounds
of material poverty alone: "To the one poor in worldly goods but
rich in vices, who is not poor in spirit and not rich toward God,
God says: 'Detach yourself from the alien possessions that are in
your soul, so that you may become pure in heart and see God.'"[34]
Recall where and how you've heard notions of the "worthy" and
"unworthy" poor being discussed in your life. Did you hear these
messages while growing up? How do images of the "unworthy" poor
get used in national and international politics today? Lastly, reflect
on whether Jesus made a distinction between the "worthy" and
"unworthy" poor.

Endnotes

1 Beard, *SPQR*, 444.

2 Beard, *SPQR*, 440.

3 McGuckin, *The Path of Christianity*, 1026.

4 Annaliese Parkin, "'You Do Him No Service:' An Exploration of Pagan Almsgiving," in *Poverty in the Roman World*, ed. E.M. Atkins and Robin Osborne (Cambridge, England: Cambridge University Press, 2009), 68.

5 Parkin, "'You Do Him No Service," 62.

6 McGuckin, *The Path of Christianity*, 1027.

7 Juvenal 3.153-4, tr. Neville Morley, in "The Poor in the City of Rome," *Poverty in the Roman World*, 35.

8 I clearly have it out for Clement of Alexandria. For a much more charitable read of his work, I recommend Justo González's summary in *Faith and Wealth*.

9 Matthew 19:16-30; Mark 10:17-31; Luke 18:18-30

10 González, *Faith and Wealth*, 112.

11 González, *Faith and Wealth*, 112.

12 MacCulloch, *Christianity*, 147.

13 MacCulloch, *Christianity*, 149.

14 "Clement of Alexandria, The Rich Young Ruler," in *Wealth and Poverty in Early Christianity*, ed. Rhee, loc. 844, (Kindle).

15 "Clement of Alexandria, The Rich Young Ruler," *Wealth and Poverty in Early Christianity*, loc. 764, (Kindle).

16 "Clement of Alexandria, The Rich Young Ruler," *Wealth and Poverty in Early Christianity*, loc. 793, (Kindle).

17 "Clement of Alexandria, The Rich Young Ruler," *Wealth and Poverty in Early Christianity*, loc. 844, (Kindle).

18 Joost W. Hengstmengel, "Wealth," in *Brill Encyclopedia of Early Christianity Online*, ed. Hunter, van Geest, and Peerbolte.

19 Hengstmengel, "Wealth."

20 "Clement of Alexandria, The Rich Young Ruler," *Wealth and Poverty in Early Christianity*, ed. Rhee, loc. 793, (Kindle).

21 Translation by González, *Faith and Wealth*, 113.

22 Luke 16:9.

23 Hennie Stender, "Economics in the Church Fathers," in *Oxford Handbook of Christianity and Economics* (Oxford: Oxford University Press, 2014), 27.

24 "Clement of Alexandria, The Rich Young Ruler," *Wealth and Poverty in Early Christianity*, loc. 804, (Kindle).

25 "Clement of Alexandria, The Rich Young Ruler," *Wealth and Poverty in Early Christianity*, loc. 774 (Kindle).

26 González, *Faith and Wealth*, 112.

27 MacCulloch, *Christianity*, 149.

28 Roberto Goizueta, "Liberation Theology 1: Gustavo Gutierrez," in *The Blackwell Companion to Political Theology*,(Hoboken, New Jersey: Blackwell Publishing, 2004), 283.

29 Goizueta, "Liberation Theology 1," 283.

30 The Book of Common Prayer, Confession of Sin, 41.

31 Beard, *SPQR*, 440.

32 McGuckin, *The Path of Christianity*, 1026.

33 "Clement of Alexandria, The Rich Young Ruler," *Wealth and Poverty in Early Christianity*, loc. 844, (Kindle).

34 "Clement of Alexandria, The Rich Young Ruler," *Wealth and Poverty in Early Christianity*, loc. 804, (Kindle).

IN THE
PUBLIC
SQUARE

In the Public Square

There is an important turning point in texts from these first centuries. In many of the prior texts, poor people still had names. There is Mary, Martha, Lazarus, Andrew, John, Paul, Barnabus, Chloe, etc. Even Hermas, the central figure of *The Shepherd of Hermas*, was a former slave who had gained wealth and then lost much of it amidst the persecution of Christians. Over time, however, one ceases to hear about the individual names and stories of people but instead begins to hear of "the poor" as a construct as seen from afar, a generalization to be dealt with either positively or negatively.

The father of Latin American Liberation Theology, Gustavo Gutiérrez, describes this Christian tendency to speak of "the poor" in the abstract as inflicting spiritual and psychological harm. He believes that a marker of liberation is when "the poor" are no longer merely *acted upon* but have names, identities, stories, and agency within history.[1] As you will recall from the discussion of Paul's compensation as a form of proximity, Gutiérrez defines solidarity as rooted in friendship with actual communities—that is, people with names and stories and contradictions—as opposed to an ideology or generalized political progressiveness.

While this tendency to speak of "the poor" was already occurring, it became especially prevalent as Christianity underwent a radical transformation in the fourth century. The fourth century is when the previously fledgling and persecuted faith was unexpectedly embraced by Constantine the Great, the first Christian emperor of Rome. Constantine would forever change the warp and woof of Christianity as it became the religion of the Roman imperial elite.

Such a dramatic change in fortunes required Christianity to develop or elaborate on prior ideas of wealth and power so that it could accommodate the powerful families that now made up its ranks. The conversation suddenly turned from being an internal debate about whether the wealthy and powerful could become a part of the church toward a discussion of Christianity's powerful role in the public square. Now Christians began to shape imperial decrees and receive state support for charitable institutions. In short, Christians became deeply intertwined with the state in imagining and structuring what a faithful society should look like, and "the poor" were discussed as if seen from a balcony overlooking society below.

Contrast this with where this story began, in a gospel setting in which it is Lazarus whose name we know and the rich man who remains a generalized figure (though Christian tradition later names him Dives), a proclamation of good news wherein the wealthy and beautiful people are sidelined. In this form of early Christianity, Paul speaks to specific communities and mentions people by name, sharing their conflicts and stories. By the fourth century, Christianity moves further and further away from these types of relationships, a sign of what gets lost as wealthy and powerful Christians take center stage in this evolving story.

13 Constantine's Imperial Benefits (Many Strings Attached)

While in college, I studied the Roman Catholic Social Justice tradition and was shaped by the witness of people like Archbishop Óscar Romero (1917-1980), a one-time conservative and diffident faith leader who transformed into one of the most outspoken advocates on behalf of the poor amidst El Salvador's violent civil conflict.

Archbishop Romero's personal transformation and the sermons he ultimately delivered, broadcast throughout the countryside, are a striking example of a bishop rising to the occasion and risking everything for the sake of truth and justice. In a violent and chaotic time, Romero's homilies were considered one of the few trusted sources of accurate information about what was actually happening. His efforts to get as much information as possible about what happened to *los desaparecidos* (those who had been "disappeared" by the state) stands as an example of a church leader leveraging their position to uncover truths that many would have preferred to remain in secret. All of this brought about repeated threats on his life, and he was ultimately assassinated by a right-wing death squad while saying mass in 1980.[2]

Examples like Archbishop Romero helped me to understand what the church's prophetic role in the public square could be, and more recent examples of leaders like Bishop William Barber and the Rev. Liz Theoharis of the Poor People's Campaign, Bishop Mariann Budde of the Episcopal Diocese of Washington, and my colleague Dean Kelly Brown Douglas of Episcopal Divinity School at Union, have all affirmed for me what Christianity looks like when faithfully speaking truth to power in the public square.

But for every one of these courageous and prophetic voices, the painful reality of Christianity in America today is that there are also powerful Christians like Ralph Drollinger, a one-time athlete and sports evangelist from California who led weekly Bible studies in President Trump's White House for cabinet secretaries.[3] By spring of 2018, Drollinger's Bible studies, some of which took place in the West Wing, included regular participation from eleven of fifteen cabinet secretaries with former Vice President Mike Pence occasionally in attendance.[4]

Drollinger has stated that "a movement for Christ among governing authorities holds promise to change the direction of a whole country," and this includes advising at the highest level on issues of wealth and poverty. Journalist Katherine Stewart notes, "In a Bible study titled, 'Toward a Better Biblical Understanding of Lawmaking,' [Drollinger] cites 1 Peter 2:18-21, 'Servants, be submissive to your masters with all respect, not only to those who are good and gentle, but also to those who are unreasonable.' Here Drollinger explains, 'The economy of Rome at the time of Peter's writing was one of slave and master. The principle however, of submitting to one's boss carries over to today.'"[5] Similarly, Drollinger is a strong advocate for limiting the right to vote of the poor, arguing "if there is not a change to a flat tax soon, citizens who are now both on government subsistence programs and paying no income tax should have the privilege of voting curtailed until their case proves otherwise."[6]

Clearly, Drollinger's voice represents a very different sort of Christian witness in the public square than those who use their positions to "speak truth to power" about the injustices experienced by the most vulnerable members of society. Christianity's role in the public square is a contradictory one, to say the least, with multiple visions competing over how society should be structured, especially around issues of wealth and poverty. What's fascinating for me, then, is to see the way these contradictions can be traced all the way back to that transformational period in the fourth century when Christianity first emerged onto the public square.

For the first few centuries, Christians were a persecuted, insular, and secretive group within the empire. One humorous detail from the period before Constantine is that many Christians in the city of Rome were so averse to public engagement that they were said to have had a certain "sweet" smell, a delicate way of describing the result of their careful avoidance of the public baths. This inward focus also shows up in how Christianity thought about wealth and poverty. Christianity's care for the poor—expressed through *koinonia*—was primarily carried out within and among Christian assemblies and was therefore primarily directed to the vulnerable members within the community.

This inward focus changed dramatically in the fourth century with the rise of Constantine and imperial Christianity. Under Constantine, Christianity was forced out into the public square. Christianity was officially recognized, vast churches began to be built, clergy received tax exemptions, and the liturgy itself began to reflect the splendor of imperial households. Bishops were suddenly charged with being "lovers of the poor" and were made magistrates of an appeals court system, the church was assigned the role of offering charity toward the Christian and non-Christian poor alike, and previously established charitable networks became subsidized by the state. All of these benefits and newfound responsibilities were in exchange for loyalty to the emperor and, according to historian Peter Brown, required Christian clergy to practice the Roman virtue of *verecundia*—namely, the art and practice of knowing one's place.

Looking at this transformational period offers an opportunity to reflect on how Christianity currently engages in issues of wealth and poverty in the public square today. What one sees, both in the fourth and fifth centuries as well as today, is the emergence of competing versions of Christianity in the public square. On the one hand, some Christians would use their newfound proximity to power to serve as chaplains to the wealthy and build up the church's own wealth and influence. On the other, some Christians leveraged their public roles to "speak truth to power" on the suffering of the most vulnerable members of Roman society. It was schizophrenic right from the start, in other words, and this may have been in no small part a result of the contradictory and conflicted person and personality of the first Christian emperor, Constantine.

The Emperor Constantine was a violent, capricious, and paradoxical figure, "an autocrat who never ruled alone; a firm legislator for the Roman family, yet who slew his wife and eldest son and was perhaps, himself, illegitimate; a dynastic puppet-master, who left no clear successor; a soldier whose legacy was far more spiritual than temporal."[7] His conversion and military victories as a newly converted Christian helped forge an imperial Christianity that oftentimes had very little to do with the humble life and teachings of Jesus of Nazareth. And yet, at the same time, Constantine embraced the church's charism for caring for the poor, a *koinonia* that had been practiced between and among Christians but now became the public responsibility of bishops who now oversaw a church subsidized by imperial wealth.

Constantine's faith likely had its origins in his mother, Helena, who was a Christian from her youth and had already opened the future emperor to "the inner life of the communities, which he admired for its monotheism and practicality of morals."[8] He was also influenced by his tutor, the Christian philosopher-rhetorician Lactantius, who first joined Constantine while he was an imperial hostage in Nicomedia and then later became an adviser on religious matters to the emperor. Lactantius's teachings on justice and the equality of all people in the eyes of God may have shaped Constantine's decision to make Christian bishops magistrates over appeals courts, thereby expanding access to Rome's court system to the poor.[9]

Surpassing the influence of his mother Helena and Lactantius, however, was Constantine's own staggering ambition to imperial power and his (somewhat surprising) belief that worshipping the god of the Christians would ensure military success. Brown notes that Constantine's conversion to Christianity "was an act of supreme willfulness, such as only a charismatic Roman emperor could have undertaken" and one in defiance of the majority of citizens of the empire. In converting to Christianity, "[Constantine] put himself under the protection of the Christian God, and in so doing, he deliberately chose a God as big and as new as himself," one that was "an all-powerful and transcendent deity who owed nothing to the past."[10]

Constantine took a convoluted route to becoming sole emperor of Rome. His journey began in the year 306 CE as his father, Constantius I, who was the emperor of the western half of the Roman Empire, lay dying in what is now York in Britain.

The prior Roman Emperor Diocletian had divided the Roman Empire into east and west in 295 and appointed a "tetrarchy" composed of two senior emperors, who were each accompanied by junior emperors-in-training. This essentially resulted in four different rulers constantly vying for legitimacy and power. The shortcomings of this approach became apparent soon after Diocletian's abdication in 305.

Diocletian's renunciation of the throne set the stage for civil war. When Constantius I died in 306, his troops defied imperial authorities and declared his son, Constantine, emperor of the west. The military's support for Constantine went against the tetrarchy's desires and resulted in a civil war in which Constantine would eventually defeat Maxentius, who, through many twists and turns, had become his chief rival for control of the western portion of the Roman Empire.

Constantine's crucial victory over Maxentius occurred at the battle of the Milvian Bridge in Rome in 312. A new, military-grade version of Christianity was thought to have played a key role in this for "during what became a crushing victory for Constantine, his troops bore on their shields a new Christian symbol, the *Chi Rho*, the first two letters of Christ's name in Greek combined as a monogram."[11] "The Christians ever after attributed the startlingly 'easy' conquest of Rome to the 'new god' who had instructed Constantine to draw on the cross as the new palladium of Rome."[12]

Having defeated his rival in the western half of the empire, Constantine continued his quest to become sole emperor of all of Rome through a protracted challenge of the remaining emperor of the east, Licinius. With Constantine's rise to power closely tied to Christianity, Licinius acquiesced to the Edict of Milan in 313, the first imperial edict of religious toleration granting Christianity legal status and rights in Rome.[13] However, over the course of the following ten years, as Constantine began to offer generous financial support for Christian clergy and churches, Licinius became increasingly anxious that Christians generally—but especially his Christian troops—would shift their loyalties to his rival Constantine. As a result, Licinius began sporadic persecutions of Christians, which "became the substantive cause of the final war with Constantine, who was, no doubt, glad of the excuse which they provided for him."[14]

In 324, 18 years after his father's troops had declared him emperor of the western half of the empire, Constantine defeated Licinius, completing his quest to become the sole emperor of Rome, and he did so under the banner of the new, military-styled God of the Christians.

Constantine's version of the Christian faith represented a radical and occasionally perplexing reinterpretation of Christian teachings through the lens of his own military quest for imperial power. Many scholars have noted that the supposedly Christian God who Constantine called upon before his battle at the Milvian Bridge in 312 has a lot more in common with the military god Sol Invictus (Unconquered Sun) than with Jesus's life and teachings.

Gone is the Jesus who urged his followers to turn the other cheek; earlier traditions that had forbidden Christians from serving in the military were soon replaced not only by Christian troops but also with military chaplaincy.[15] Money undoubtedly played a role in smoothing these matters over, for despite Constantine's hodgepodge approach, "as he began showering privileges on the Christian clergy, it is unlikely that many of them considered whether the emperor should be given a theological cross-examination before they accepted their unexpected gifts."[16]

Those very unexpected gifts and privileges offered to Christian clergy marked an important turning point in how Christians thought about wealth and power.

The material benefits of Constantine's reign for Christians began even before Constantine became sole emperor. Christian clergy in the west were made exempt from taxation and other civic duties; slaves were able to be manumitted before a gathering in the presence of a bishop; Sunday was declared a day of rest; and penalties against celibacy and childlessness were rescinded, an easing of prior restrictions on Christian clergy.[17] The Edict of Milan of 313 also "officially acknowledged what had been a *de facto* reality of the church's ownership of buildings, cemeteries, gardens, and other movable and immovable properties throughout the third century by ordering their restoration."[18]

Significantly, and as a harbinger of things to come, among these various benefits was also the legal privileging of Christians over and against Jews. A new imperial prohibition stating that "Christians may not be insultingly called Jews" signaled a new era in which legal distinctiveness of Christianity was established by revoking the privileges previously extended to Judaism.[19] Jews were no longer permitted to own Christian slaves; they were to refrain from harassing members of their communities who converted to Christianity; they were also no longer permitted to enter imperial service; and the building of synagogues was to cease.[20] Constantine, therefore, embraced Christians' resentments toward Jewish communities and codified them into law.

Such privileging and prioritization of Christianity represented a stunning change of fortunes for a religion that not so long ago had been fiercely persecuted by one of Constantine's predecessors, the Emperor Diocletian. Prior to Constantine, Christianity had managed to grow from a small Jewish sect in the first century to somewhere between 7 to 10 percent of the imperial population by the third.[21] While 7 to 10 percent of the Roman population was substantial, little could have prepared the Christian community for the transformation that occurred when Constantine rose to power. Rhee notes, "When Constantine seized the imperial power (in the West) with the power of the Christian God (312 CE), the church had been functioning as a formidable social and economic institution with massive operation of charity," but the impact of Constantine suddenly granting religious freedom, financial subsidies, and clerical exemption from taxes "was nothing less than revolutionary."[22]

The material impact of this transformation can be seen most easily through the church architecture and buildings of this period. Before Constantine, "Christians had not developed a distinct architecture for their public buildings for the simple reason that they did not have many," and those that Christians did possess "were, by and large, private dwellings converted for the purpose."[23] In the city of Rome, at least 25 pre-Constantinian Christian communities met in converted premises, humble venues that had been confiscated during the prior Emperor Diocletian's persecutions.

Constantine both restored these properties to Christians after his victory over Maxentius and began Christianity's love affair with architecture through an empire-wide building campaign, for humble venues no longer "befit a religious community now in imperial favour."[24] Famous examples of churches built during this period include St. Peter's and the Basilica of St. Laurentius (outside the walls) in Rome, the Golden Church in Antioch, the Church of the Twelve Apostles in Constantinople, and churches on the supposed sites of Golgotha, of Christ's resurrection, and at Mamre for the theophany to Abraham.[25] Constantine also proclaimed in stone how he understood his own role in Christian history by constructing a mausoleum for himself seven years before his death. In what would become the Church of the Holy Apostles in Constantinople, this church was "intended to be endowed with memorials of all twelve apostles" wherein "he would lie as the thirteenth and last of the messengers of God."[26]

Other innovations came in the form of what was on display during the worship that took place within those buildings. Constantine supplied the funds for 50 copies of the Bible, two of which remain today called the *Codex Vaticanus* and the *Codex Sinaiticus*. These 50 Bibles represented "an extraordinary expenditure on creating deluxe written texts, for which the parchment alone would have required the death of around five thousand cows (so much for Christian disapproval of animal sacrifice)."[27] Constantine's wealth also transformed how bishops and clergy dressed during worship, giving rise to the ornate liturgical vestments that are still seen today. "The copes, chasubles, mitres, maples, fans, bells, censers of solemn ceremony throughout the church from East to West were all borrowed from the daily observances of imperial and royal households. Anything less would have been a penny-pinching insult to God."[28]

In addition to these architectural liturgical displays of wealth, Brown's work in *Eye of the Needle: Wealth, the Fall of Rome, and the Making of Christianity in the West, 350-550 AD*, offers a detailed look at Constantine's decision to release bishops and clergy both from taxes as well as forms of public service. "From 313 onward," he notes, "Constantine granted to bishops and clergymen the same privileges that had always been accorded by Roman emperors to those who furthered the cultural and religious ends of Roman society," which "consisted of exemption from many forms of public service and even (but more grudgingly) from certain forms of personal taxation."[29]

This resulted in clergy gaining enviable leisure that allowed them to devote themselves wholeheartedly to study and worship. Constantine's pious son Constantius II would later state that such leisure helped ensure that Christian clergy would offer the form of right worship that safeguarded the continuing strength of the empire. It also certainly helped to strengthen a sense of loyalty among Christian clergy to said empire.[30]

To understand the day-to-day significance of this decision to grant tax exemptions and leisure to the clergy, Brown explores the ways that taxes and duties were collected at the time. The Roman Empire functioned as a minimal state in which many tasks of government were delegated to local authorities, particularly town councillors (the curiales) and the trade associations (the collegia and the corpora) of the cities. "Imperial demands for labor bit into the time of town councillors—and even, for the average townsman (who was subject to corvée labor), into their own bodies—quite as deeply as the imperial taxes bit into their pockets. To receive exemption from such duties was to step into an altogether enviable oasis of leisure."[31]

The newly granted benefits of tax exemptions and clergy leisure were immediately and repeatedly contested by the curiales, collegia, and corpora who had to then pick up the slack. In this zero-sum game, "the more members each group lost through some of their number receiving personal exemptions, the more 'official duties, physical toil, and sweat' would be left to be borne by the few who remained."[32] This set up a competitive dynamic between town councils, trade associations, and Christian communities who were all now seeking moderately wealthy plebians to fill positions. As a result of Constantine's tax exemptions for clergy, Christians were now competitively poised to draw from the moderately wealthy who would otherwise have been pressured into service as town councillors and heads of trade associations. The ranks of the clergy began to fill with the moderately wealthy.

This represents a remarkable transformation when one considers the low view prior emperors had of Christianity. The Emperor Domitian (51-96 CE) had violently persecuted Christians on the grounds that Christianity was "a religion of the lower classes, advocating the worship of a condemned criminal who had taught a revolutionary idea of love and freedom: dangerous ideas that had no regard for traditional religious rites, the divine authority of kings, or the sustenance of the status quo."[33] Now Christianity was buckling beneath the weight of imperial largesse and was drawing clergy from families with significantly more refined backgrounds.

And yet the freedoms and privileges, the building campaigns, vestments and liturgical objects, the tax exemptions and leisure—namely, all the wealth and privileges which now very publicly flowed into Christian churches—came with many strings attached. For "with imperial largesse, Constantine made the church not only officially visible (much more so than before) but also accountable to the public for the very public gifts it received."[34] This included a newly imposed, public responsibility for caring for Rome's poor.

Within the span of a few decades, Christians had gone from being a persecuted minority—a religion whose stories of crucifixion and martyrdoms were at the hands of imperial Rome—to being a faith suddenly receiving an outpouring of wealth from the first Christian emperor and publicly refashioning itself in accordance with the gifts received. The wealth that was now flowing to clergy and churches was to be justified to the Roman public by Christians taking on a new and public role of caring for the poor, both Christian and non-Christian alike, all the while practicing the Roman virtue of *verecundia*, the art of keeping one's head down and knowing one's place.

Prior to Constantine, the Christian church's collections for the poor had been primarily for the poor within and among the Christian assemblies, both in congregations or as gifts sent to other Christian communities who were suffering a particular hardship such as famine. Rhee writes, "Up to this point, the church received offerings from the faithful, especially the middling group and the wealthy, because it primarily cared for the poor of its own, i.e., Christians."[35] Now the very public gifts which Christian churches received came with a newly imposed, public responsibility of caring not only for their own poor but also for the publicly registered poor, both Christian and non-Christian alike.[36] Significantly, during this period a new and universal interpretation of Matthew 25:31-45 began to surface, one in which it was understood that Christ appeared in every person, not just fellow Christians, who were hungry, thirsty, strangers, naked, and imprisoned.[37]

This new, public role for the church manifested itself in many different ways, but I will focus on discussing just three: namely, the new role of bishops as magistrates of an appeals court, the all-important food distribution, and the imposed agreement that Christian clergy not only be loyal but that they also keep their head down (*verecundia*), focus on helping the poor, and avoid being pushy.

Constantine elevated the role of Christian bishops to that of local magistrates of an appeals court that ran parallel to the Roman system, an important milestone for those interested in Christianity's engagement in the justice system. Constantine was keenly aware of the strength of Christianity's administrative structures, particularly the way the church divided its regions into dioceses and appointed bishops as "overseers." By elevating these "overseeing" bishops to the role of local magistrates, he opened a judicial court system to a greater number of Roman citizens, expanding access to the poor. Rhee writes that this was, essentially, "an ecclesiastical court for appeals cases, open to both Christians and non-Christians, especially for the poor and the powerless, that granted bishops the final judicial authority in arbitrating civil suits."[38] Historian John McGuckin adds: "This meant that poorer people could for the first time feel confident about having access to Roman law, with a chance of receiving equity and justice from someone who possibly knew them and their family and was committed to pastoral care and moral values, without desire for corrupt profit."[39]

In addition to this new role for bishops, churches became imperially subsidized distribution points for food and clothing. Rhee writes, "Constantine delegated distribution of grain dole and clothing to the bishops for the continuing care of widows, orphans, the elderly, and the poor who were registered on the church lists as the 'official' poor; and the church in Antioch, for example, received 36,000 measures of grain, an amount sufficient for supporting a thousand people for a year."[40]

Constantine's nephew and imperial successor, Julian the Apostate (331-363), later griped about the way this food and clothing distribution became so closely identified with the Christians and their churches. Julian tried in his very brief reign to return the Roman Empire to the traditional gods worshipped prior to Constantine. Referring to Christians as Galileans and atheists, Julian complained, "For it is disgraceful that, when no Jew ever has to beg, and the impious Galilaeans support not only their own poor but ours as well, all men see that our people lack aid from us."[41] As I'll discuss in a future chapter, part of Julian's plan to undermine Christianity involved replicating such distribution of food and clothing to the poor through the Hellenic temples he was newly subsidizing, an act that revealed a begrudging admiration for the administrative structures that Christians had put into place.

With this new public responsibility to care for the poor came an additional imperial requirement for Christians to keep their head down, not draw clergy from the wealthiest and most powerful families, and to practice the virtue of "knowing one's place." Brown notes that in Constantine's mind the church's "business was to look downward to the poor. As Constantine explained in an edict issued in 329: 'The wealthy must be there to support the obligations of the secular world, while the poor are maintained by the wealth of the churches.'"[42]

Christians were to offer their unfailing loyalty and support to the Roman emperor and clergy were expected to practice *verecundia*, a virtue of sub-elites. In this, Christian bishops and priests joined "experts such as schoolteachers, grammarians, and doctors [who] were expected to show *verecundia* in the presence of their social superiors. For all the indispensable skills they communicated to their patrons, they remained 'social paupers' compared with the real leaders of society. They were not to be 'pushy.'"[43]

Many Christians (including myself) have long thought of Constantine's conversion and his subsequent transformation of Christianity in exclusively negative terms, a turning point in which the church sold its soul for imperial subsidies, tax exemptions, grand basilicas, and those golden-threaded vestments still being worn by clergy today. This still seems basically true to me. And yet, insomuch as a goal of writing this book is to nuance simple narratives, this story must also include the fact that it is during this same period when Christianity went from a highly insular, inward-looking faith toward having responsibilities in the public square.

The financial benefits that Christians received meant that, for the first time, Christians (and bishops especially) were responsible for caring for the poor, both Christian and non-Christian alike. Frankly it's difficult to imagine the riveting sermons of later figures like Basil of Cesarea, John Chrysostom, and Gregory of Nyssa—all of whom offered searing critiques of Roman society—without Constantine's imposing on the church generally and bishops in particular this new public role as "governors" and "lovers" of the poor. The question that emerges for me is whether this is one aspect of Constantine's legacy that the church today should espouse. What would it mean for priests and bishops, especially, to embrace a public role as advocates for justice and for the poor?

Discussion Questions

Take some time to look closely at the Nicene Creed, originally adopted at the first ecumenical council in 325, a gathering of Christian bishops held under the watchful eye of the Emperor Constantine at his summer retreat of Nicaea. Which aspects of Jesus are emphasized in this statement of correct belief? Which aspects of his ministry are downplayed or have gone entirely missing?

Money has a way of changing everything. How do you see Christianity changing as a result of the sudden influx of wealth flowing to churches and clergy? What vestiges of this imperial faith remain from this period?

What do you think about the various privileges afforded to Christian churches today including tax exemptions and, increasingly for some, federal funding for charitable efforts (faith-based initiatives)? In Constantine's time, the influx of funding came with significant and explicitly stated *quid pro quos*. Do you sense any *quid pro quos* occurring around churches, tax exemptions, and federal funding today?

A Next Step

Learn more about a fairly recent shift in policy around federal support for faith-based initiatives. In 2003, then-President Bush stated, "Governments can and should support effective social services provided by religious people, so long as they work, and as long as those services go to anyone in need, regardless of their faith."[44] This initially caused alarm among those who saw this as a blurring of the constitutional line separating church and state. Nevertheless, by March of 2005, the White House reported having given more than $2 billion in grants the prior year to social programs operated by faith communities, possibly "the most money the federal government had given in one year to religious charities."[45] Compare and contrast this recent example of state support for faith-based charity with Constantine's approach to Christianity.

Endnotes

1 Goizueta, "Liberation Theology 1: Gustavo Gutiérrez," 284.

2 I want to commend Julio Torres's recent psychological biography of Romero entitled *Oscar Romero: A Man For Our Times* (New York: Seabury Books, 2021).

3 Stewart, *The Power Worshippers*, 34.

4 Stewart, *The Power Worshippers,* 41.

5 Stewart, *The Power Worshippers*, 48.

6 Stewart, *The Power Worshippers,* 49.

7 Bill Leadbetter, "Constantine," in *The Early Christian World: Volume 1* (England: Routledge Worlds, 2000), 996.

8 McGuckin, *The Path of Christianity,* 281.

9 McGuckin, *The Path of Christianity,* 280-281.

10 Brown, *Through the Eye of a Needle,* 31.

11 MacCulloch, *Christianity*, 189.

12 McGuckin, *The Path of Christianity*, 280-281.

13 McGuckin, *The Path of Christianity*, 338.

14 Leadbetter, "Constantine," 1001.

15 Leadbetter, "Constantine," 1005.

16 MacCulloch, *Christianity*, 191.

17 Leadbetter, "Constantine," 996.

18 Rhee, *Loving the Poor, Saving the Rich*, loc. 4213-4240 (Kindle).

19 Leadbetter, "Constantine," Theodosian Code 16.8.9.

20 Leadbetter, "Constantine," Theodosian Code 16.9.3, 16.8.5, 16.8.24, 16.8.27.

21 McGuckin, *The Path of Christianity*, 336.

22 Rhee, *Loving the Poor, Saving the Rich*, loc. 4213-4240 (Kindle).

23 Leadbetter, "Constantine," loc. 1003 (Kindle).

24 Leadbetter, "Constantine," loc. 1003 (Kindle).

25 Rhee, *Loving the Poor, Saving the Rich*, loc. 4213-4240 (Kindle).

26 Leadbetter, "Constantine," loc. 1004 (Kindle).

27 MacCulloch, *Christianity*, 191-192.

28 MacCulloch, *Christianity*, 199.

29 Brown, *Through the Eye of a Needle*, 35-36.

30 Brown, *Through the Eye of a Needle*, 35-36.

31 Brown, *Through the Eye of a Needle*, 35-36.

32 Brown, *Through the Eye of a Needle*, 35-36.

33 McGuckin, *The Path of Christianity*, 123.

34 Rhee, *Loving the Poor, Saving the Rich*, loc. 4240 (Kindle).

35 Rhee, *Loving the Poor, Saving the Rich*, loc. 4240-4257 (Kindle).

36 Rhee, *Loving the Poor, Saving the Rich*, loc. 4240-4257 (Kindle).

37 Rhee, *Loving the Poor, Saving the Rich*, loc. 4240-4257 (Kindle).

38 Rhee, *Loving the Poor, Saving the Rich*, loc. 4213-4240 (Kindle).

39 McGuckin, *The Path of Christianity*, 296

40 Rhee, *Loving the Poor, Saving the Rich*, loc. 4240-4257 (Kindle).

41 A.M. Harmon, tr., *The Works of the Emperor Julian, Volume III*, Loeb Classical Library (Cambridge, Massachusetts: Harvard University Press, 1913).

42 Brown, *Through the Eye of a Needle*, 43-44.

43 Brown, *Through the Eye of a Needle*, 44-45.

44 David Stout, "Bush Pushes Faith-Based Agenda," *The New York Times*, February 10, 2003.

45 Elisabeth Bumiller, "Bush Says $2 Billion Went to Religious Charities in '04," *The New York Times*, March 2, 2005.

14 Lactantius on Justice, Equality, and Mercy

Justice, equality, and mercy are important terms for thinking about Christianity's witness in the public square. I have recently heard philosopher and theologian Cornel West define justice as "what love looks like in public." Several years ago, I heard Bryan Stevenson, founder of the Equal Justice Initiative in Montgomery, Alabama, speak extensively on just mercy. I have also recently heard the terms racial justice and racial equality used interchangeably at two separate meetings of Episcopal organizations. All three of these words get used when discussing Christianity's responsibilities toward the poor and so it's worthwhile looking at how these words were used and defined in the first few centuries of the church.

North African lay rhetorician-philosopher-theologian Lactantius (c.250-325) is believed to be the first Christian thinker to subject the idea of societal justice to serious analysis.[1] Justice, equality, and mercy are key ideas in his work, *The Divine Institutes,* which is a manifesto written to the first Christian emperor about what a Christian society should look like and prioritize. It represents the first time a Christian theologian is appealing to a Christian emperor to recast society in a way that is in greater alignment with the values of the faith.

In *The Divine Institutes*, Lactantius makes a compelling case that a Christian society grounded in God's justice is comprised of two parts: 1) piety toward Christ and 2) a valuing of the *aequitas* (equality) of all people as made in the image of God. To exercise "justice," therefore, means creating a more compassionate and merciful society in which all people—including groups who were largely considered expendable by Roman society—were treated in a humane way. Interestingly, the groups Lactantius names remain among the most marginalized even in the twenty-first century. Lactantius argues a Christian society is one that is compassionate in its treatment of the hungry, immigrants and refugees, captives, children and widows in need, the sick, and strangers and beggars in need of burial.[2] Grounding this argument is his remarkable restatement of the Golden Rule for the public square: "The whole nature of justice lies in our providing for others through humanity what we provide for our own families and relatives through affection."[3]

Born in North Africa in 240, Lactantius was the official chair of Latin rhetoric at the imperial summer residence of Nicomedia, in what is now modern-day Turkey.[4] It was there around 300 CE that Lactantius first taught a young Constantine who was, at that time, being held there in comfortable captivity. The future emperor's captivity was to ensure that his father, Constantius I, then stationed in York, behaved well as junior caesar of the western half of the empire.[5]

It is unclear exactly when Lactantius converted to Christianity—whether before he arrived in Nicomedia or after—but he was most certainly a Christian when the Emperor Diocletian began the Great Persecution in 303 and purged all Christians from the imperial court. Lactantius fled and spent the next fourteen years hiding in exile, during which time he wrote the majority of *The Divine Institutes*. This text sought "to rebut ideas that had justified a policy of torture and death for professing Christians on behalf of imperial polytheism, which was supposed to insure imperial unity and security."[6] It is a text, then, that smarts from the pain of Diocletian's persecution and the use of violence against Christians.

As noted in the previous chapter, a dramatic transformation took place during the fourteen years Lactantius was in exile. Through a great deal of bloodshed and a succession of military victories, Lactantius's former student Constantine rose to become emperor of the western half of the empire in 312 and then defeated his eastern rival Licinius to become sole emperor of a united Rome in 325. At some point,

Constantine summoned Lactantius to serve in his administration, though exactly when Lactantius reappeared at Constantine's side is disputed.[7] Constantine eventually made his former teacher Lactantius an advisor on religious matters and a tutor for his son Crispus. Lactantius died around 320.

While Lactantius was serving as Constantine's religious advisor, he realized the text he had composed during exile could speak to the new imperial age in important ways. He therefore lightly revised *The Divine Institutes* and directed it toward its single most important reader, the Emperor Constantine. Constantine was, therefore, "not only the most highly placed, most august reader but the principal agent, providentially raised up, for the imperial transformation put forward by *The Divine Institutes*."[8] In this sense, it is an appeal to the emperor to transform Roman society on the new terms of Christianity.

Similar to many other thinkers of his time, Lactantius believed there was a prior period in Rome's history in which "all were equally well off because abundant and generous giving was done by those with to those without."[9] Lactantius believed that this Golden Age ended, however, when people turned away from the monotheistic worship of Saturn and began to also worship Jupiter. According to Lactantius, the turn toward polytheism resulted in greed and inequality, and this inequity was the source of all society's evils. In this age of greed, "not only did they who had a superfluity fail to bestow a share upon others, but they even seized the property of others, drawing everything to their private gain; and the things which formerly even individuals laboured to obtain for the common use of men, were now conveyed to the houses of a few."[10]

Polytheism, therefore, is inextricably linked in Lancantius's mind to the empire's highly differentiated and unequal society centered on caste and status. Such inequality was inextricably tied to societal injustice. He writes, "Therefore, neither the Romans nor the Greeks could possess justice because they kept people distinct in different levels from the poor to the rich, from the humble to the powerful, from common people to the highest authorities of kings. Where people are not all equal, there is no equality; and inequality excludes justice of itself."[11] *The Divine Institutes*, then, is an appeal to Constantine to return Roman society to a state of greater equality so that justice could prevail.

Lancantius sees the solution to society's ills as 1) equally held (or shared) worship of Christ and 2) recognition of the equality of all people as made in the image of God. "The two veins of justice are piety and equality (*aequitas*); all justice springs from these fountains. While piety forms its source and origin, equity provides all its energy and method."[12]

For Lactantius, the promise of Christian monotheism means that all people—no matter the station in life—would come to see themselves as judged equally by God. This equal judgment of all people is key to understanding Lactantius's fervor for a society united by worship, for God alone could see that all people were spiritually equal to one another. "With [God] no one is a slave and no one is a master; for if he is the same father to all, we are all his children with equal rights."[13]

But while Lactantius begins with a meditation on how polytheism had resulted in societal inequality, he is also careful to say that this spiritual equality no longer necessarily leads to shared wealth and property held in common. Indeed, modern-day libertarians love to quote Lactantius because he is clear that spiritual equality should not impinge upon people's right to private property. Instead, Lactantius echoes Paul and the ancient Christian notion of *koinonia* in saying that all people are called to bring about God's justice through *voluntary* offerings of charity and service to those in need. Historian Helen Rhee notes, "Because Lactantius understands private property and economic distinctions to be compatible with Christian justice and aequitas, the key to achieving and acting out Christian justice and *aequitas* in the present (in his society) is service to fellow humans."[14] Lactantius believes that a just society lives out right worship and honors the *aequitas* of all people through voluntary acts of mercy.

Lactantius argues that compassionate giving and voluntary acts of mercy are a shared responsibility by all in society, thus the impact on each individual is minimized as a result of it being shared. He writes, "All this instruction is not for you alone but for all the people who are united in mind and hold together as one," and "Do not think that you are being advised to reduce or exhaust your property now, but rather to convert to better uses what you would spend on excesses."[15] He goes on to say that support for the poor should come from what the wealthy would have used to buy wild animals and gladiators with, transforming waste into great sacrifice on behalf of society.

It is worth pausing here to acknowledge both the advance this represented in a society that regularly considered vast categories of the poor as expendable as well as the significant limitations of this approach in effecting concrete change. In terms of an advance, we should recall the way inequality was perceived in Roman society. Historian John McGuckin notes, "It was a widespread belief in Hellenistic society that the (often wretched) disparity of lot was simply how things were in the greater cosmic order. Imbalances were not injustices."[16] Therefore, Lanctantius's arguments for people's essential equality before God still represented a radical cultural shift and significant advance.

And yet, there is a big gap between saying that all people are spiritually equal in God's eyes and taking steps to order a society in such a way wherein this is honored and recognized. One horrific example leaps to mind. As a result of his faith, the Emperor Constantine prohibited the widespread practice of tattooing enslaved people on their faces, a technique used to make it easier to identify slaves' owners and return those who had run away. Constantine is said to have ended this practice because he believed the human face reflected the image of God. This recognition that enslaved people's faces reflected the image of God, however, did not result in Constantine —or Lactantius, for that matter—calling for the enslaved population's freedom (though Constantine did allow for occasional release from slavery by Christians). It would take Gregory of Nyssa (c.335-c.394 CE) to put all the pieces together and preach the only known homily from this period to call for the ending of slavery altogether.

The most generous reading here is that Lactantius's argument for the spiritual equality of all people and for a society characterized by voluntary acts of mercy sows the seeds for later change. The Jesuit priest Thomas Hughson argues that while Lactantius didn't propose specific policies to Constantine, "Book V [of *The Divine Institutes*] presents equity as a norm and virtue with a political dimension in its exercise, in the sense that equity challenged Constantine and imperial government to move in the direction of protecting the poor from exploitation by the wealthy and powerful. Equity, like social justice, was not only a virtue in persons but also a desired societal goal."[17]

Lactantius movingly sums up his views on what a Christian society would look like by saying, "The whole nature of justice lies in our providing for others through humanity what we provide for our own families and relatives through affection."[18] He argues that a Christian society grounded in justice is marked by a recognition that all are made in the image of God, and therefore it feeds the poor, offers hospitality to immigrants and refugees, ransoms captives, defends children and widows in need, looks after the sick, and provides for burial of strangers and beggars.[19]

This description of what justice looks like in society reveals Lactantius's concern for the most vulnerable members of society as well as a core belief that compassion (*humanitas*) and mercy (*misericordia*) are a source of protection for these groups.

In a moving passage, Lactantius observes that whereas animals have been given various means of protecting themselves from the dangers of the natural elements, humans were made by God to be comparatively helpless against nature. What God has given humanity, instead, is a shared sense of mercy, compassion, and kindness as its best protection. Lactantius states that when we can recognize our common ancestry and basic equality with one another, we build a society that cares for the most vulnerable in dangerous times:

> For God, who has not given wisdom to other animals, has made them more safe from attack in danger by natural defenses. But because He made man naked and defenseless, that He might rather furnish him with wisdom, He gave him, besides other things, this feeling of kindness; so that man should protect, love, and cherish man, and both receive and afford assistance against all dangers. Therefore kindness (*humanitas*) is the greatest bond of human society; and he who as broken this is to be deemed impious.[20]

The truth of this statement has become profoundly apparent to me amidst the COVID-19 pandemic, and especially so when stated in the negative: society is left unprotected and highly vulnerable when people have lost a sense of shared compassion for one another. The basic lack of a feeling of compassion and responsibility for one another has exponentially increased the dangers of this natural disaster.

This core belief that a sense of compassion and kindness toward one another is society's best protection leads Lactantius to critique Roman society's praise of *apatheia* (freedom from emotion) and *autarchia* (self-sufficiency). He contends these traditionally Stoic attitudes—somewhat similar to our "Pull yourself up by your own bootstraps" mentality—are actually extremely dangerous, creating a society and culture in which mercy, compassion, and kindness are maligned as forms of weakness.[21]

Lactantius had a bone to pick with the Stoics and Cicero in this regard. He critiques the long philosophical tradition and elite culture that denigrated feelings of mercy toward the less fortunate. Historian Justo González notes, "By making it a virtue not to feel, the Stoics make it a virtue not to be moved by the distress of others, and they therefore glorify inhumanity."[22] Lactantius counters, "And though they [the Stoics] generally admit that the mutual participation of human society is to be retained, they entirely separate themselves from it by the harshness of their inhuman virtue."[23] Lactantius argues that *apatheia* goes against humanity's natural sense of mercy and compassion, which ultimately serves as our best bet against the capriciousness of life and the dangers of natural disaster.

While many today would rightly critique Lactantius's definition of justice as impartial and imperfect and its enthusiasm for an imperially imposed monotheism doesn't align with our embrace of a pluralistic and multireligious world, there is much to be said for this first attempt to ground a Christian society in the understanding of all people equally made in the image of God. Lactantius's subsequent restatement of the Golden Rule for the public square—namely, that

"The whole nature of justice lies in our providing for others through humanity what we provide for our own families and relatives through affection"—remains an ideal to strive toward.[24]

In his appeal to Constantine, Lactantius argues that a Christian society is one that is more equal, just, and merciful. He critiques Rome's philosophical and cultural indifference toward the poor and argues that the highest form of justice is mercy to those on the margins and giving to those who can never repay. González observes that Lactantius was a critic of a prevailing culture (so very alive still today) in which "some are 'suitable' and some are 'unsuitable' to be helped—or, as some would say today, that one must distinguish between the 'worthy poor' and those who are not, giving only to the former."[25] Lactantius argues that God does not make this distinction and so neither should society.

Instead, Lactantius posits that God has granted humanity a feeling of kindness (*humanitas*) toward one another as our greatest source of protection in a frightening world, and he warns of the dangers of those cultural traditions which see caring for the most marginalized members of society as a form of weakness. Although there is much within Lanctantius's vision that we might critique as insufficient to contemporary understandings of justice and equality, there is also a great deal that can continue to challenge and inspire our justice and advocacy work as well.

Discussion Questions

Lactantius defines a Christian society as one that reflects God's justice—that is, a society that is characterized by 1) piety toward Christ and 2) the *aequitas* of all people as made in the image of God. While I am downright fearful of any theocratic society (this Latino gay guy wouldn't survive very long a white-evangelical vision of a Christian nation), Lactantius's vision nevertheless captures what much Christian advocacy in the public square is based upon. There is a connection between worship, spiritual practices, and the long-term work of struggling for a more just and equitable future that treats marginalized communities as made in the image of God. What do you see as the connections between worship, spirituality, and this kind of justice work?

In his definition of justice, Lactantius appears to echo and adapt the Golden Rule for the public square when he states, "The whole nature of justice lies in our providing for others through humanity what we provide for our own families and relatives through affection."[26] What do you make of this statement as a vision of a just society?

In advocacy work, a theory of change describes how and why a desired change will come about in a particular setting. One might say that Lactantius's theory of change was that society would be transformed when the wealthy began drawing from their excess riches and making voluntary acts of compassion to the most vulnerable. What do you see as the strengths and weaknesses of this theory of change?

Lactantius critiques Roman society's valuing of *apatheia* (freedom from emotion) and *autarchia* (self-sufficiency). He contends these traditionally Stoic attitudes are extremely dangerous, leaving society vulnerable and unprotected. Do you agree? How do you see this playing out in society today? What do you think of Lactantius's description of a sense of compassion, empathy, and kindness as a God-given means of protection?

A Next Step

Lactantius assures his readers, "Do not think that you are being advised to reduce or exhaust your property now, but rather to convert to better uses what you would spend on excesses."[27] He goes on to say the Roman wealthy should calculate what would have been used to buy wild animals and gladiators with and instead give that money to feeding the poor, offering hospitality to immigrants and refugees, ransoming of captives, defending children and widows in need, looking after the sick, and providing for burial of strangers and beggars.

If you are fortunate enough to have taken a vacation (or vacations) in the past year, come up with a true estimate of what you spent on those trips. Once you have an amount in hand, imagine giving an anonymous donation of that same amount toward an organization that works with the most vulnerable populations in society (Lactantius's list of marginalized groups is still depressingly current). As a former therapist of mine liked to say, observe what emotions come up for you as you engage in this exercise. Are you excited by the prospect? Afraid? Angry? Can you imagine taking the next step and making such a donation?

Endnotes

1 Thomas Hughson, "Social Justice in Lactantius's *Divine Institutes,*" in *Reading Patristic Texts on Social Ethics: Issues and Challenges for Twenty-First Century Christian Social Thought,* eds. Johan Leemans, Brian J. Matz, and Johan Verstraeten (Washington, D.C.: The Catholic University of America Press, 2011), 185-205.

2 Lactantius, *The Divine Institutes*, 6.12.

3 Lactantius, *The Divine Institutes*, 6.12.

4 Rhee, *Loving the Poor, Saving the Rich*, loc. 325-332 (Kindle).

5 McGuckin, *The Path of Christianity*, 129.

6 Hughson, "Social Justice in Lactantius's *Divine Institutes*," 189.

7 Dennis E. Trout, Book Review of *The Making of a Christian Empire* by Elizabeth DePalma, in *Church History*, Vol. 69, No. 4 (Cambridge: Cambridge University Press, 2000), 869–71.

8 Hughson, "Social Justice in Lactantius's *Divine Institutes*," 193.

9 Lactantius, *The Divine Institutes*, Book 5.5.

10 Lactantius, *The Divine Institutes*, Book 5.6.

11 Lactantius, *The Divine Institutes*, Book 5.14.

12 Lactantius, *The Divine Institutes*, Book 5.14.

13 Lactantius, *The Divine Institutes*, 5.14.

14 Rhee, *Loving the Poor, Saving the Rich*, loc. 3278-3339 (Kindle).

15 Lactantius, *The Divine Institutes*, 6.12.

16 McGuckin, *The Path of Christianity*, 1026.

17 Hughson, "Social Justice in Lactantius's *Divine Institutes*," 199.

18 Lactantius, *The Divine Institutes*, 6.12.

19 Lactantius, *The Divine Institutes*, 6.12.

20 Lactantius, *The Divine Institutes*, 6.10.

21 Parkin, "'You Do Him No Service,'" 62.

22 González, *Faith and Wealth*, 140.

23 Lactantius, *The Divine Institutes*, 6.10.

24 Lactantius, *The Divine Institutes*, 6.12

25 González, *Faith and Wealth*, 141.

26 Lactantius, *The Divine Institutes,* 6.12.

27 Lactantius, *The Divine Institutes,* 6.12.

15 Julian's Begrudging Respect for Christian Charity

Shortly after the reign of Constantine, the first Christian emperor of Rome, was the Roman Empire's last pagan one. Flavius Claudius Julianus tried during his very short reign to return Rome to its former religious traditions. This emperor is more well-known as Julian the Apostate, a name given to him by his later Christian detractors who resented those efforts. His two-year reign from 361-363 offers an intriguing window into the light and shadow, strengths and weaknesses of Christianity during this critical transition point as it was in the process of becoming the religion of the Roman Empire.

Christian Bishop Gregory of Nazianzus would later describe Julian's reign as little more than a passing cloud. But what an interesting cloud. In the two years before his death-by-spear in 363 in a battle against Persia, Julian issued edicts and wrote treatises against the Christians (or Galileans, as he often called them) that revealed his views of the new faith and his plans to undermine it. His efforts are fascinating in part because of the insight they offer about Christianity during this period, not to mention raising the prospect of what might have been had he lived longer and been more successful in his efforts.

Despite Julian's antipathy toward Christianity, embedded in these very same campaigns to restore Rome to its prior religious traditions is a begrudging respect for Christianity's organizational structure and its now expanded, imperially subsidized model of charity. Just prior to his death, Julian began to restructure Roman paganism in a way that closely resembled Christianity, even to the point of describing himself as the head of the pagan church—a pagan pope.[1] Further, Julian understood Christian charity to be among the causes of the new faith's rapid spread, and in a letter to Arsacius, the pagan high priest at Galatia, Julian urged that Hellenic temples adopt Christians' model of charity and indicated he was prepared to send supplies of food and materials to enable them to do so. That this was written by an emperor seeking to undermine Christianity reveals how important charity and other acts of mercy were in Christianity's spread.

Julian's words in his letter to Arsacius have been a source of pride for Christians for generations. Referring to Christians as atheists, he gripes "Why do we not observe that it is their benevolence to strangers, their care for the graves of the dead, and the pretended holiness of their lives that have done most to increase atheism?"[2] Before Christians exult too much in this aspect of our legacy, however, it's worth exploring some of Julian's other critiques of Christianity— particularly as this new faith took on the trappings of imperial wealth and power—as they are remarkably relevant still today.

Julian's life was framed by the violence of imperial Christianity. Julian was the nephew of the first Christian emperor, Constantine the Great, who decriminalized Christianity in 313 with the Edict of Milan and presided over its transformation into Rome's imperial religion before his death in 337. Constantine understood himself as the 13th and final of Jesus's apostles and built the Church of the Holy Apostles in Constantinople so to enshrine himself as such for posterity.[3] Constantine's self-proclamation as Jesus's final apostle speaks to the way faith and imperial power had become aligned, a transformation that resulted in fairly obvious contradictions between the power, violence, and wealth of imperial Christianity and the poverty, nonviolence, and the coming of Jesus as "one who serves."

With the sole exception of Julian, Constantine and his imperial successors would all be Christians from this point on. These Christian emperors would eventually make Roman paganism illegal, close pagan temples, and redirect the pagan temple financial resources to building Christian churches and supporting Christian clergy. In 357, a few years prior to Julian's reign, imperial Christians successfully removed the pagan Altar of Victory from the Roman Senate—a symbol of Christianity's newfound strength in Rome.[4]

Julian, however, appears to have been repelled by Rome's transition to this version of Christianity. Born into a Christian family, he secretly converted from Christianity to Roman Neoplatonism in 351 at the age of 19, a personal detail he kept hidden until becoming emperor ten years later. Although it's not clear what exactly led to his conversion, I'm partial to the view that having one's father, brother, and many other family members murdered by people calling themselves Christians may have led to his dim view of the faith.[5] He also had a mentor and teacher who had not converted to Christianity and who was a powerful influence on him.

Julian became a successful general in the Roman army, was declared Caesar over the western provinces of Rome by the pious Christian Emperor Constantius II in 355, and after a key battle against Germanic armies, was declared Augustus by his troops in 360. This action likely would have resulted in a protracted civil war against the Emperor Constantius had the emperor not died shortly thereafter, naming Julian as his successor.

With Constantius's death, Julian became sole emperor of Rome in 361. It is only at this point that Julian revealed himself to not be a Christian, a revelation that shocked the ruling classes who had seen the way the wind was blowing and had begun converting to Christianity. Julian began acting rapidly at that point: he declared his reign to be in the style of the philosopher-emperor Marcus Aurelius, grew a controversial beard, defended said beard, and returned the Altar of Victory to the senate. He also began to devote a significant amount of time to undermining imperial Christianity.

As a former Christian, he did this effectively and with an insider's knowledge of the contradictions of the faith, many of which Christians still wrestle with today. For instance, unlike his aversion to Christianity, Julian held a profound respect for Judaism—at one point even seeking to rebuild the temple in Jerusalem—and he saw Christianity as an offensive upstart that disregarded the wisdom of both Jewish and Greco-Roman religious traditions. In Julian's (now lost) essay "Against the Galileans," likely written in Antioch during the winter of 362/3, the emperor asserted that Christians had "rejected all that is good in the traditions of Greeks and Jews alike, and speak out of deep ignorance." The man wasn't wrong, of course. His criticism of Christianity's anti-Judaism is just one of the many points where we realize Julian understood Christianity's faults much more deeply than many Christians do today.

Julian also banned Christians from teaching Greek and Roman literature and philosophy. This occurred through an edict in 362 that ruled Christian teachers should be disqualified on the grounds that "proper education entails not merely expertise in language and letters, but a 'healthy disposition'" and that Christians who believe one thing while teaching another could not be said to be able to truly educate their pupils.[6] He also recognized Christians' long associations with burial rites and used this knowledge against them by decreeing in 363 that funerals could not be carried out in broad daylight, as was the Christian custom.[7]

Beyond this, there was the issue of money. Under Constantine, "vast sums were spent on the building of basilicas, and there were grand endowments of land given to the church. That land, moreover, was to be exempt from tax. Clerics were excused from the burden of costly public offices, even personally subsidized. There were food allowances for Christian widows and nuns."[8] Constantine also encouraged precious metals once stored in the ancestral pagan temples to be used in the building up of Christian churches. Julian was aware of how these benefits and access to resources played a role in strengthening imperial Christianity, and so he went about reversing this financial support and these privileges. In the book, *Julian's Gods: Religion and Philosophy in the Thought and Action of Julian the Apostate*, Rowland B.E. Smith writes that in February 362, Julian issued a new edict that:

> Decreed that temples of the gods that had been put to improper use should be rededicated, and that those which had been destroyed by the Christians should be rebuilt at the church's expense. Owners of land which had formerly belonged to the temples were to give it back, and a special tax was levied on those who had used the fabric of sacred buildings in the construction of new ones. Christian clergy tax exemptions were suddenly revoked, and their judicial power and exemption from service withdrawn.[9]

Philip Daileader, professor of history at the College of William and Mary, recounts that when bishops and clergy contested the removal of these privileges, the Emperor Julian replied that he had once heard Jesus's statement that it was easier for a camel to go through the eye of a needle than for a rich man to enter the kingdom of heaven. Therefore the bishops and clergy should be thanking him for helping them get closer to their heavenly goal.[10] Once again, the man wasn't wrong. One might say the so-called "apostate" Julian perceived the contradiction between the message of the gospels and the wealth and power of imperial Christianity quite keenly.

Perhaps Julian's most deft (and embarrassing) strategy, however, was to simply step back and allow Christian factionalism to do the work of undermining Christianity for him. In 363, Julian proclaimed freedom of worship for all religions. Whereas Constantine and his pious son Constantius II had patrolled the Christian episcopate and councils to ensure unity of belief and right worship, Julian intentionally included all forms of Christianity, thereby removing Roman support and sponsorship from catholic Christianity and placing other factions such as Arianism on equal footing. Rather than being a strategy for multiculturalism, however, this decree has been understood as a strategy for undermining catholic Christianity's strength and unity, as he well knew the viciousness of the internal divisions among Christians (still a characteristic of Christians today) and how such factionalism would lead to its general weakening.

Julian's efforts to revive paganism ended with his death in 363, at the age of 31, having been emperor for a mere 20 months. While it is unclear who actually killed the emperor, embittered Christians quickly claimed a Christian soldier had thrown the spear that pierced the emperor's liver, and they widely celebrated his death. That spear killed the last pagan emperor of Rome. Julian's successors were all Christian; his anti-Christian policies were rolled back; the Altar of Victory was once again removed from the senate; and the later emperor, Theodosius, effectively outlawed paganism by making pagan sacrifices illegal and ordering the closing of all pagan temples.[11]

Along with seeing and understanding Christianity's weaknesses—its anti-Judaism, factionalism, and hypocrisy around wealth and power— Julian also begrudgingly recognized some of the strengths that had led to its growth. Indeed, many of his efforts to restore traditional religious traditions betray a respect for Christianity's organizational structures. He saw the way that bishops, priests, and deacons overseeing regional networks of churches allowed Christians to move resources from one community to another and make distributions in times of need, a practice already evident in Paul's Jerusalem Collection and Justin Martyr's emphasis on a collection for the poor, which had become an imperially subsidized system during Constantine's reign.

In *The Last Pagan Emperor,* H.C. Teitler notes,

> By his own pious and modest way of life Julian hoped to be a shining example for his subjects, but he realized that more needed to be done to halt the progress of Christianity. For that reason he developed means to found a pagan church. He himself would be its leader, as pontifex maximus. Under him high priests would be in charge of the priests consigned to them. For priests there was a key role in store (the comparison with the organizational structure of the Christian church urges itself upon us), and Julian devised guidelines for them. Their conduct must be impeccable; banal pleasures (races, circus, theater) should be avoided. The reading of frivolous poetry was prohibited. Priests should bury themselves in philosophical works, preferably those of Pythagoras, Plato, Aristotle, and the Stoics. Their most important duty was of course to conduct the service of the gods, but—and this was new—the care for the poor and the sick should concern them, too, for it was through poor relief and charity that the "Galilaeans" had won many adherents.[12]

With Constantine, the very public gifts that Christian churches received under Constantine and his son came with a newly imposed, public responsibility of caring for the publicly registered poor, both Christian and non-Christian alike.[13] Historian John McManners notes that by "the mid-third century the Roman church was feeding 155 church officials of various grades, and more than 1,500 widows and distressed persons. At Antioch in Syria late in the fourth century, the number of destitute persons being fed by the church had reached 3,000. It became common for a register or matricula of names to be kept." Church funds were occasionally used for the purchase and emancipation of slaves, although unfortunately this doesn't seem to have been a widespread practice.[14] This notion of the church—and bishops especially—as having a particular responsibility in caring for the poor would eventually lead to bishops like Basil of Caesarea and Gregory of Nyssa articulating one of Christianity's public roles as making visible the needs of the poor to a distracted and wealth-obsessed society.

Even Julian "the Apostate" could see, then, that Christian charity and this public role of caring for the poor were genuine strengths and the likely cause of many conversions. Thus, in a remarkable letter to Arsacius, high priest of Galatia, Julian expresses frustration that paganism wasn't recovering in popularity as quickly as he would like and argues that pagan temples should serve the destitute in the same way Christians have. He also pledges to shift imperial support from Christian churches in order to enable such aid. He refers to the way bishops have used imperial grain allowances to create charitable provisions for local communities—an allowance he would now be ending and redirecting toward the Hellenic temples.[15]

Referring to Christians as both atheists and Galileans, Julian writes,

> Why, then, do we think that this is enough, why do we not observe that it is their benevolence to strangers, their care for the graves of the dead and the pretended holiness of their lives that have done most to increase atheism? I believe that we ought really and truly to practice every one of these virtues. I have but now made a plan by which you may be well provided for this; for I have given directions that 30,000 modii of corn shall be assigned every year for the whole of Galatia, and 60,000 pints of wine. I order that one-fifth of this be used for the poor who serve the priests, and the remainder be distributed by us to strangers and beggars. For it is disgraceful that, when no Jew ever has to beg, and the impious Galilaeans support not only their own poor but ours as well, all men see that our people lack aid from us. Teach those of the Hellenic faith to contribute to public service of this sort, and the Hellenic villages to offer their first fruits to the gods; and accustom those who love the Hellenic religion to these good works by teaching them that this was our practice of old. Then let us not, by allowing others to

outdo us in good works, disgrace by such remissness, or
rather, utterly abandon, the reverence due to the gods. If I
hear that you are carrying out these orders I shall be filled
with joy.[16]

Despite Julian's short rule, his actions show a keen insight into both
the weaknesses and strengths of Christianity—patterns of behavior
that continue today. In the same way one can still sit in basilica-like
buildings and watch clergy celebrate the eucharist weighed down by
Roman imperial robes, the administrative and charitable structures of
Christianity are also still in operation.

I'll never forget, for instance, a visit I made with the Episcopal Church
Foundation (ECF) to rural Cuba in 2014. On one of the many stops
in the Cuban countryside, we had the opportunity to visit with
five elderly women who were the vestry members (congregational
council) of their local parish. The main sanctuary had burned down
30 years prior, and so we met in the sole part of the church building
that was still standing. This is where worship services had continued
to be held for the past 30 years and where, on that day, the parish's
children gathered to sing a song for the visitors from abroad.

This meeting reminded me of the stubborn strength of church
structures and the resilience of the women lay leaders, for the vestry/
council still met periodically, they had their plans for rebuilding one
day, and the congregation continued ministries to the most vulnerable
members of the surrounding community, including a children's
ministry and regular visiting of the homebound. This is to say that
despite all odds, including fire and a repressive regime, an organized
ecclesiastical structure with a relationship to the bishop and a sound
reputation in the wider community was still in place in this remote
part of Cuba.

This speaks to what has become a widely recognized strength of faith-
based (not just Christian) non-governmental organizations (NGOs).
A recent report on the importance of faith-based NGOs across
the globe in the development and relief sphere noted that "Local
religious leaders are critical to humanitarian responses in many areas,

particularly where the reach or legitimacy of the state is weak. In this context, faith-based and local NGOs are unique players in the international humanitarian space: rooted in their local or religious communities, they have a global reach."[17] The trust created by the fact that these communities have been around for years is key here, as the network of relationships they represent cannot be quickly replicated by outside visitors or NGOs. This network of relationships and the resilience of this distributional network are an organizational wonder—a miracle, really, in and of its own right.

I find it helpful to be reminded of this from time to time. As someone who works for the church, I admit that it is occasionally easy to forget the value of bishops, standing committees, dioceses, deaneries, parishes, clericus meetings, and vestries when one is confronted over and over again by the glacial pace and inefficiency with which ecclesiastical bodies move. I know I am not alone in occasionally looking with jealousy at new and innovative nonprofits who manage to make major impacts in their communities in short amounts of time. And yet, I've also come to appreciate how even ecclesiastical sluggishness can be a surprising strength because like a barnacle firmly attached to the shipwreck of society, church structures have a way of sticking around through even the worst of times.

Through thick and thin, decade after decade, amidst fires, revolutions, and pandemics, the church remains ploddingly present, and this oftentimes means that it is the church that is there in the most difficult-to-reach communities when other agencies (and even entire governments) come and go. Very often one finds churches doing the quieter, unexciting work that rarely makes the local news: holding a fragile community together, offering pastoral care, hosting soup kitchens, visiting the isolated and homebound, establishing prison ministries, developing youth programs, distributing clothing, and holding annual charity fundraisers.

Further, these structures have a way of springing into action in times of sudden disaster, in part because they have built up trust through the quieter labor of addressing the daily disaster of poverty. For example, by mid-2021, for example, the news media and celebrity focus on the Flint, Michigan water crisis had largely moved on, yet the interdenominational network of faith leaders and faith communities within Flint is still there. As the needs have shifted, so too have the nature of the efforts. From an initial focus on distributing safe drinking water, various congregations are now moving their attention to the long-haul effort of providing nutritious food to children and youth to try to mitigate the long-term effects of lead poisoning. In this case, the occasionally frustrating lethargy of the church means it will be continuing its work even as national attention and more flashy efforts drift away.

The church—in its plodding and gloriously inefficient way—will be sticking around for generations. Such charitable, long-term presence, I believe, is something to both be grateful for and constantly seek to strengthen.

Discussion Questions

Both Constantine and Julian addressed Christianity's relationship to Judaism, albeit in very different ways. Whereas Constantine implemented decrees to privilege Christianity over Judaism, Julian considered Christianity to have insultingly disregarded both Jewish and Hellenic wisdom and sought to rebuild the Jerusalem Temple. What do you make of these emperors' contrasting opinions on Christianity and Judaism during this period?

While not the cause of all conversions to Christianity, it is clear there was a perceived connection between the material care for the poor extended by Christians and the spread of Christianity. What do you make of Julian's complaint that "the Galileans" are increasing because they "support not only their own poor but ours as well"?

Despite his sharp critiques of Christianity, Julian the Apostate retained a begrudging appreciation for the way that Christianity's ecclesiastical structures facilitated its charitable distribution of food and basic necessities to the poor. Are church administrative structures oriented toward this purpose in your region? What would it mean for them to become more so?

A Next Step

Take time to research the interdenominational and interfaith networks at the local and state level addressing issues of poverty and injustice. For instance, in Flint, Michigan, critical work was done during the lead water crisis by a longstanding interdenominational alliance called Concerned Pastors for Social Action. In New York City, the Interfaith Assembly on Homelessness and Housing helps bring leaders of many faiths into a united voice on the crisis of homelessness. If your congregation hasn't joined such networks already, explore what it would mean to join and participate regularly.

Endnotes

1   Hans-Ulrich Wiemer and Stefan Rebenich, ed., "A Companion to Julian the Apostate," in *Brill's Companions to the Byzantine World*, edited by Wolfram Brandes (The Netherlands: Brill, 2020), Volume 5, 2020.

2   *The Works of the Emperor Julian, Vol. III*, Loeb Classical Library, 1913.

3   Leadbetter, "Constantine," loc. 1004 (Kindle).

4   Philip Daileader, "Early Middle Ages," Class offered by The Great Courses.

5   E. Christian Kopff and Stewart Henry Perowne, "Julian," in *Encyclopedia Britannica*, September 24, 2009.

6   Rowland B.E. Smith, *Julian's Gods: Religion and Philosophy in the Thought and Action of Julian the Apostate* (London: Routledge, 2012), 199.

7   H. C. Teitler, *The Last Pagan Emperor: Julian the Apostate and the War against Christianity* (Oxford: Oxford University Press, 2017), 67-68.

8   Smith, *Julian's Gods*, 211.

9   Smith, *Julian's Gods*, 211.

10   Daileader, "Early Middle Ages."

11   Daileader, "Early Middle Ages."

12   Teitler, *The Last Pagan Emperor*, 28-29.

13   Rhee, *Loving the Poor, Saving the Rich*, loc. 4240-4257 (Kindle).

14   John McManners, *The Oxford Illustrated History of Christianity* (Oxford: Oxford University Press, 2001), 37-39.

15   Smith, *Julian's Gods*, 212.

16   *The Works of the Emperor Julian*, Vol. III, 1913.

17   "The Rise of Faith-Based NGOs and Local NGOs," Inter-Agency Research and Analysis Network, iaran.org/future-of-aid-drivers-blog/the-rise-of-faith-based-ngos-and-local-ngos.

16 Life of Antony: A Silent Protest and Legacy of Anti-Blackness

Julian's efforts to undermine imperial Christianity proved to be little more than a passing cloud, a brief pause in Christianity's eventual embrace of both imperial wealth and power. But Julian was not the only one protesting this transformation of the faith. In *Christianity: The First Three Thousand Years,* Diarmaid MacCulloch describes monasticism's development in Syria and Egypt as a form of "silent protest" and an implied criticism of the church's decision to become a large-scale and pervasive organization.[1] Monasticism became an alternative to and refuge from proximity to imperial power, monarchical bishops, and a wealth-obsessed church—a way of life that aimed to remain faithful to Jesus's literal imperative to dispossess one's self of wealth.

In the third and fourth centuries, the first Christian ascetic hermits enacted this protest by stepping out of society—quite literally walking into the nearby desert in many cases—and by following Jesus's advice to leave their lives behind. These ascetics rejected interpretations that had exclusively spiritualized Jesus's call to dispossession and ultimately preserved material dispossession as a model and ideal for the church today. Further, they managed to thread the needle of developing this alternative model while remaining under the authority of the bishop and therefore part of the orbit of the wider church.[2] This meant monasticism remained part of the wider church but not of it, a relatively non-threatening form of silent protest against the church's concurrent embrace of imperial wealth and power.

The themes and tensions in this approach are found in the life of Antony of Egypt (c.250-356), frequently called the father of monasticism. *The Life of Antony* was written by Athanasius, bishop of Alexandria, shortly after Antony's death around 356 and "became one of the most popular Christian texts in antiquity and was responsible for making [Antony] paradigmatic for later monastic theory, both in regard to the solitary life and that of the small community."[3]

The Life of Antony outlines many themes that will come to characterize monastic spirituality: a preservation of Jesus's call to rid oneself of material wealth; a withdrawal into the desert; what one scholar called "failed solitude" (more on this later); a battle with demonic forces, including money, sexual temptation, and kinship ties; and an emphasis on both discerning and battling evil spirits.

To this list of more well-known attributes, as a person of color, I must add the origins of Christian anti-Blackness, a less well-known aspect of monastic spirituality that Christian admirers of this tradition must come to terms with, particularly as the church and society takes stock of the history and sources of racism and anti-Blackness. Even as the *Life of Antony* became foundational to monastic life and spirituality, it also held the first-known Christian reference to the devil as a Black boy. The sheer popularity of this text meant that the image of the devil's true self as a Black Ethiopian boy—later called the Prince of Darkness—would be exported and repeated over and over again in other monastic writings.[4]

Any Christian who appreciates the way monastic spirituality offers an alternative to a worldly and power-hungry church must also come to terms with its binaries of light versus darkness and how it introduced an anti-Blackness that remains a disturbing aspect of Christian spirituality still today.

Athanasius's *The Life of Antony* is considered to be "the most successful and widely imitated hagiographical text of all time" and "the most read book in the Christian world after the Bible," firmly establishing Antony of Egypt as the "father of monasticism."[5][6] As a hagiography, it is not strictly a historical record: "Athanasius painted a portrait of Antony that suited his own purposes: an ascetic who was soundly opposed to Athanasius's opponents, the Arians and was as firm a supporter of bishops as Athanasius himself."[7] Part of Athanasius's agenda was the assertion of Egypt's spiritual prowess, and he was successful in making Egypt and its desert fathers a center and model for all later monastic life and spirituality.[8]

In Athanasius's *The Life of Antony*, Antony undergoes a profound conversion experience shortly after his parents' deaths that centers on the dispossession of his inherited wealth and property. Indeed, the first sections of *The Life* serve as a kind of review of the New Testament's greatest hits and argue for Christians to have a very different approach to wealth and the economy.

Born into a Christian family that "possessed considerable wealth," Antony was left alone at "18 or 20" by his parents' death to care for himself and his sister. About six months later, while walking to church, "he communed with himself and reflected as he walked how the apostles left all and followed the Savior (Matthew 4:20); and how they in the Acts sold their possessions and brought and laid them at the apostle's feet for distribution to the needy (Acts 4:35)."[9] As we discussed in earlier chapters, this passage from Acts refers to the *koinonia*—economic fellowship and sharing—that was such a critical aspect of the early church in Acts and Paul's letters.

Antony then entered a church and arrived just in time to hear the gospel passage: "And the Lord said to the rich man, 'If you wish to be perfect, go, sell your possessions, and give the money to the poor, and you will have treasure in heaven; then come, follow me' (Matthew 19.21)."[10] Interpreting this as a heavenly sign, Antony then "went out immediately from the church, and gave the possessions of his forefathers to the villagers"—possessions that amounted to 300 acres, "productive and fair," and sold all else, giving the money to the poor. Upon returning to church another time, he heard the gospel passage in which Jesus said, "Do not worry about tomorrow" (Matthew 6:34), at which point he immediately left and gave even more of his wealth to the poor and handed his younger sister off to be raised by "known and faithful virgins." Free at last of his possessions (and, well, his sister), "he henceforth devoted himself outside his house to discipline, taking heed to himself and training himself with patience."[11]

One of the mysteries of Christian monasticism is where the earliest monastics like Antony learned their ascetic practices from.[12] *The Life* notes that Antony had imitated pious hermits even in his youth and that he spent a period learning from the wisdom of these men before departing for the desert.[13] Later, *The Life* says that an angel visited Antony to give him his monastic rule. The historian John McManners, however, offers an additional possibility: he notes that Antony's ability to leave his sister with a community of "faithful virgins" suggests women's Christian monasticism likely preceded what Antony and Pachomius are given credit for.[14] "Antony's innovation was to move from the inhabited area into the remove of desert; but, long before he or Pachomius had ever thought of adopting asceticism, there already existed in Egypt structured communities of what today would be termed nuns." McManners concludes, "Too often, in ancient as in modern times, monastic history has been written exclusively from a masculine point of view."[15]

Antony's dramatic conversion story and especially his fierce battles with the devil made *The Life* "an immediate success, soon translated into Latin (in two versions) and several other languages, and eagerly read in both the Christian east and west."[16] No other non-biblical Christian text has enjoyed so wide a circulation or been so influential a model for spiritual biographies or in the development of monastic spirituality, a fact that elevated Egypt as a foundational site of Christian spirituality and helped preserve a tradition of material dispossession for Christianity today.

Nearly every stage of Antony's life as depicted in *The Life* established aspects of monasticism that still exist in the twenty-first century. This includes "first and foremost, the idea of monasticism as a life of withdrawal into the desert."[17] Antony's original withdrawal into the desert has been "reimagined again and again to include life on rocky outcroppings off the Irish coasts, in the silent vastness of Russian forests and amidst the desolation of modern urban centres."[18]

Another key theme is that of the monastic as "a failed solitary," as Antony is described in John Wortley's *An Introduction to the Desert*

Fathers. Antony and subsequent solitaries did not and could not isolate themselves completely. "For those who placed themselves in solitary confinement, there was always some casement through which they could receive the necessities and life and communicate with their fellow beings."[19] Further, solitaries like Antony became famous and ended up attracting many visitors. In Antony's case, "a growing number installed themselves willy-nilly not so far away from where the solitary lay" in what would become the first steps toward communal (*cenobitic*) monasticism.[20]

This *cenobitic* monasticism represents a reawakening of that older notion of *koinonia* described in Acts and Paul's letters, for the term *cenobitic* is the Latin rendering of the *koinonia* (common life) that was characteristic of the early church.

Especially important for Anglicanism, historian John McGuckin notes:

> Antony's many different exempla in *The Life* and the sayings attributed to him in later monastic manuals taught Christian monks to balance their lives in the desert with a pattern of prayer and psalms through the night and the dawn, then rest in the morning with eating and labor, followed by sleep in the afternoon, then study, prayer, and dinner at dusk, and prayers again in the coolness of the night. This formula of daily variety between oral and mental prayer, physical labor, and rest, was said to have been revealed to him by the visitation of an angel since he had no one else to show him standards of "desert polity."[21]

Or perhaps Antony was simply recalling the patterns of prayer and work that the women monastics had established long before him.

Returning, then, to the notion of monasticism as a form of silent protest, *The Life of Antony* offered an attractive alternative for Christians who sought refuge from the imperial, wealthy, and increasingly power-hungry church. This narrative included the initial conversion story and literal dispossession, withdrawal to the desert, emphasis on receiving visitors, and different modes of organizing "desert polity." In my own tradition, monastic spirituality is deeply admired and has been foundational in shaping the spirituality and daily patterns of the offices found within the Book of Common Prayer. Yet there is a tendency to overlook the negative legacy of asceticism, including *The Life of Antony's* anti-Blackness and the imprint of racism it would leave on Christianity for centuries to come. This strikes me as especially important today as Christians explore the origins of anti-Blackness within our religious traditions and its continuing hold over how the church thinks about God and holiness.

In Antony's first spiritual battles with demons in the desert, an exhausted devil is described as finally casting off his many disguises and appearing to Antony at last "as his true self"—a Black boy, taking a visible shape with the color of his mind."[22] This is an erotically charged encounter as the boy describes himself as "the friend of fornication" and "the spirit of lust." David Brakke, whose research I've drawn on extensively for this section, notes that in portraying the devil's true self as a Black boy, Athanasius's *The Life* is affirming Egyptians' longstanding fears and stereotypes about their darker-skinned Ethiopian enemies, who they and the wider Roman Empire stereotyped as hypersexual and dangerous.

The unconquered Ethiopians neighboring the Egyptians had long been a source of both fascination and fear for the Roman Empire generally and for Egyptians in particular. But "while persons elsewhere in the Mediterranean may have been able to romanticize the mythic military power of the Ethiopian people, Egyptians had a more palpable sense of an 'Ethiopian threat' and thus were more likely to scapegoat darker-skinned persons in their midst."[23]

The impact of this depiction—with the binaries of light and darkness, goodness and evil, now projected onto skin color—is hard to overstate. From the fourth century through the medieval period, monastics in both the east and west embraced and expanded upon *The Life's* anti-Blackness. As Kelly Brown Douglas notes in her book, *Resurrection Hope: A Future Where Black Lives Matter,* the intertwined anti-Black and anti-Ethiopian narrative even shows up in Gomes Eanes de Zurara's oft-cited description of the first captive Africans to arrive on Portuguese soil in 1444, captives whom he describes "as Black as Ethiops, and so ugly, both in features and in body, as almost to appear (to those who saw them) the images of a lower hemisphere."[24] Douglas notes that "Comments regarding aesthetic 'Blackness' are historically fraught with assumptions about character and temperament," and such characterizations proved essential to the rationale for the economically driven practice of capturing and enslaving Africans.

This perception has its roots in the Christian ascetic tradition. Black boys and Black women were regularly depicted as demons that monks had to resist or violently overpower. Brakke writes:

> [*The Life of Antony*] was not the last time the devil or one of his demons would appear with black skin to an Egyptian monk, according to tales preserved in the monastic literature from the fourth and fifth centuries. A young monk beset by thoughts of sex encountered an Ethiopian woman with a foul smell. An older monk found an Ethiopian girl he remembered seeing in his youth sitting on his knees; driven mad, he struck her, and a foul odor adhered to his hand. Afflicted by pride, another monk was divinely instructed to reach for his neck, where he found a small Ethiopian, which he cast into the sand. A monk who disobeyed his elder discovered an Ethiopian lying on a sleeping mat and gnashing his teeth. Ethiopian or Black demons continued to tempt or frighten Christian ascetics into the medieval period.[25]

The Blackness of Ethiopian demons came to serve multiple purposes in monastic spirituality. First, Blackness became a useful way of illustrating a monk's powers of discernment in a morally complicated world. "The Blackness of the demons, by providing an unmistakable sign of evil at work, confirms the clarity of vision given to the 'man of God.'"[26] In the *Dialogues* of Gregory the Great, for instance, Benedict of Nursia discerns the presence of a Black demon when no one else can. As other monks struggle to understand why one of their brothers is never able to make it through his prayers, Benedict alone can see a Black boy pulling on the monk's cloak during worship.[27]

Second, monastic stories regularly relied on the stereotype of Ethiopian hypersexuality. When Athanasius depicted the Black boy in *The Life of Antony* as "fornication's lover" and the "spirit of lust," he was building on longstanding Roman fears and fascinations about the erotic power of Ethiopian men and women. Significantly in terms of depictions of homosexuality, the Prince of Darkness is described not only as Black but also as having an erotic power over Antony, which the monk must resist. This section of *The Life of Antony* is characterized by both fascination and fear.

Third, in a step that strikes me as critical for the ongoing association of lighter skin with spiritual purity ("Fairest Lord Jesus," as one still-frequently sung hymn goes), the contrast of white and Black became a way of demonstrating monastic spirituality's power to transform. These stories hinge on the notion that even dangerous Blackness can be tamed through the power of monastic spirituality, with darkness becoming light and Blackness becoming as white as snow. Tragically, this monastic emphasis on white and light ignores the scriptural descriptions of God's holy presence in darkness, such as when "Moses drew near to the thick darkness where God was" at the giving of the commandments on Mount Sinai (Exodus 20:21). This begs the question of how our spirituality can recover darkness and Blackness as holy, beautiful, and a fecund space from which God speaks.

The Egyptian story of Moses the Black (330-405), also known as Moses the Robber, is illustrative of the continuing monastic embrace of all things light, bright, and white. Moses begins his spiritual journey as an Ethiopian slave dismissed by his master on account of many thefts. When Egyptian monks complained about his arrival among them, the Ethiopian Moses says to himself, "They have acted rightly concerning you, you ash-skinned one, you Black one. You are not a human being, so why do you go among human beings?"[28] Later, in a scene that could easily come from those American movies that revel in the reformation of Blackness (e.g. *Dangerous Minds, The Blind Side, Freedom Writers*), the abbot of the monastery takes Moses to the roof to watch the first light rays of dawn come over the dark horizon. Watching light overtake the previous night's darkness, the abbot tells him, "Only slowly do the rays of the sun drive away the night and usher in a new day, and thus, only slowly does one become a perfect contemplative."[29] Moses the Black's story rests on repeated associations of black skin with the darkness of his violent past, as well as the certainty that such darkness could be driven away by the pure, bright light of monastic spirituality.

Finally, Blackness in monastic literature came to symbolize a Christian monk's power over the demonic. In cases like the story of Moses the Black, the focus is on the power of the Egyptian monks to reform Blackness, but other stories hinge on the monk's power to banish or even violently destroy the Black demon. Demons regularly appear in ways that suggest utter powerlessness. They are depicted as little boys, or "foul-smelling" women, and in some cases, they are even held down in chains. In *The Life*, Antony ultimately tells the boy, "You are very despicable then, for you are black-hearted and weak as a child. Henceforth I shall have no trouble from you, 'for the Lord is my helper, and I shall look down on my enemies.'"[30]

A particularly graphic example of violent banishing comes from the fourth-century, apocryphal collection of stories called the *Acts of Peter and Paul*. Told from the perspective of a man named Marcellus, the text relates Peter's spiritual contests with a contending spiritual leader named Simon Magus. Marcellus has a dream in which he sees "a very ugly woman, according to her appearance an Ethiopian, not Egyptian, but very Black, clad in filthy rags, but with an iron chain about the neck and a chain on her hands and feet; she danced." In this dream, the apostle Peter tells Marcellus to behead the woman, but Marcellus objects, saying that as a senator of noble race, he has never even killed a sparrow. Peter then calls out to "our true sword, Jesus Christ" to "cut off not only the head of the demon, but break all her members in the presence of all these, whom I have tested in thy service." At once an angel comes "with a sword in his hand and knock[s] her down."[31]

By the fourth century, then, monastic spirituality reveled in and exported an anti-Blackness that persists in Christianity today. Whereas biblical imagery in both the Old and New Testament previously contrasted light and darkness and is replete with associations of darkness and the color black with evil, Athanasius's *Life of Antony* and the subsequent monastic literature it inspired takes the additional step of affixing evil to dark skin.[32] The Egyptians monks' fears and stereotypes about their black-skinned neighbors, the Ethiopians, were incorporated in *The Life of Antony* and then exported widely as this monastic literature inspired new generations of monks across Eastern and Western Christianity.

Antony's journey begins with a call to material dispossession. He hears the gospel and on two occasions gets rid of his property and possessions so that he could step out of society and follow Christ. He also gives his sister over to a community of nuns. The monastic movement that grew from his example would eventually form an attractive alternative to imperial faith, monarchical bishops, and a wealth-obsessed church, but its legacy is a fraught one. I appreciate Diarmaid MacCulloch's description of monasticism as a form of "silent protest" insomuch as it depicts how this way of life is both a retreat from society and a positive alternative that nevertheless manages to stay within the bounds of the church's hierarchy.

Yet if we are going to continue to admire and draw from the wisdom and insights of this monastic tradition, we have to wrestle with the entirety of its legacy. This means that contemporary admirers of monastic spirituality—including the cottage industry of uncritical literature it inspires—need to take more seriously the troubling aspects of this spiritual tradition and what it has wrought today. Indeed, even the most foundational impulse to retreat and form an alternative to corrupt society can be wielded in troubling ways.

In recent years, for instance, anti-LGBTQIA+ activist Richard Dreher has argued in *The Benedict Option* for conservatives to follow the sixth-century monastic example of Saint Benedict of Nursia by retreating from what he views as a sexually corrupt society and creating a network of institutions based on the purity of Christian values. This too can be read as a form of "silent protest" against the rise of what he perceives as an overly inclusive church and society. Inspired by Benedict, Dreher writes, "Rather than wasting energy and resources fighting unwinnable political battles, we should instead work on building communities, institutions, and networks of resistance that can outwit, outlast, and eventually overcome the occupation."[33] The journalist Emma Green notes in *The Atlantic* that this movement is true to the spirit of monasticism in that "It is a radical rejection of the ties between Christianity and typical forms of power, from Republican politics to market-driven wealth."[34] This disturbing version of monasticism is about retreating from a seemingly corrupt, multiethnic, and pluralistic society in favor of a vision of sexual and racial purity.

In addition to weighing the motives for Christians' retreat from the complexities of society, the anti-Blackness tradition deeply embedded in this spirituality still needs to be seriously addressed. It's telling, for example, that even Thomas Merton couldn't bear to bring himself to face this aspect of monasticism's legacy and so his description of Moses the Black in *The Wisdom of the Desert Fathers* avoids the entire issue by portraying him as simply wearing a long black robe.[35]

I write all of this as someone who deeply appreciates many aspects of monastic spirituality, especially the way it preserved the gospel's focus on the literal dispossession of wealth. In fact, a critical part of my own formation was six months spent living in a convent with nuns in Querétaro, Mexico, during my junior year of college. The pattern of prayer and work, focus on a life of simplicity, vision of faith in community, and the need for a retreat to the desert against a wealth- and power-hungry society continue to inspire and shape my own vocation. Nevertheless, if we are going to embrace these positive aspects of the tradition, we must address the entirety of this inheritance, especially the binary of light versus darkness and dualistic outlook that so much of this tradition rests upon. As Christians continue to wrestle with the spiritual evil of racism, I believe we must look deeply at the long history and origins of anti-Blackness within Christianity. This work must be done if ever we are to begin to build a church and spirituality that embraces rather than retreats from the vibrant diversity of our world.

Discussion Questions

Monasticism is characterized by a withdrawal from a corrupt society and has served as a form of silent protest against an imperial Christianity that is at ease with both wealth and power. What do you see as the strengths and drawbacks of this approach?

Antony's conversion story hinges on his hearing a series of crucial texts in the New Testament wherein Jesus advises would-be disciples to dispossess themselves and follow him. His conversion foreshadows how monastic spirituality would both become the means through which dispossession of wealth gets preserved but also the way this aspect of Christianity would become relegated only to those who "wish to be perfect." What do you think about this aspect of monastic spirituality and the way it was increasingly applied only to ascetics?

The biblical binary of light versus darkness became an entry point through which virulent anti-Blackness entered the Christian tradition. Indeed, the black-skinned Ethiopian boy became the symbol of demonic sexuality, and figures like Moses the Black (also known as Moses the Robber) perpetuate stereotypes of Ethiopians' violence and danger. How might a deep study of this aspect of monastic spirituality lead to a critical reevaluation about its legacy?

A Next Step

Study the images of people in your church's sanctuary. These oftentimes include Jesus, his apostles, saints, and angels. How often do you see light, whiteness, and purity associated with one another? Are there any images of people with darker skin color depicted? If Jesus is depicted as Anglo, how and why do you think that happened? One of the Episcopal parishes I am a member of is beginning a long and careful, congregational process of discussing the whiteness of the images in our sanctuary and of selecting another image to add that reflects the diversity of the members of the congregation.

Endnotes

1 MacCulloch, *Christianity*, 200-206.

2 MacCulloch, *Christianity*, 201-202.

3 McGuckin, *The Path of Christianity*, 394.

4 MacCulloch, *Christianity*, 205.

5 "Anthony the Great," in *The Early Christian World: Volume 1*, ed. Philip Francis Esler (London: Routledge, 2000) 1010.

6 MacCulloch, *Christianity*, 205.

7 MacCulloch, *Christianity*, 205.

8 MacCulloch, *Christianity*, 205.

9 *The Life of Antony: St. Athanasius,* tr. H. Ellershaw, (Kindle edition), Parts 1-2.

10 *The Life of Antony: St. Athanasius*, Part 2. Refers to Matthew 19:21.

11 *The Life of Antony: St. Athanasius*, Part 2.

12 John Wortley, *An Introduction to the Desert Fathers* (Cambridge: Cambridge University Press, 2019), 16-27.

13 *The Life of Antony: St. Athanasius*, Part 3.

14 McManners, *The Oxford Illustrated History of Christianity*, 132-133.

15 McManners, *The Oxford Illustrated History of Christianity,* 132-133.

16 "Anthony the Great," *The Early Christian World: Volume 1,* 1011.

17 "Monasticism," *The Early Christian World: Volume 1,* 312.

18 "Monasticism," *The Early Christian World: Volume 1,* 312.

19 Wortley, *An Introduction to the Desert Fathers,* 18.

20 Wortley, *An Introduction to the Desert Fathers*, 18.

21 McGuckin, *The Path of Christianity,* 395-396.

22 *The Life of Antony: St. Athanasius*, Part 6.

23 David Brakke, "Ethiopian Demons: Male Sexuality, the Black-Skinned Other, and the Monastic Self," *Journal of the History of Sexuality*, Vol. 10, No. 3/4, Special Issue: Sexuality in Late Antiquity (July-October 2001), 501-535.

24 Kelly Brown Douglas, *Resurrection Hope: A Future Where Black Lives Matter* (Maryknoll, New York: Orbis Books, 2021), 23. She is citing Edgar Prestage's *The Chronicles of Fernão Lopes and Gomes Eanes de Zurara* (Watford, England: Voss and Michael Ltd., 1928), 86.

25 Brakke, "Ethiopian Demons," 501-535.

26 Brakke, "Ethiopian Demons," 501-535.

27 "Gregory the Great," *Dialogues 2.4.*

28 Brakke, "Ethiopian Demons," 501-535.

29 "History of St. Moses the Black Priory," web.archive.org/web/20110829205900/http://stmosestheblackpriory.org/about_history.html.

30 Athanasius, *Vita Antonii 6*, Section 6.

31 Bernhard Pick, "Acts of Peter," in *Apocryphal Acts of Paul, Peter, John, Andrew and Thomas* American Theological Library Association Historical Monographs, 1909.

32 Brakke highlights Genesis 1:3-4, 1 Thessalonians 5:5, Revelations 6:11, 7:13.

33 Emma Green, "The Christian Retreat from Public Life," *The Atlantic,* February 22, 2017.

34 Green, "The Christian Retreat from Public Life," *The Atlantic.*

35 Thomas Merton, *The Wisdom of the Desert* (New York: New Directions, 1960), 36; cf. Apophthegmata patrum Moses 8 (65:286).

17 Evagrius Ponticus on Love of Money

One of the most compelling voices to emerge from the silent protest of asceticism was that of Evagrius Ponticus. A monk who lived in the second half of the fourth century, he carefully noted, categorized, and struggled against a world he believed was beset by demons. His rigorous self-scrutiny and self-revelation gave birth to a new form of Christian literature centered on the intense searching of the soul.[1] His conflicts with evil—including the deadly sin of greed and the demon he named Love of Money—resulted in the most sophisticated demonology of early Christian monasticism, if not in ancient Christianity as a whole.[2]

Among Evagrius's various works is a short treatise called *Talking Back* on tactics for defeating the eight demons that assail monastic life: gluttony, fornication, love of money, sadness, anger, listlessness, vainglory, and pride. Evagrius advised *antirrhēsis,* which involved a monk reciting relevant passages from the Bible to thwart these demons' various suggestions.[3]

Talking Back is both pointed and expansive when it comes to the demon Love of Money. Evagrius addresses the customary sins of financial corruption and lack of generosity to the poor but also saw the demon's work behind how monks sometimes confused sufficiency—the ascetic ideal of having just enough—with the temptation to build economic security for themselves. Instead of seeking economic security, Evagrius urges a bare-bones existence, insisting monks strive for a minimalist self-sufficiency and give everything else to the poorer, elderly monks of their community. His vision of economic vulnerability recalls that of Jesus in the gospels telling the disciples to go out two-by-two with nothing but the shirt on their backs, relying entirely on the kindness of the people they encounter along the way (Luke 9:3). For Evagrius, there was to be no stockpiling of goods for leaner times nor even the accumulation of savings for old age. Monks were to attain "the death of Jesus" by embodying complete economic vulnerability and dependence on God and others in their community.[4]

Evagrius was born to a "country bishop" in 345 in Pontus in Asia Minor and was seemingly destined for a prominent ecclesiastical career from an early life. His early years intersected with many of the great philosophers and theologians still studied today. Ordained a lector by Basil the Great in Pontus as a young man, he traveled to Constantinople and was made a deacon by Gregory of Nazianzus around 380. His later teachings as a monk in Nitria and Kellia in Egypt drew the interest of John Cassian who, in turn, greatly influenced Benedict of Nursia.

Yet despite this aura of ecclesiastical promise, Evagrius appears to have always also had a tortured and self-destructive edge to him. One catches a glimpse of this from an early period in Constantinople. Not long after he became the protege to Gregory of Nazianzus, Evagrius became entangled in a romantic affair with a married woman and had to flee quickly when he was warned in a vision of her husband's impending revenge. He fled to Jerusalem and wandered the streets of the Holy City until he suffered a mental and physical breakdown. He found refuge in 383 at the monastery of Melania the Elder (c.342-410), a wealthy woman, intellectual, and ascetic. Melania's monastery on the Mount of Olives was one of the great centers for the study and dissemination of the works of Origen of Alexandria, and Evagrius's time there profoundly impacted his theological outlook and spirituality.[5] Following Melania's urging, at around the age of 38, Evagrius left Jerusalem to become a monk in Nitria and Kellia in Egypt.

The form of monasticism that Evagrius found in Egypt has been described by scholars as "semi-eremitic," meaning that "the monastery" was actually a loose cluster of individual hermits living in proximity to one another. The monks lived in individual residences (the place "Kellia" eventually gave its name to "cells"), were under the supervision of an abba, and they came together regularly for teaching, meetings, and fellowship.[6] "Nitria was the site where intending monks were inducted into desert, living in small communities designed to supervise them and test their vocations," and Kellia was "a loose association of monastic settlements covering many square miles of the desert" where more advanced monks could escape irritating monastic newcomers.[7]

Evagrius eventually became a renowned spiritual teacher at Nitria and Kellia. He consciously modeled himself and his community along the lines of the ancient philosophical *schola*, where "intellectual labor, study, deep meditative reflection, and the development of the states of inner peace and wordless prayer were given a higher priority over the traditional forms of ascetical labor and vocal prayer services (psalms and exclamations) favored by the earlier, less intellectual monks."[8] A centerpiece of this teaching was his sophisticated demonology, borne out of his spiritual battles with the various demonic forces that plagued his existence.

Yet along with recognizing his brilliance, Evagrius's brother monks appear to have been troubled by his unceasing battles with demons. Soon the elders of the monastery began warning him about his extreme asceticism. His brethren found many of Evagrius's theological viewpoints unsettling even as he became the community's most renowned member.[9]

When Evagrius left Jerusalem for Egypt, he was joining a silent protest against the church's embrace of wealth and power as well as against the societal instability of the second and third centuries. However, as Evagrius would discover, it was impossible for monks to separate themselves completely from society and particularly from the temptations of money. In the semi-eremitical monastic communities he joined, monks were directly responsible for their own financial affairs. David Brakke notes: "Thus monastic renunciation complicated his relationship to money and possessions, rather than ending it completely."[10] He goes on to state that monks' close involvement in their own financial affairs is likely why the demon Love of Money appears more often in the writings from semi-eremitical monastic settings than in monasteries where finances were managed collectively by just a few individuals. Evagrius therefore advised a monastic beginner: "Give thought to working with your hands, if possible both night and day, so that you will not be a burden to anyone, and further that you may be able to offer donations, as the holy apostle Paul advised."[11]

It was in this setting that a monk named Loukios wrote to Evagrius requesting a practical treatise for dealing with the demons that undermined monastic life. This took place at some point in the last decade of the fourth century. *Talking Back* was Evagrius's response to this request, reflecting his rigorous observations on how demons plagued both his own existence and that of his community, for "[Evagrius] scrupulously attended to his thoughts and, based on these observations, prepared a dossier of verses from scripture to be cast in the face of attacking demons."[12]

Talking Back was originally written for small groups of immediate and intimate disciples.[13] It addresses monks' physical drives toward sexuality and their desire for increase of wealth and comfort and advises fasting, hard labor, and redirection of thought in the face of these demonic influences. When a demon attacked, the body "was given the tasks of weaving with the hands, plowing the earth, while all the time the mind repeated a simple phrase in sotto voce. If conflicting thoughts and distractions became unmanageable, the phrase was repeated aloud for some minutes until the order of things had been reestablished."[14]

Evagrius especially worried about the monks' over-involvement in financial affairs as he saw how Love of Money could distort the spiritual priorities of the community. Evagrius writes that to "talk back" against the demon Love of Money means fighting "against the thought that anxiously serves in business affairs on the pretext that the money has run out, and now there is nothing left of it, and it cannot be regained," and "against the inner thoughts that want to acquire riches and to consume the intellect with anxiety about them."[15]

Evagrius argues that anxiety about money and lust for owning and protecting property undermine the goals of monastic life. His writings on this topic are strikingly relevant for the church today, for he warns monks against laboring so much that they neglect prayer and study:

> Against the thought of love of money that, on account of the desire for wealth, drove us to perform manual labor night and day, and so deprived us of reading the Holy Scriptures and prevented us from visiting and ministering to the sick: Wealth does not profit on the day of wrath, but righteousness delivers from death (Proverbs 11:4).[16]

He also sees monks exploiting others in the name of creating wealth and warns "against the thought that demanded more manual labor from a brother than he is capable of..." and "against the thought that, on account of love of money, leads us to afflict with the burden of many labors a brother who has recently become a disciple."[17] Interestingly, he condemns neglect of prayer and exploitation of paid and unpaid labor in the name of financial security; I would not be the first to say these things still haunt the church today.

Evagrius is equally piercing when he addresses the drive to own property and possessions, and I imagine he likely had imperial Christianity's various church building efforts in mind. He rejects the comforting notion that property can be put to holy use, a position that will later be central to Augustine of Hippo and his church building campaigns. "Against the demon that said to us, 'Property can, when a person acquires riches, serve the Lord': No one can serve two masters; for a slave will either hate the one and love the other, or be devoted to the one and despise the other. You cannot serve God and wealth" (Matthew 6:24).[18] Instead, Evagrius views property ownership as rooted in the sexual desire "to possess", and that it is a form of lust that drives people (and institutions) to seek to own and manage more and more. He also perceives an animalistic anger behind how individuals and communities protect their property. For "if we have property, then we become like a dog that barks at and attacks people because it wants to protect its things." For Evagrius, the epitome of this is monks suing one another over property, as well as in those who misuse resources intended for the good of the whole community.[19]

To defeat Love of Money, Evagrius instructs monks to practice complete dispossession, both of one's material wealth as well as of the inner desire for financial security. His advice goes well beyond simplicity and extends to his warning against holding onto wealth so as to avoid poverty in old age: "Against the soul that seeks more than food and clothing and does not remember that it entered the world bare and it will leave it naked. For we brought nothing into the world, so that we can take nothing out of it; but if we have food and clothing, we will be content with these (1 Timothy 6:7-8)."[20]

In choosing economic vulnerability, monks were to send all surplus wealth to the elderly monks who were the poor of the monastic communities. Yet even here Evagrius warns of a spiritual danger. For even as he encourages such generosity—"Against the thought of love of money that withheld compassion from a brother who asked out of his need and that advised us to store up for ourselves alone…"[21]—and skewers monks who give and then regret such generosity as well as those who make loans only to the monks who could repay, he warns about generosity becoming a point of pride and itself a cause for seeking riches. In *Foundations of the Monastic Life*, Evagrius warns, "Do not desire to possess riches in order to make donations to the poor, for this is a deception of the evil one that often leads to vainglory and casts the mind into occasions for idle preoccupations."[22] The temptations of the demon Love of Money were (and are) everywhere.

Contemporary admirers of Evagrius's work have often noted the monk's psychological acuity, and this is certainly the case in regard to describing money's addictive and transforming qualities. While thinkers like Clement of Alexandria and Augustine of Hippo wrote of wealth as a neutral tool, one whose moral value depended entirely on how it was used, Evagrius observes that this tool has dynamic properties and that it changes the behavior and outlook of the monks who interact with it on a regular basis. Evagrius, then, helps to raise the question of what is money, anyway.

In *Mind Over Money*, a book that surveys 263 recent psychological studies on money from across the globe, author Claudia Hammond presents the findings that money functions psychologically similarly to both a tool and a drug in our daily lives. Reflecting on the way our brains light up in MRI machines when dealing with money, Hammond notes, "Money is acting like a drug, not chemically but psychologically. Money hasn't existed for long enough in evolutionary terms for humans to develop a specific neural system to deal with it. So it seems as though a system usually associated with immediate rewards has been co-opted to deal with money."[23] And "Yet, at the same time, we desire money because it helps us to accomplish what we want in life. In other words, money is a tool: a way of getting the things we want."[24]

Her descriptions of both the drug- and tool-like qualities of money are not simply metaphor. For people living in poverty, a gain of a significant amount of money has been shown to have the unsurprising result of immediately decreasing the stress hormone cortisol, with levels of happiness and life satisfaction rising and levels of stress and depression falling.[25] This is an important finding as other studies have shown that families living in poverty, including toddlers, have higher cortisol levels on account of the strain and stress that comes with trying to make ends meet.[26] That an influx of money alone can decrease immediate stress and help diminish what scholars call "a neurobiological poverty trap" speaks to the medicinal quality of money in particular cases and at specific doses. In the next chapter on Basil of Caesarea's homilies during a time of natural disaster, I note how he refers to wealth as medicine for people who are suffering from hunger and that people were dying for want of this medicine.

On the other hand, for those who are not living in poverty, psychological studies also show that regular, close association with money may have the sort of harmful, addictive, and distorting effects that Evagrius described in his treatise. Constantly thinking about and managing money has been shown to lead to a decreased willingness to help others, a tendency toward self-isolation, and a reduction in enjoyment of simple pleasures.[27] Among the 50 (sometimes delightfully quirky) studies conducted by the psychologist Paul Piff is the finding that those who earn more than $200,000 per year are more likely to say they would have deserved to be on the first lifeboat on the Titanic. This same group was also 44 percent less proportionally generous than those earning less than $25,000 per year (a finding that will come as no surprise to anyone who has worked for the church). Further, "In another study, when asked to choose between circles of different sizes to represent either themselves or 'other' people, the wealthier a person was, the more likely they were to choose a bigger circle. Richer people were also more likely to agree that they were good at everything and never wrong, and to check their appearance in a mirror before having their photo taken."[28]

Further studies have shown that people who are more exposed to money are negatively impacted: for instance, "economics students give less to charity, with one study showing that the number who admitted to giving nothing at all was double that of students in disciplines such as architecture and, yes, psychology," a finding that held true across the entirety of students' years of study. Even as students studying other subjects became slightly more generous as they approached graduation, "economics students remained at the same less-generous level throughout."[29]

All of these are fascinating studies about how money distorts our thinking, but perhaps my favorite has to do with the lies we tell ourselves regarding the randomness of being born into privilege. In one study, subjects playing Monopoly were randomly assigned advantages over the other players. This included starting the game with twice as much money, getting to throw two dice instead of one, and receiving $400 rather than $200 every time the player went past Go.[30] Not surprisingly, the advantaged players consistently won the game. More surprising, however, was how the winners responded when asked why they won it. Hammond notes that "they talked of the effort they'd put in and the wise decisions they'd made but none mentioned that they had an advantage from the start."[31] Perhaps the demon Love of Money's greatest trick is to simply blind us to our own privilege. Such self-delusion was something that Evagrius observed and knew well, and it speaks to the power of the human mind to justify ongoing inequality, including the randomness of wealth-by-inheritance.

I include these studies here because they offer a corrective to the widely accepted view of money as a morally neutral tool that can be used for either good or evil. Both Evagrius and these psychological studies suggests that we have a much more complicated and dynamic relationship to money. If Christians wish to accept the notion that wealth is a tool, then we should be aware that this tool operates more like a drug in that it can have medicinal qualities in certain cases and doses but can become highly addictive and harmful in other situations. I find this to be a far more accurate description of the strange way I see people (including myself) thinking and acting around money. Yes, wealth can serve a purpose, but I'm oftentimes in meetings and conversations where I suspect something akin to an addiction to this substance is playing a larger role than most people realize. I have seen and known personally Evagrius's observation of the way that obsessing after wealth undermines the goals of Christian community.

When reading *Talking Back*, I occasionally had the sense of being trapped in the thicket of Evagrius's deeply perceptive but haunted mind. The imperiling whisper of demonic forces appears at every turn and his life is a pitched battle against many forces. To combat Love of Money, Evagrius advises monks to live right on the edge of not just simplicity but chosen poverty. His rigor deserves the overused word "radical" and is tied to his striving to attain "the death of Jesus." Indeed, in *Talking Back*, he warns "Against the soul that wants to attain the death of Jesus while retaining some wealth and forgets how Elisha the prophet, when he renounced the world, divested himself of all that he had."[32]

This pursuit of the death of Jesus ultimately resulted in a dangerous physical regimen that would be his physical undoing. Augustine Casiday notes, "[Evagrius] ate only once per day. When he did eat, his diet was extremely limited. He assiduously abstained from lettuce, green vegetables, fruit, grapes and meat; he refrained from bathing and took no cooked food; eventually, he ruined his digestive tract and probably suffered from urinary tract stones. He slept no more than a third of the night, devoting the rest of his time to prayer, contemplation and study of scripture."[33]

This regimen proved so harsh that Evagrius's elders in Kellia began warning him to moderate his practices, warnings he willfully ignored. This strikes me as a profoundly tragic decision for someone who so carefully observed how we delude ourselves. Evagrius died of a ruined digestive tract on the feast of Epiphany in 399, a relatively early death widely thought to have been the result of his extreme asceticism.

What Evagrius left behind in his writings on money, however, raises the question of the psychological effects of money on both individuals and institutions. Money, after all, is not just an abstract way of defining value; this definition is far too intellectual to describe the emotional intensity of how people act around money. No, it is a much more deeply psychological phenomenon. If money is a tool, then this tool happens to act much more like a drug in that it has both transformative and addictive qualities.

Evagrius's observations raise all sorts of questions that we should ask about ourselves and the institutions we are part of. Are we addicted to money? Are our institutions? To what extent is anxiety about money distorting and undermining the values of the communities we are a part of? In the name of financial security, have we forgotten the gospels' emphasis on chosen simplicity and economic vulnerability? Evagrius's warning to his fellow monks about the power of Love of Money still rings painfully true, for he warns us all "against the thought that anxiously serves in business affairs on the pretext that the money has run out, and now there is nothing left of it, and it cannot be regained," and "against the inner thoughts that want to acquire riches and to consume the intellect with anxiety about them."[34]

Discussion Questions

Evagrius Ponticus viewed Love of Money as a demonic force, a deceptive spirit that was always seeking to undermine the monastic life. Love of Money showed up in all sorts of ways including as a distracting anxiety over financial matters, as a lust for wealth that led monks to work all day and night, and even in the claims of would-be philanthropists who said they were becoming wealthy in order to give more to the poor. How do you see the demon Love of Money undermining Christianity and the life of faith today?

Evagrius considered property ownership to be particularly dangerous and considered it self-delusion when monks claimed owning property was justified on the grounds it could be used for holy things. "Against the demon that said to us, 'Property can, when a person acquires riches, serve the Lord': No one can serve two masters; for a slave will either hate the one and love the other, or be devoted to the one and despise the other. You cannot serve God and wealth (Matthew 6:24)." While recognizing that Evagrius was often extremist in his viewpoints, does he nonetheless have a point? How and when do we as individuals and faith communities end up serving our property and possessions rather than God?

In *Mind Over Money*, author Claudia Hammond presents the findings that money functions psychologically similarly to something like both a tool and a drug in our daily lives. Money functions as dynamically as medicine, which can be extremely helpful in particular cases and doses but which can also be addictive and poisonous as well. What do you think of this psychological definition of money?

A Next Step

Evagrius counseled a bare-bones existence and radical simplicity of life. He warned monks against the tendency to confuse sufficiency—having enough—with economic security and instead urged Christians to embrace voluntary poverty and give all surplus to the poor. In doing so, he believed monks became more open and generous. What would it mean for you and your faith community to practice greater simplicity and increased generosity? What would be a significant first step in this process?

Endnotes

1 McGuckin, *The Path of Christianity*.

2 *Talking Back: A Monastic Handbook for Combating Demons,* Evagrius of Pontus; tr. and Introduction by David Brakke (Collegeville, Minnesota: Liturgical Press, 2009), 2.

3 *Talking Back: A Monastic Handbook for Combating Demons*, 2.

4 David Brakke, "Care for the Poor, Fear of Poverty, and Love of Money: Evagrius Ponticus on the Monk's Economic Vulnerability," in *Wealth and Poverty in Early Church and Society*, 77-78.

5 McGuckin, *The Path of Christianity*, 908.

6 Augustine Casiday, *Evagrius Ponticus* in Early Church Fathers (London: Routledge, 2006), 10.

7 McGuckin, *The Path of Christianity*, 396.

8 McGuckin, *The Path of Christianity,* 398.

9 McGuckin, *The Path of Christianity,* 398.

10 Brakke, "Care for the Poor, Fear of Poverty, and Love of Money," 76-87, 77.

11 Brakke, "Care for the Poor, Fear of Poverty, and Love of Money," 76-87, 82-83.

12 Casiday, *Evagrius Ponticus,* 13.

13 McGuckin, *The Path of Christianity*, 870.

14 McGuckin, *The Path of Christianity,* 872.

15 "Concerning the Love of Money," *Talking Back,* 97-98.

16 "Concerning the Love of Money," *Talking Back*, 97-98.

17 "Concerning the Love of Money," *Talking Back*, 97-98.

18 "Concerning the Love of Money," *Talking Back*, 97-98.

19 Brakke, "Care for the Poor, Fear of Poverty, and Love of Money," *Wealth and Poverty in Early Church and Society*, 76-87, 79-80.

20 "Concerning the Love of Money," *Talking Back*, 97.

21 "Concerning the Love of Money," *Talking Back*, 85.

22 "Concerning the Love of Money," *Talking Back*, 76-87, 84.

23 Claudia Hammond, *Mind over Money: The Psychology of Money and How to Use It Better* (New York City: Harper Perennial, 2016), 10.

24 Hammond, *Mind over Money*, 11.

25 Hammond, *Mind over Money*, 202.

26 Hammond, *Mind over Money,* 228.

27 Hammond, *Mind over Money,* 233-234, 201.

28 Hammond, *Mind over Money,* 239.

29 Hammond, *Mind over Money,* 259-260.

30 Hammond, *Mind over Money,* 240.

31 Hammond, *Mind over Money,* 240.
32 "Concerning the Love of Money," *Talking Back*, 88.
33 Casiday, *Evagrius Ponticus*, 13.
34 "Concerning the Love of Money," *Talking Back*, 97-98.

18 Basil of Caesarea Preaches to the Wealthy in a Time of Natural Disaster

Whereas Evagrius warned about Love of Money's addictive and distorting effects on Christian communities, the bishop Basil of Caesarea (330-379) spoke about wealth's power to serve as a form of medicine to those in desperate need. Indeed, the idea of wealth as medicine in suffering people's lives would become a theme in both his preaching and ministry, which relied on donations to build a hospital to serve the poor.

Basil's forceful preaching and advocacy on behalf of the destitute of his city brings us back to how the Emperor Constantine and the rise of the imperial church gave rise to a new and public role for bishops and the church as a whole: that of caring not only for the Christian poor but also for the publicly registered poor, both Christian and non-Christian alike.[1] But whereas Constantine expected bishops and clergy to carry their responsibilities out while practicing the *verecundia*—the virtue of knowing one's place—later interpreters of this public role would bring it closer to prophetic advocacy. Basil of Caesarea is a particularly good example of this as he aimed to make visible the suffering of those who were dying in a time of natural disaster.

A milestone in Basil's advocacy occurred in 369 in Caesarea, in what is now modern-day Turkey. The winter rains had refused to fall that year, and this resulted in food shortages, panic among the rich, and hunger among the most vulnerable citizens, immigrants, and slaves. By 370, fear had taken root among the city's landowners, many of the wealthiest citizens had fled the city, and the price of food skyrocketed in markets as a result of the wealthy hoarding grain in their storehouses. Into this calamity, the still-relatively new bishop began preaching in a way that expressed how he understood his role to be a "lover of the poor."

In Basil's homily "In a Time of Famine and Drought," he describes what happens when a person dies by starvation before declaring to a disquieted congregation that "the person who can cure such an infirmity and refuses one medicine because of avarice, can with reason be condemned a murderer."[2] Such a statement surely shocks the wealthy, yet Basil presses on, believing that the salvation of the rich is also at stake. In his "Homily to the Rich," Basil says, "Yet while it is uncertain whether you will have need of this buried gold, the losses you incur from your inhuman behavior are not at all uncertain… And I think that when it comes to this, as you are burying your wealth, you entomb it with your own heart."[3]

As a "lover of the poor," Basil lays bare the suffering that could just as easily have been ignored by a public that perceives wide swaths of the population as expendable. During a famine, he raised funds for a soup kitchen and what is now considered the first hospital in history. The Basiliad, as it would later be called, was staffed by physicians and clergy and offered medical treatment and trade skills to the impoverished sick of the region for centuries to come. In this case, Basil's belief that wealth could be medicine quite literally helped to form the hospital.

Basil's homilies to the elite of Caesarea are troubling, direct, and remain compelling for their force and clarity, and they represent a socially focused response to the complex questions that Christian bishops were facing in fourth-century Rome. Looking at his life offers us a chance to return to the question of the public role of a Christian bishop both during a time of natural disaster as well as the more day-to-day disaster of ongoing inequality and injustice. Did the church have anything to say to the wealthy as poverty and hunger overwhelmed the city? Were Christians to be exclusively concerned with their own poor, or did they also have a responsibility to the impoverished and hungry in the wider public as well?

Basil's passionate sermons for the wealthy to release their stores of grain and riches to the poor were the fruit of lifelong, spiritual wrestling with issues of wealth and poverty. Born to a family of wealthy Christians in 330 in Caesarea, capital of Cappadocia, Basil's classical education included a year of study in Athens, where he met Gregory of Nazianzus, who became a lifelong friend. Basil practiced as a lawyer after his return from Athens until a chance encounter with the Christian monk Eustathius of Sebaste rekindled an earlier interest in hermetic asceticism. Through the guidance and encouragement of his sister Macrina, Basil subsequently left his law practice and embarked on a radically new path.

In 357, Basil traveled to Palestine, Egypt, Syria, and Mesopotamia to learn more about ascetic practices and distributed his personal fortune to the poor along the way. While in Egypt, he visited Pachomius, an abbot who is credited with bringing solitary ascetics into an organized form of communal monasticism for the first time. Basil's travels and visit with Pachomius's community inspired him to abandon the solitary life of hermetic asceticism and to found a monastic community on his family's estate. Once again, his sister Macrina proved to be influential in both this decision and then as a leader in the community itself. Basil drew heavily from his visit with Pachomius when he wrote his *Larger Rule and Shorter Rule*, texts that remain as foundational to Eastern monasticism as Benedict of Nursia's Rule is to Western monasticism.

Basil's contributions to Christian doctrine were significant. He was an early and influential supporter of the Nicene Creed at a synod in Constantinople in 369, and he played an important role in resolving the Arian controversy that threatened to divide the church at the time. Partly because of his theological leadership at these synods and amidst these controversies, Basil was made a deacon in 362, a priest in 365, and then bishop of Caesarea just five years later.

As a new bishop, Basil stepped into a precarious public leadership role that required balancing the practices and traditions of Christian assemblies with the pressing expectations of imperial Rome. In *Poverty & Leadership in the Later Roman Empire,* historian Peter Brown writes, "Beneath the gaze of the emperor and his highly placed officials, Basil created publicly acclaimed systems of poor relief that justified the wealth and tax exemptions of the church of Caesarea."[4] Yet, it is also clear that for Basil, this was about more than just imperial tax exemptions. Basil's prior experience of living in a monastic community had profoundly shaped his understanding of the social purpose of wealth. He therefore urged the rich to take up the monastic ideals of sufficiency, simplicity, and communal distribution of their riches.[5] This came to a head in 370 as the new bishop began urging the wealthy in bracing terms to open their storehouses of grain so the hungry might eat and so the wealthy might gain their own salvation.

Basil preached several homilies about the famine and drought that had befallen Caesarea, texts that sparkle with such intensity that you can almost hear his voice as he rallies support for relief efforts. These homilies remain striking for the direct and confrontational manner that he speaks to the wealthy, beginning with how he places blame for the drought and subsequent famine as God's punishment for the lack of concern the wealthy held for the poor: "No, the reason why we are not governed in the usual way is clear and self-evident: We receive, but give to nobody; we praise good works, but do not practice them toward the needy…" and "Our barns and granaries are too tight for what we store in them, and yet we ourselves do not have compassion for those who suffer from tight circumstances."[6]

Basil describes famine as the worst possible kind of suffering to befall humanity and offers a visceral description of what happens to the human body through starvation: "Of all human calamities, famine is the principal one; and the most miserable of deaths is, no doubt that by starvation." He goes into detail when describing the effects of famine on the body: "The flesh clings to the bones like a cobweb. The skin has no color… The belly is hollow, contracted, formless, without weight, without the natural stretching of the viscera, joined to the bones of the back."[7]

He also describes how the prospect of this terrible death resulted in the hungry having to make unimaginable decisions, including parents deciding which of their children to sell into slavery. In "Pull Down Your Barns," Basil depicts a father's internal wrestling over which of his children to sell so he might have enough money to purchase food for the rest of his family:

And what are [the father's] thoughts at such times? "Which should I sell first? Which will please the corn merchant best? Should I take the eldest? He has rights of the firstborn I dare not violate. The youngest then? I pity his youth, still innocent of misery. This one is his parents' living image; this other is ripe for schooling. What hopelessness! What am I to do? Can I turn against any of them? Can I become a brute beast? Can I forget the bond of nature? If I cling to them all, I will see them all wasting away with hunger. If I sacrifice one, with what face can I look at the others? They will suspect me of treachery at once. How can I stay in a household which I myself have orphaned? How can I sit down to my table with food when these are the means of filling it?"[8]

Lest anyone believe this nightmarish scenario is far in humanity's past, I'll note that in December 2021 the *LA Times* ran an article entitled "As hunger and poverty worsen in Afghanistan, desperate parents are selling their children." The article tells of an Afghan father making the same excruciating decision Basil described in the fourth century, selling a "10-year-old girl into marriage without telling his wife, taking a downpayment to help feed his family of six children. Without that money, he told her, they would all starve. He claimed he had to sacrifice one to save the rest."[9] In January 2022, UN Secretary-General António Guterres spoke out forcefully on the hunger that had settled over Afghanistan, which had resulted in "babies being sold to feed their siblings."[10]

Amidst the nightmare of famine, Basil insisted the wealthy of Caesarea were hoarding the very medicine that could alleviate the starvation and horror he so vividly described, and their refusal to help placed their salvation in peril. In perhaps the most pointed line from this homily, Basil states, "The person who can cure such an infirmity and refuses one's medicine because of avarice, can with reason be condemned as a murderer."[11]

Basil goes about making a moral argument against the accumulation of wealth through several moves. First, like Evagrius, Basil was profoundly aware of the peculiar temptations that come with wealth. He describes the madness of the wealthy who have so much yet who remain addicted to hoarding more and more. He invokes the parable of the rich fool (Luke 12:13-21) to describe those who are so wealthy

that they must pull down their barns to build still larger ones in order
to store all that they have, even as people all around them suffer:
"[The rich fool] added continually new to old, swelled his plenty with
annual increase, and came at length to the hopeless dilemma where
greed prevented him from letting the old be brought out, yet he had
no room to store the new." [12] Even abundance ended up as a source of
misery for the rich, for "What heartens others distresses the miser.
It does not cheer him to have his granaries filled within; his heart is
wrung by the overflow of wealth; he fears it may reach the folk outside
and thus help to relieve the destitute."[13] In this same homily, Basil
describes what could be done with this wealth if only it were given
away, "yet you keep it all locked away behind doors and sealed up;
and then the thought of it keeps you awake at nights; you take counsel
about it inwardly, and your counselor is yourself—a fool!"[14]

Basil also joins in the now lengthy tradition of reinterpreting the
Gospel of Luke's vexing parable of the unjust steward. In contrast to
the way the church speaks of stewardship today, Basil emphasizes that
a transformed steward sends money flowing out rather than in. That
is, *the unjust and faithful steward is transformed from being a steward
of his master's wealth to redirecting this wealth toward the alleviation of
debts of the poor.* He therefore urges the wealthy to stop serving wealth
by building larger and larger barns to store their riches and instead
repent and serve God by becoming stewards of humanity, sharing
their wealth for the good of the wider community:

> You have been made the minister of a gracious God, steward
> for your fellow servants. Do not suppose that all these things
> were provided for your belly. The wealth you handle belongs
> to others; think of it accordingly. Not for long will it delight
> you; soon it will slip from you and be gone, and you will be
> asked to give strict account of it.[15]

Basil then begins describing a form of almsgiving that will likely make
many contemporary Christians wince. He argues that releasing the
grain from their barns is a transaction with God that assures wealthy
people of their salvation: "If you give to the hungry, the gift becomes
your own and comes back to you with increase. As the wheat falling
on the ground brings forth a gain for the one who scatters it, so
the grain bestowed on the hungry brings you profit a hundredfold
hereafter," and "You must leave your money behind whether you will

or not, but your honor coming from the glory of good works will take you to the Master."[16]

Does this suggest that Basil linked salvation with works (that is, almsgiving) as opposed to grace? Yes. Does it suggest a highly transactional God? Yes. Did it generate donations for people who were desperately hungry? Seemingly, also yes.

Basil's argument—one made amidst the urgency of famine—represented a synthesis of longstanding Jewish and Christian traditions of caring for the poor with the philanthropic practices of fourth-century Rome. These philanthropic practices hinged on prior patronage practices and so in Basil (and many others') reframing, God was like a patron with whom one was transacting. This patron God was granting salvation to the rich in exchange for their gifts to the poor. Brown speaks about Basil and others' efforts in this area dramatically: "To put it bluntly: in a sense, it was Christian bishops who invented the poor."[17] That is, the destitute, who were seen as having nothing material to offer the wealthy in exchange, were finally seen as worthy recipients of their gifts because bishops preached that a more significant exchange was taking place with God.

Basil's argument that building wealth is akin to hoarding medicine while many around the world die for lack of it is relevant to the world we live in today. Indeed, one of the most bizarre events of the very strange year of 2021 was that of two billionaires, Richard Branson and Jeff Bezos, heading into space aboard privately funded rockets. The images of these ultra-wealthy men taking off in great view of the public and the estimates of how much wealth they gained during the pandemic and subsequently spent on their joyrides ignited an all-too-brief public debate about the ethical responsibilities that come with wealth.

As people reacted to these billionaire space flights, some insisted that outside of breaking the law, the wealthy held no social responsibility to use their riches to alleviate the suffering of others. Many others (likely the majority) at least entertained the question of what good could have been done with this wealth had it been directed toward the alleviation of suffering, including feeding the hungry. United Nations Secretary-General António Guterres sounded like Basil when he criticized Bezos and Branson for "joyriding to space while millions go hungry on earth."[18]

Still a smaller group (and I imagine Basil would actually have been among these) questioned a society in which some individuals could accumulate so much wealth in the first place, arguing that such inequities reflect a form of societal madness and that to use this wealth as they did as so many others suffered from hunger was an evil act, akin to a doctor withholding medicine from a dying patient.[19] Basil, as you'll recall, had few qualms about calling such people murderers.

For Basil, however, these debates were not simply taking place on social media nor were they hypothetical meditations focused on other people's wealth. Basil's homilies reflected what he was doing with his own wealth as well. Basil had already given away his personal fortune by the time he preached his homilies in 370, and he would later donate his family's wealth to establish a soup kitchen and to build a hospital for the indigent sick of Caesarea. In a letter to Amphilochius, Basil is recorded as inviting the bishop of Iconium to come and visit his newly built "church of the hospital (or poorhouse)" on the outskirts of Caesarea.[20] The Basiliad existed for centuries after Basil's death.

The questions Basil faced as the new bishop of Caesarea continue to resonate today: is it moral to accumulate wealth in the face of so much suffering? At what point do wealthy people, institutions, and nations have a social obligation to help the most vulnerable?

For the church, what is the public role of a Christian bishop in the face of rampant inequality and growing destitution, particularly during a time of natural disaster? Does the church have anything to say to the wealthy who withhold the much-needed medicine of wealth in a time of disaster? Amidst the COVID-19 pandemic, what did the church say as pharmaceutical corporations refused to follow in the footsteps of the Jonas Salk, developer of the polio vaccine, who in 1955 insisted the patent should be owned by all, stating, "Could you patent the sun?"[21]

Basil's homilies to the rich are a startling reminder that Christianity has not always had such an obsequious relationship to the rich, that bishops have not always stayed tactfully mum on issues of economic justice, and that there have been Christian leaders who spoke out clearly and forcefully about the obligations of the wealthy in times of great need.

Discussion Questions

Whereas Evagrius warned about the demon Love of Money's addictive and distorting effects on Christian communities, Basil of Caesarea spoke about wealth's power to serve as a form of medicine in a time of famine. In his homily, "In a Time of Famine and Drought," he declares that "the person who can cure such an infirmity and refuses one medicine because of avarice, can with reason be condemned a murderer."[22] What do you think of his description of wealth as a form of medicine being withheld from a suffering patient?

Basil reinterprets the parable of the unjust steward noting that the transformed steward sends money flowing out rather than in, going from being a steward of his master's wealth to redirecting this wealth toward the alleviation of debts of the poor. Speaking to the wealthy, he argues, "You have been made the minister of a gracious God, steward for your fellow servants. Do not suppose that all these things were provided for your belly. The wealth you handle belongs to others; think of it accordingly. Not for long will it delight you; soon it will slip from you and be gone, and you will be asked to give strict account of it."[23] What do you think of this notion of "the wealth you handle belonging to others" and becoming "stewards of humanity?"

Basil of Caesarea ends up embodying the ancient notion of a bishop's role as "lover of the poor." Historian Peter Brown speaks about Basil and others' efforts in this area dramatically: "To put it bluntly: in a sense, it was Christian bishops who invented the poor."[24] That is, he and other bishops understood their role to be raising the suffering of the poor to public awareness and rallying support for relief efforts. What would it mean for bishops today to understand this as part of their role?

A Next Step

Conduct a Bible study on the parable of the rich fool (Luke 12:13-21), one in which Jesus criticizes those who are so wealthy that they must pull down their barns to build still larger ones in order to store all that they have. Basil notes, "[The rich fool] added continually new to old, swelled his plenty with annual increase, and came at length to the hopeless dilemma where greed prevented him from letting the old be brought out, yet he had no room to store the new." [25] In a time of natural disaster, he notes that even abundance ends up as a source of misery for the rich, for "What heartens others distresses the miser. It does not cheer him to have his granaries filled within; his heart is wrung by the overflow of wealth; he fears it may reach the folk outside and thus help to relieve the destitute."[26] What does the parable of the rich fool mean to you?

Endnotes

1 Rhee, *Loving the Poor, Saving the Rich*, loc. 4240-4257 (Kindle).

2 "Homily 8: In Time of Famine and Drought," *Wealth and Poverty in Early Christianity*.

3 "Homily 7: To the Rich," *Wealth and Poverty in Early Christianity*.

4 Peter Brown, *Poverty and Leadership in the Later Roman Empire,* (Lebanon, New Hampshire: University Press of New England, 2002), 39.

5 *Wealth and Poverty in Early Christianity*, ed. Rhee, loc. 424 (Kindle).

6 "Homily 8: In Time of Famine and Drought," *Wealth and Poverty in Early Christianity*.

7 "Homily 8: In Time of Famine and Drought," *Wealth and Poverty in Early Christianity*.

8 "Homily 6: I Will Pull Down My Barns," *Wealth and Poverty in Early Christianity*.

9 Elena Becatores, "As Hunger and Poverty Worsen in Afghanistan, Desperate Parents Are Selling Their Children," *The Los Angeles Times*, December 31, 2021.

10 "Secretary-General's Press Encounter," United Nations. https://www.un.org/sg/en/node/261394.

11 "Homily 8: In Time of Famine and Drought," *Wealth and Poverty in Early Christianity*.

12 "Homily 6: I Will Pull Down My Barns," *Wealth and Poverty in Early Christianity*.

13 "Homily 6: I Will Pull Down My Barns," *Wealth and Poverty in Early Christianity*.

14 "Homily 6: I Will Pull Down My Barns," *Wealth and Poverty in Early Christianity*.

15 "Homily 6: I Will Pull Down My Barns," *Wealth and Poverty in Early Christianity*.

16 "Homily 6: I Will Pull Down My Barns," *Wealth and Poverty in Early Christianity*.

17 Brown, *Poverty and Leadership in the Later Roman Empire*, 8.

18 Seth Borenstein, "Billionaires Rocketing into Space Draw UN Chief's Red Glare," Associated Press News, September 21, 2021.

19 "Poverty and Shared Prosperity 2020: Reversal of Fortune," World Bank, worldbank.org/en/publication/poverty-and-shared-prosperity.

20 Thomas Heyne, "Reconstructing the World's First Hospital: The Basiliad," *Hektoen International,* Spring 2015.

21 "Could You Patent the Sun?" New York Public Radio, December 12, 2016. wnycstudios.org/podcasts/takeaway/segments/retro-report-patenting-sun

22 "Homily 8: In Time of Famine and Drought," *Wealth and Poverty in Early Christianity*.

23 "Homily 6: I Will Pull Down My Barns," *Wealth and Poverty in Early Christianity*.

24 Brown, *Poverty and Leadership in the Later Roman Empire,* 8.

25 "Homily 6: I Will Pull Down My Barns," *Wealth and Poverty in Early Christianity*.

26 "Homily 6: I Will Pull Down My Barns," *Wealth and Poverty in Early Christianity*.

19 Against Predatory Lending

One frequently raised critique of social justice-focused Christianity is that this prophetic and socially attuned version of the faith represents something new, a recent development born out of the World Wars, identity politics, and liberation theologies of the twentieth century. I hope it is clear by now that when it comes to Christianity's history of condemning exploitation of the poor, this is patently untrue. Especially on issues such as usury, the predatory lending of money at exorbitantly high interest rates to the poor, faith leaders can reach all the way back to the Old and New Testaments, as well as church fathers such as Basil of Caesarea, John Chrysostom, and Ambrose of Milan, for precedent in condemning this form of exploitation. These ancient roots are apparent in a single homily preached by Basil of Caesarea.

Basil delivered his "Homily on Psalm 14" while he was bishop of Caesarea. His opening lines speak to his low level of patience with the wealthy of his city at that point: "You rich! Listen to the advice that we give to the poor in view of your inhumanity: Bear any suffering than the calamity that will come from usury."

In crying out against "you rich," Basil is speaking directly to the wealthy landowners who were the primary lenders in his community. He denounces their lending practices from the pulpit stating, "Indeed, it is extremely inhuman that some have to beg for the most basic necessities to support their lives while others are not satisfied with the capital they have, but excogitate ways of increasing their opulence at the expense of the poor in distress." He continues, "The poor ask for medicine and you offer them poison; they beg for bread and you give them a sword; they plead for freedom and you subject them to slavery; they implore to be freed from their bonds and you entrap them in an inescapable net."[1]

Inspired by Basil's homily, the fourth-century bishop Ambrose of Milan (339-397) later offers equally searing words about "the inescapable net" of predatory lending in his homily "On Tobit." Ambrose even echoes Basil's forceful opening line: "You rich, such are indeed your favors!... For you even the poor are a source of profit. You subject the poor to usury; you know how to oblige them to pay you interest even when they do not have enough to look after their basic needs."[2]

It is difficult for me to imagine preachers today standing in a pulpit and inveighing against the predatory lending practices of bankers, mortgage, student loan, credit card, and payday loan industry executives as forcefully as these two bishops did in the fourth century. This is likely because such lending has become depersonalized, the actions of banks and payday lending companies rather than that of a small group of wealthy landowners sitting in the congregational assembly. Even so, such preaching is still necessary as predatory lenders have never ceased "excogitating ways to increase their opulence at the expense of the poor in distress," as Basil preached. As faith leaders, we need to reacquaint ourselves with Christianity's ancient history of condemning lending with interest as the basis for advocacy against lending at predatory interest rates. This includes exploring the Old and New Testament's abhorrence of predatory lending, the early church councils' forceful prohibitions on usury among clergy and laity alike, and the writings of figures like Basil of Caesarea and Ambrose of Milan, among many others, from the first few centuries of the church.

Basil's words in his "Homily on Psalm 14" still leap off the page today. In the homily, Basil reflects on the psalmist's condemnation of the "evildoers who eat up my people as they eat bread" (Psalm 14: 4) and sees the charging of interest on the poor as a form of enslavement. Instead of practicing usury, he urges the wealthy to lend their surplus money to the poor without any interest at all: "Give your surplus money, do not burden it with interest, and both you and your debtor will fare well... But if you look for interest, be satisfied with those given by the Lord. He will pay, through the poor, the due interest."[3] Significantly, Basil grounds his argument in Jesus's radical teaching on lending found in the Gospel of Luke: "Now what does the Lord advise? 'Lend to those from whom there is no hope of repayment.'"[4]

Basil's choice to cite Jesus's teaching is important because I've come across a recurring misperception that the New Testament is silent on the topic of usury.[5] This could not be further from the truth. Indeed, theologian Douglas Meeks argues: "Probably the most consequential economic saying of Jesus for the history of the West is 'Lend, expecting nothing in return' (Luke 6:34-35, cf. Matthew 5:42). This command, together with that of Deuteronomy 23:19, impelled the Christian tradition through the Reformation to condemn the injustice of usury."[6]

Jesus's teaching on lending occurs in a very important part of the Gospel of Luke. It forms part of his Sermon on the Plain, which begins with Jesus saying that it is the poor, the hungry, and the weeping who are blessed.[7] Jesus goes on to state, "If you lend to those from whom you hope to receive, what credit is that to you? Even sinners lend to sinners, to receive as much again. But love your enemies, do good, and lend, expecting nothing in return. Your reward will be great, and you will be children of the Most High; for he is kind to the ungrateful and the wicked," (Luke 6:34-35). I'll only add here that while it's well-known (though not well-practiced) that we are to love our enemies, it's far less well-known that in the very same breath, Jesus commands us to express this love through how we lend to one another—that is, free of interest. This lending and borrowing of money without interest again speaks to Christianity's early vision of economic fellowship, the sharing of resources and trying to help one another face extremely challenging circumstances.

In addition to Jesus's command, Basil's homily also draws on the extensive Old Testament traditions that abhor predatory lending to the poor. This is especially apparent in Basil's description of debt and indebtedness as a form of "slavery" and "an inescapable net."[8]

The ancient association of usury and enslavement is perhaps best expressed in Leviticus 25:35-38. This passage connects the experience of indebtedness of the poor with the slavery experienced by the Hebrew people in Egypt:

> If any of your kin fall into difficulty and become dependent
> on you, you shall support them; they shall live with you as
> though resident aliens. Do not take interest in advance or
> otherwise make a profit from them, but fear your God; let
> them live with you. You shall not lend them your money
> at interest taken in advance, or provide them food at a
> profit. I am the LORD your God, who brought you out of
> the land of Egypt, to give you the land of Canaan, to be
> your God.

This notion that one is to never take financial advantage of those who have fallen into desperate straits, whether through lending with interest or even by providing food at a profit, is a frequently overlooked yet radical theme within Old Testament scripture. The memory of slavery has ethical obligations for a people, including a prohibition against lending with interest.

The connection between usury and slavery is repeated elsewhere in the Old Testament, and creditors are described as coming to take away debtors' children as slaves (2 Kings 4:1). The Book of Nehemiah describes the horrific results of families having to borrow money on their own fields to pay the king's tax: "We are forcing our sons and daughters to be slaves, and some of our daughters have been ravished; we are powerless, and our fields and vineyards now belong to others," (Nehemiah 5:4-5). In Psalm 15, it is only those who do "not give money in hope of gain, nor does [they] take a bribe against the innocent" who are allowed to abide in God's tent.[9]

The main thrust of the prohibition against predatory lending, then, is that it is an act of kicking people while they're already down and taking advantage of the poor while they are in desperate need; it is an act of enslavement of the very people God once liberated. The biblical witness repeatedly condemns those who see the desperation of others as an opportunity for a stronger profit margin, an outlook so breathtakingly out of step with the rapacious logic of predatory lending (and, well, much of the US economy) that those who engage in this practice are described as enslavers of the poor and adversaries to God's liberative action in the world.

Basil's condemnations of usury builds on Jesus's radical teaching to lend without interest. Jesus roots this teaching in Old Testament traditions, which held that usury was a form of enslavement of the poor. This biblical abhorrence of usury was then picked up and expanded upon by early Christian assemblies and eventually appeared in some of the earliest Christian councils' church laws (called canons). While not exactly a part of Basil's homily, it's still worth reviewing these briefly because they show how central this issue once was in the mind of the church and how solidly Basil stood on tradition when he condemned the wealthy landowners who "excogitate ways of increasing their opulence at the expense of the poor in distress."

In the twentieth canon from the Council of Elvira (c.306), the first church council from which canons are extant, there is a prohibition against usury for all Christians, both clergy and laity alike. Elvira was then followed by similar condemnations in the councils of Arles (314), Nicaea (325), and Carthage (348), continuing through to Pope Leo the Great's (440-461) *Nec hoc quoque* that forbade Christian clergy from engaging in the sin of usury and condemned laity who made money through such lending as guilty of shameful gain. At many of these councils, both clergy and laity who were found to be engaged in usury were condemned, although the punishments for clergy were frequently much harsher.

The Council of Elvira is a good example of this. Held near modern-day Granada, Spain, the council aimed to restore order and discipline after a period of persecution by adopting 81 canons that were remarkable in their moral rigor. Elvira produced church laws recommending expulsion from the church for idolatry and repeated adultery and divorce as well as usury. As we'll see in a later chapter, it also describes a disturbing incident about a Christian slave owner. On the topic of usury, Canon 20 reads:

> If any clergy are found engaged in usury, let them be censured and dismissed. If a layman is caught practicing usury, he may be pardoned if he promises to stop the practice. If he continues this evil practice, let him be expelled from the church.[10]

This was followed by later conciliar prohibitions, including that of the First Council of Nicaea in 325. Nicaea—from which Christians have the Nicene Creed—was the first ecumenical council of the Christian church and met in what is now modern-day Iznik, Turkey. This gathering was called by Constantine, who hoped a general council would solve the tensions and rivalries created in the Eastern church by the priest Arius and the theological movement of Arianism. This council is well-known for producing an early version of the Nicene Creed and condemning Arianism as heresy. Less well-known is the fact that it set forth a new church law concerning clerics who practiced usury. Canon 17 reads:

> Forasmuch as many enrolled among the Clergy, following covetousness and lust of gain, have forgotten the divine Scripture, which says, He has not given his money upon usury, and in lending money ask the hundredth of the sum [as monthly interest], the holy and great Synod thinks it just that if after this decree any one be found to receive usury, whether he accomplish it by secret transaction or otherwise, as by demanding the whole and one-half, or by using any other contrivance whatever for filthy lucre's sake, he shall be deposed from the clergy and his name stricken from the list.[11]

Unfortunately, the frequency with which usury has been addressed speaks to its prevalence and how often both clergy and laity alike were engaged in such lending. In Robert P. Maloney's essay, "Early Conciliar Legislation on Usury: A Contribution to the Study of Christian Moral Thinking," he concludes, "In both East and West, ecclesiastical legislation prohibited what civil legislation allowed. Severe penalties were threatened against violators of the law. Yet even so, lending at interest went on. Both clerics and laymen ignored prohibitions and sought profit from their loans."[12]

Despite extensive biblical teaching, the conciliar prohibitions, and voices of those like Basil the Great, the reality of usury is rarely spoken of today as an issue of concern within most churches. Why is that?

One reason for Christianity's muted witness on this issue likely has to do with questions around what counts as usury today. If we equate usury solely with lending money at interest, it becomes much harder to see what the church can do at this point. That horse has left the barn, as it were. Indeed, one of the few contemporary sermons I have found on usury—aptly entitled "The Sin We Stopped Feeling Sorry For"—describes usury as so intrinsically intertwined with our economy that condemnations of lending with interest no longer make sense:

> Do you have an interest-bearing account at a bank? You are loaning the bank money at interest. You are a usurer. Do you have a retirement account, a 401K, a 403B? You might hold mostly stocks, but I bet the part of your portfolio is in bonds as well. Interest-bearing, usurious bonds and Treasury bills. It is inescapable. To be part of modern middle-class life in America is to be involved in usury. And even if you somehow have avoided every opportunity to charge interest to someone else, you are almost surely still guilty of paying interest in some way: on a mortgage, on a car loan, on a credit card. In willingly agreeing to pay interest, you are giving your creditor an occasion to sin. You are tempting someone else to do that which displeases the Lord, according to Psalm 15 and all of the Bible.[13]

The above paragraph sets the preacher up for explaining why this is a sin the church stopped feeling sorry for. His point: interest-bearing loans are such an essential part of the modern economy that it is difficult to imagine any church seriously encouraging stopping all lending with interest. That said, I believe equating usury with general lending with interest obscures the more particular concern that the biblical tradition expresses around predatory lending practices. An unwillingness to address the difference has meant the church is largely silent about the most exploitative forms of lending still prevalent today.

If we narrow our focus on usury to predatory lending practices, it is clear the church's voice on this issue is still very much needed. This is perhaps most obviously the case in the form of payday lending. To cite just one very recent example: prior to 2016, the average interest on payday loans in South Dakota was 652 percent per year. It's not difficult to imagine the impact such an interest rate would have on a South Dakotan family that had to borrow $100 to make rent. Tragically, after a brief period in which these kinds of payday loans were banned in the state, a permanent loophole for payday lenders was created that rendered South Dakota's 2016 ban moot.[14] The payday loans are back, and insomuch as this is just one of many examples of payday lending, we remain in a country in which God's people are forever being "eaten up as bread" as Psalm 14 puts it.

Yet modern-day usury is hardly confined to the payday loan industry. Some of the most disturbing stories from the 2008 financial crash involved the predatory lending practices of major banks such as Wells Fargo and Bank of America and how they targeted low-income communities of color for subprime mortgages.[15] It is now proven that Wells Fargo sent bank employees to Baltimore's Black churches to sell subprime mortgages, and in Memphis, this same bank also intentionally targeted elderly African Americans because they were perceived as less likely to understand the terms of the agreements.[16]

As a result of such tactics and the demographics of poverty in this country, low-income communities of color disproportionately bore the brunt of foreclosures during the financial crash. Richard Rothstein, author of *The Color of Law: A Forgotten History of How Our Government Segmented America*, notes, "Many of the victims were in California, and of Mexican origin. Those in the East and Midwest were mostly African American. Although not specifically detailed in the government's complaint, many lost their homes to foreclosure when they were unable to meet the harsh repayment terms to which they had agreed, mostly unwittingly."[17]

Those foreclosures and the cultural fallout that ensued also revealed Americans' peculiar perspective on who should be held responsible for such debt. In stark contrast to the biblical and early church tradition that places the moral onus on the lender rather than the debtor for having trapped people in "inescapable nets" of poverty, many Americans maintain a pro-business and fiscally puritanical view of these matters and have tended to stigmatize and shame debt-holders in the harshest of terms.[18]

This attitude was starkly embodied on the floor of the Chicago Board of Trade in February 2009. In a videoed rant that ultimately helped inspire the rise of the Tea Party, CNBC reporter Rick Santelli scorned the notion that the US government should help subsidize "the losers' mortgages," remarks that were received with applause from traders all around.[19] Of course, we now know that many of those who Santelli referred to as "losers" were targeted by unscrupulous lenders. In part because of voices like Santelli's, those homeowners never received debt relief, and "despite the biggest housing collapse in post–Great Depression American history, indebted homeowners were left drowning underwater with only minimal assistance from the government."[20]

Basil tells the wealthy who are lending money in Caesarea: "If you take from the poor, you commit the worst crime of inhumanity: you derive profit from miseries, you gain money from tears, you oppress the needy, you starve the hungry. You have no mercy whatsoever, you do not realize the bond you have with those who suffer."[21] Tragically, many parts of Basil's "Homily on Psalm 14" could just as easily be directed today at payday loan industry, credit card, and bank executives in light of their companies' predatory lending tactics. Where is the church on this issue?

Perhaps the most important Christian witness against lenders and debt today comes from the evangelical financial guru David Ramsey, who in October 2020 hosted the third-largest talk radio program in the country. Suffice to say, Ramsey is a provocative figure. On the one hand, he echoes the Old Testament tradition in his insistence that debt is a type of slavery: "Ramsey believes that as long as you have one red cent of debt—credit card debt, student loans, car payments, mortgages, medical bills—you can never be free."[22] Much like Basil (though somewhat less eloquently), he has choice words for lenders: "credit card companies (scum), payday lenders (the scum of the earth), and debt collectors ('some good people', but largely 'complete scum')."[23] Yet unlike the Old Testament and Basil, he ignores the systemic reasons so many Americans are in debt and regularly speaks of personal indebtedness, including medical debt, as a personal failing of the debtor. He therefore teaches that people need to bootstrap themselves out of debt, even to the point of urging people to decline available government assistance.

The fact that Ramsey remains so enduringly popular speaks to a real need that he and parts of the evangelical tradition are addressing far more effectively than mainline churches. While I can barely stomach five minutes of listening to the guy, the fact remains that at least he is offering people *something* in the way of much-needed, practical advice on how to emerge from crushing debt.

For this Episcopalian, a more promising example (at least initially) came from the Church of England. In 2013, the Archbishop of Canterbury, Justin Welby, surprised many when he began speaking out forcefully against the payday loan industry in England. Since he was a former oil industry executive with extensive knowledge of the finance industry, this was an exciting development. That the titular head of the second-largest Christian communion was talking about predatory lending in the twenty-first century would have made Basil of Caesarea proud.

The backlash from the financial industry, however, was swift and forceful and served as a kind of reminder of how powerful the financial interests are in keeping the church out of these matters. The *Financial Times* revealed shortly after Welby's statements that the Church of England was itself invested in England's leading payday lending company, Wonga, a company that charged annual percentage rates of more than 5,000 percent.[24] The flagrant hypocrisy of it all led the archbishop to publicly recommit to divesting the Church of England from the payday lending company and encourage church members to join existing or church-founded credit unions. Even so, I believe it's fair to say the credibility of his voice and that of the church on this issue was somewhat diminished.[25]

In any case, it is very likely that local leadership on this issue matters a great deal more than churchwide statements (though these are important too). What would it look like to preach about the biblical perspective on usury and debt? How might one integrate the prophetic and the pastoral in the pulpit, simultaneously calling out the way that predatory lending traps people in "an inescapable net" while recognizing how much shame American culture piles onto people who are trapped in it? People may be surprised to discover just how much the Old and New Testaments have to say on this issue—

and where scripture places moral responsibility for this form of exploitation. Bible studies on these passages would be opportunities for people to explore both what the tradition has to say about the predatory charging of interest on loans to the poor and to begin to share their own experiences about the reality of debt in their lives.

Finally, I'm struck by the line that Basil wields at the wealthy: "You rich, listen to the advice that we give to the poor in view of your inhumanity: Bear any suffering than the calamity that will come from usury." While this mention of "advice" might have been rhetorical flourish, there is indeed a role for the church to play in being a source of wisdom in view of the inhumanity of predatory lenders. In my neighborhood in Brooklyn, there are municipal signs pasted everywhere on trashcans and bus stops reminding people that student loans are not free money; that they must eventually be paid back. When I buy clothes, I am often surprised (and a bit confused, honestly) when I'm offered a store credit card as a matter of course during checkout. What is the real product being sold at such places? Amidst the proliferation of opportunities for quick credit and intentionally confusing messaging, financial literacy programs—especially about credit and debt—can help people avoid getting entrapped by unscrupulous lenders. There is a desperate need for thoughtful sources of truth, education, and clarity on these issues.

Beyond education, the church can also help establish sound lending alternatives. Like so much else about Jesus's teaching, most of us can only approximate the ideal Jesus sets forth in his Sermon on the Plain to lend without any interest at all. Therefore, we should look to inspiring examples like the credit union created in the Episcopal Diocese of Los Angeles.

In the wake of the Rodney King riots, Dr. Gloria Brown, the Diocese of Los Angeles, and Episcopal Relief & Development established the Episcopal Federal Credit Union to help devastated communities avoid the payday loan and pawn shops that were the only lenders left when major banks abandoned the hardest-hit areas.[26] Nearly 30 years later, this credit union is still going and recently proved to be a bulwark against the economic impacts of COVID-19. Over the past 30 years it has continued to offer low-interest, small loans to struggling families, and at the end of March 2020, as the pandemic devastated Los Angeles, they announced an emergency cash fund for churches whose cash flow had dropped and a 50 percent reduction in their customary interest rate for congregational loans.[27] I see these lending models as abiding in the spirit of what the scripture was saying—providing lending that is liberative rather than entrapping, a way of drawing closer to Jesus's ideal of helping others out by lending without any interest at all. What would it look like for the church to strengthen and/or replicate this model in other parts of the country?

Basil of Caesarea's fourth-century writings and the biblical tradition he invokes speak to how central economic justice issues have historically been to Christianity. The world still needs the church's witness on exploitative and predatory lending practices, and there is real opportunity for the church to make a significant impact on people's daily lives by advocating against predatory lending, establishing lending alternatives, and developing financial literacy programming to help vulnerable families avoid "the inescapable net."

Discussion Questions

Basil of Caesarea rails against a world in which "some have to beg for the most basic necessities to support their lives while others are not satisfied with the capital they have, but excogitate ways of increasing their opulence at the expense of the poor in distress." What does it mean to scheme up ways of increasing one's own wealth at the expense of the poor? Where do you see examples of this today?

Basil draws upon profound scriptural tradition in arguing that the charging of interest on loans to the poor is akin to enslavement. What do you think about this connection between debt, slavery, and forms of predatory lending? Is it fair to say that engaging in predatory lending is similar to being an enslaver of the poor?

How might the church be a source of truth, education, and clarity on debt and predatory lending?

A Next Step

In 2020, St. Bede's Episcopal Church in Santa Fe, New Mexico, did something extraordinary. They used $15,000 they had collected in donations to wipe out the $1.4 million dollars of medical debt of 782 households.[28] This was done in partnership with RIP Medical Debt, a New York based nonprofit that buys debt at a fraction of the amount owed for households with incomes at less than twice the poverty level, and subsequently erases this debt through donations from places like St. Bede's. The rector, Rev. Catherine Volland, notes that St. Bede's was able to make this donation because 10% of every gift made to St. Bede's is set aside for community outreach. "I don't know if this parish has ever funded a program with such a great impact," Volland said. Consider whether this is an effort your community of faith might take up.

Learn more about your state's protections for borrowers, including if there are strong caps in your state on the payday loan debt trap. The Center for Responsible Lending maintains an updated map of the US Payday Interest Rates which can be found here: responsiblelending.org/research-publication/map-us-payday-interest-rates. Partner with organizations who are seeking to strengthen the protections for lenders.

Endnotes

1   "Basil's Homily on Psalm 14," *Wealth and Poverty in Early Christianity*, loc. 419 (Kindle).

2   "Ambrose of Milan's On Tobit," *Wealth and Poverty in Early Christianity*, 108.

3   Rhee, *Wealth and Poverty in Early Christianity*, 67.

4   Rhee, *Wealth and Poverty in Early Christianity,* 67.

5   Ian Harper and Lachlan Smirl, "Usury," *The Oxford Handbook of Christianity and Economics,* ed. Paul Oslington (Oxford: Oxford University Press, 2014), 566. "In contrast to the Old Testament prohibitions against usury, the New Testament is silent on the subject. In particular, nowhere does the New Testament record Jesus teaching against the taking of interest."

6   Meeks, "Economics in Christian Scriptures," *The Oxford Handbook of Christianity and Economics*, 17.

7   Luke 6:20-21.

8   "Basil's Homily on Psalm 14," *Wealth and Poverty in Early Christianity*, ed. Rhee, loc. 419 (Kindle).

9   Psalm 15:5.

10 Samuel Laeuchli, *Power and Sexuality: The Emergence of Canon Law at the Synod of Elvira* (Philadelphia: Temple University Press, 1972).

11 "First Council of Nicæa," New Advent. newadvent.org/fathers/3801.htm.

12 Robert P. Maloney, "Early Conciliar Legislation on Usury: A Contribution to the Study of Christian Moral Thinking," *Recherches De Théologie Ancienne Et Médiévale*, Vol. 39, 1972, 145–157.

13 "The Sin We Stopped Feeling Sorry For," Holy Trinity Greek Orthodox Church, Lansing, Michigan, January 20, 2020. holytrinity-lansing.org/articles-from-father-mark-1/2020/1/20/the-sin-we-stopped-feeling-sorry-for.

14 Daniel Moattar, "Trump to Payday Lenders: Let's Rip America Off Again," *Mother Jones*, February 11, 2020.

15 Richard Rothstein, "A Comment on Bank of America/Countrywide's Discriminatory Mortgage Lending and Its Implications for Racial Segregation," Economic Policy Institute, January 23, 2012.

16 Rothstein, "A Comment on Bank of America/Countrywide's Discriminatory Mortgage Lending."

17 Rothstein, "A Comment on Bank of America/Countrywide's Discriminatory Mortgage Lending."

18   J. Oliver Conroy, "The Man Who Wants to Help You Out of Debt—At Any Cost," *The Guardian*, October 29, 2020.

19 Atif Mian, *House of Debt: How They (and You) Caused the Great Recession, and How We Can Prevent It from Happening Again* (Chicago: University of Chicago Press, 2014), 135.

20 Mian, *House of Debt,* 135.

21 Rhee, *Wealth and Poverty in Early Christianity*, 67.

22 Conroy, "The Man Who Wants to Help You Out of Debt—At Any Cost."

23 Conroy, "The Man Who Wants to Help You Out of Debt—At Any Cost."

24 Sharlene Goff and Brooke Masters, "Church of England Invests in Wonga backer," *Financial Times*, July 25, 2013.

25 Trevor Grundy, "Following Scandal, Archbishop Justin Welby Offers to Open Up Credit Unions," Religion News Service/*Washington Post*, July 26, 2013.

26 Jennifer Miramontes, "Credit Unions for Economic Justice," ECF Vital Practices, March 2020. ecfvp.org/vestry-papers/article/832/credit-unions-for-economic-justice.

27 Miramontes, "Credit Unions for Economic Justice."

28 Scott Wyland, "St. Bede's Church in Santa Fe Helps Pay Off $1.4M in Medical Debt for 782 Households," *Santa Fe New Mexican,* July 17, 2020.

20 John Chrysostom's Critique of Golden Cups

Basil of Caesarea's homily to the wealthy lenders of his city reflects the church's growing role in the public square. Amidst all the questionable aspects associated with the rise of imperial Christianity, there was also this more positive legacy of the church becoming responsible not only for the Christian poor but also for the publicly registered poor, Christian and non-Christian alike.[1] Historians have noted that it was during this period a new interpretation of Matthew 25:31-45 began to appear, one in which Christ was described as coming in all people—not just fellow Christians—who were hungry, thirsty, strangers, naked, and imprisoned.[2] This more universal interpretation of Matthew 25 is especially apparent in the many homilies that John Chrysostom (c.347-407) delivered during his priestly ministry in Antioch and then as patriarch in Constantinople. In Chrysostom's writings, he returns over and over again to "the sweetest passage" of Matthew 25:31-46 as the biblical centerpiece of his theology.

In this passage from the Gospel of Matthew, God's coming judgment of the righteous and condemned is likened to that of a shepherd separating the sheep from the goats, with the deciding factor being whether a person cared for the most vulnerable during their lifetimes. Both the righteous and condemned are surprised to discover God had been appearing to them throughout their lifetimes in the persons of the hungry, the thirsty, the stranger, and prisoners. God deems as righteous those who fed the hungry, gave a cup of water to the thirsty, welcomed the stranger, and visited the prisoners; the condemned are those who turned the poor away and refused to offer any relief. Among the many reasons why this passage is so extraordinary is that God's identification with the most vulnerable is complete. Jesus tells his disciples, "Truly I tell you, just as you did it to one of the least of these who are members of my family, you did it to me."[3]

Like those preachers who return to one passage and one sermon over and over again, Chrysostom frequently ended up preaching on Matthew 25:31-46 even when he started somewhere else. Indeed, theologian Rudolf Brändle has argued that this biblical passage serves as the overall integrative force of Chrysostom's entire theology.[4]

Chrysostom's "Homily 50" on the Gospel of Matthew, for instance, starts out as a reflection on Matthew 14:13-36, the story of Jesus walking on water and the healing of the sick in Gennesaret, but then culminates in a meditation on what it means to worship Christ's body in both the eucharist and in the bodies of "the least of these." In this homily, Chrysostom argues Christ's body is to be found in the eucharist as well as in those who are hungry, strangers, and locked away in prisons. He points out that "a great gulf" is created when Christian communities spend lavishly in devotion to Christ's body in the eucharist yet fail to see or care about this same body in the lives of the most vulnerable: "For what is the profit, when His table indeed is full of golden cups, but He perishes with hunger?"

Chrysostom is particularly focused on abuses of church wealth and liturgical splendor. On wealth stewardship, Chrysostom argues Christian communities need to prioritize the least of these in society over the building up of individual and institutional wealth. He argues that while scripture does not explicitly condemn gifts for church buildings or the beautification of worship, the "sweetest passage" of Matthew 25:31-46 clearly condemns those who refuse to make gifts to the poor during their lifetimes. He concludes that while giving toward the church as an institution might be allowable and even important, encouraging compassion for the "least of these" must take precedent as these are the gifts that determine people's eternal salvation.

As is the case with almost every figure represented in this book, I want to add that Chrysostom has a fraught legacy. Even as I highlight his example and writings around economic justice, Chrysostom is also well-known and deservedly critiqued as virulently anti-Jewish. In a series of eight sermons called "Against the Judaizers," Chrysostom critiques members of the Christian church in Antioch who were observing Jewish festivals and observances.[5] His sermons speak to the remarkable fact that "Judaizing Christians had existed from the beginning of Christianity, and despite four centuries of opposition from Christian leaders, they continued to be a visible presence in the church."[6]

As troubling as these homilies are in and of themselves, equally disturbing is how they were later used. Chrysostom's writings became touchstones for Christians' eventual blaming the Jewish people for Jesus's crucifixion and were employed by the Nazi Party in the twentieth century to justify the Holocaust among Christians in Germany and Austria. This aspect of Chrysostom's legacy has to be borne in mind even as we explore his forceful writings on charity and economic justice.

In Chrysostom, right alongside this disturbing legacy, we also find a preacher willing to speak out forcefully against Christianity's increasing comfort with wealth stewardship, luxury liturgy, and neglect if not disdain of the most vulnerable. His writings on issues of economic justice remain highly relevant today. His tendency to criticize the wealthy and bluntly point out the hypocrisies of the church ultimately resulted in his condemnation, exile, and death. It was only after he died in exile on his way to Pontus in 407 that the church began to recover an appreciation for the significance of his preaching and recognize his witness.

Born in the middle of the fourth century, Chrysostom lost his father, a high-ranking military officer, when he was just a child. Raised as a Christian by his widowed mother, he began his career by studying law with the rhetorician Libanius but ultimately left this profession to become a hermit-monk. Chrysostom returned to Antioch, however, when it became clear that his health could not sustain the rigors of this form of asceticism. He was ordained a deacon in 381 and a priest in 386 in Antioch, where he appeared to have flourished in this role.[7] Over the following twelve years, he would become known for his zealous preaching on materialism, wealth and poverty, and on matters that touched the lives of the common people of the city. This style of preaching earned him the Greek surname Chrysostom, meaning "golden-mouthed."[8] [9]

Chrysostom likely delivered "Homily 50" during the latter part of his priesthood in Antioch, and it reflects some of his culminating thoughts about a city that was both highly prosperous and as prominent a Christian stronghold as Rome, Constantinople, and Alexandria.[10] [11] Indeed, by the middle of the fourth century in Antioch, a majority of citizens were Christian, and they were well-represented on the city's council.[12] However, the presence of these Christians in key seats of power had done little to prevent extreme disparities in wealth and poverty. Rudolf Brändle notes:

> The prosperous citizens had great palaces with marble pillars and halls, decorated with statues and frescoes. Some of the walls were covered with gold, and gold could even be found on the roofs. The splendor of the houses was matched by the luxury of the furnishings. The Antiochan upper class also showed their wealth in clothing and jewelry.[13]

Chrysostom appears to have been especially rankled by ostentatious displays of luxury and how this contrasted with the lives of the poor in the city. He likely alienated more than a few wealthy Christians when he pointed out in a baptismal class that "Countless poor people have to go hungry so that you can wear a single ruby."[14]

By the latter part of the fourth century, the wealth, splendor, and luxury of Antioch's great palaces extended to the city's Christian churches. One of the finest examples of both architectural beauty and ecclesiastical splendor was the octagonal Great Church, also known as the Golden House on account of its gilded wooden dome.[15] This was likely the site where Chrysostom preached "Homily 50," which means that when he said, "For what is the profit, when His table indeed is full of golden cups, but He perishes with hunger?" and urged congregants to prioritize care for the poor over liturgical and architectural splendor, he was pointedly doing so in a highly decorated space of polished marble, brass, gold, and precious stones.[16]

Chrysostom is frequently described as eloquent, outspoken, and tactless, and these characteristics are on full display in "Homily 50."[17] With Matthew 14:13-36 as the starting point for "Homily 50," Chrysostom first dwells on the fear the disciples must have felt as they were tossed and turned in the boat on the waters. He then transitions to describing the sick in Gennesaret who came in droves to meet Jesus so that "they might touch even the fringe of his cloak; and all who touched it were healed."[18] Chrysostom sees an example of what it means to truly worship Christ's body in this story of the sick rushing to touch Jesus's cloak, and this serves as an opening for a powerful reflection on the meaning of the eucharist. In London publisher W. Smith's 1885 translation of this homily, Chrysostom states, "Let us also then touch the hem of His garment, or rather, if we be willing, we have Him entire. For indeed His Body is set before us now, not His garment only, but even His Body; not for us to touch It only, but also to eat, and be filled."[19]

Then, standing under the golden dome of Antioch's Great Church, Chrysostom urges congregants to reconnect worship of the eucharist to serving "the least of these":

> Wouldest thou do honour to Christ's body? Neglect Him not when naked; do not, while here thou honourest Him with silken garments, neglect Him perishing without of cold and nakedness. For He that said, This is my Body, and by His word confirmed the fact, This Same said, Ye saw me an hungered, and fed Me not; and, inasmuch as ye did it not to one of the least of these ye did it not to Me.[20]

Chrysostom goes on to explore the meaning of the eucharist in light of God's coming judgment of the nations as described in Matthew 25:31-46.[21] To worship the body of Christ in the eucharist means that we must also worship the body of Christ in the most vulnerable:

> For what is the profit, when His table indeed is full of golden cups, but He perishes with hunger? First fill Him, being an hungerd, and then abundantly deck out His table also. Dost thou make Him a cup of gold, while thou givest Him not a cup of cold water? And what is the profit? Dost thou furnish His Table with cloths bespangled with gold, while to Himself thou affordest not even the necessary covering? And what good comes of it?[22]

At the heart of Chrysostom's homily is a criticism of hypocrisy—or the "great gulf" as he calls it —created by the Antiochian Christians' eucharistic devotion through investments in liturgical and architectural splendor while neglecting to care for the poor. Chrysostom warns:

> Let this then be thy thought with regard to Christ also, when He is going about a wanderer, and a stranger, needing a roof to cover Him; and thou, neglecting to receive Him, deckest out a pavement, and walls, and capitals of columns, and hangest up silver chains by means of lamps, but Himself bound in chains in prison thou wilt not even look upon.[23]

Chrysostom's views on the eucharist lead him to a subtler view of institutional stewardship that I believe can still be helpful for the church today. Chrysostom doesn't ultimately condemn investing resources in church buildings and institutions but rather asks the congregants of the Great Church to prioritize helping the most vulnerable. In this, he manages to find a "middle way" that can serve as a possible pathway forward on what it means to "steward" resources.

Chrysostom asks his hearers to reconsider their priorities by imagining Jesus's reaction to the splendor of their churches and institutions: "For tell me, should you see one at a loss for necessary food, and omit appeasing his hunger while you first overlaid his table with silver; would he indeed thank thee, and not rather be indignant?" He goes on to describe Jesus as accounting such hypocrisy "an insult, and that the most extreme."[24] Similar to Niebuhr's critique of the so-called "good stewardship" of the Christian businessman who gives to his church regularly even as he exploits his factory workers (see Chapter 3), Chrysostom warns, "Let us flee then from this gulf; neither let us account it enough for our salvation, if after we have stripped widows and orphans, we offer for this Table a gold and jeweled cup."[25] In the Episcopal Church, I want to note that this critique sounds similar to Anglo-Catholic leaders who worry that this tradition has strayed from its social justice roots as an inner-city ministry to an excessive focus on "golden cups.

In addition to arguing that the sources of a church's wealth matter—whether the gold and jeweled cups on the altar are the result of exploiting widows and orphans, for instance—Chrysostom's homily suggests that part of the role of institutional leaders is to reconnect "the golden cups" with cups of water for the thirsty, the "bespangled cloth" with cloaks for people weathering the cold, and the "silver chains of lamps" with the welfare of prisoners held in chains. Jesus is indignant, he argues, when Christians overlay his table with golden cups in so-called worship of Christ's body even as they neglect his body which comes to us in "the least of these."

In this, Chrysostom is insisting the Antiochian community reflect on which investments are ultimately lasting. While capital investments are often considered long-term, "the sweetest passage" of Matthew 25:31-46 states that compassion for "the least of these" is what is truly lasting insomuch as this is what determines our eternal lives. Chrysostom also holds that while giving gifts to the building up of the church is not explicitly prohibited by scripture, what is clearly condemned is the refusal to help "the least of these." Stated positively, gifts to the institution and toward liturgical splendor are nice and all, but the worship of Christ's body is most deeply expressed through a community's love and service to the most vulnerable.

Chrysostom offers almsgiving and service as a means of bridging this embarrassing gulf, a way that a Christian community lavishly devoted to the eucharist could first and foremost lavishly worship the body of Christ who appears to us in the poor. "And these things I say, not forbidding such offerings to be provided; but requiring you, together with them, and before them, to give alms. For He accepts indeed the former, but much more the latter."[26] In light of more recent, on-point critiques of charity that serves the poor but fails to address the systems that cause the poverty, I would want to add advocacy for economic justice as a means for Christian institutions fulfilling "the sweetest passage's" emphasis on "the least of these."

This seems as good a time as any to briefly address one of the more misguided concerns I've encountered during my wanderings around the church: namely, that the church has become confused about its role in society, becoming overly involved in public advocacy and running the risk of being a social services provider. I recall one crusty Episcopalian lamenting, "We're called to worship Christ, not be social workers!" This is a surprisingly prevalent (and profoundly dull) position that is widely held in the church, a view that ignores the ancient tradition of the church as a voice of justice and charity in the public square. Indeed, in Antioch—that is, in the very city where followers of Jesus were first called Christians—the Great Church eventually came to represent how the church can be a place that brings together both worship and what might be described as social services. [27]

In part as a result of Chrysostom's preaching and leadership, the Great Church became known as a site of both liturgical beauty and service to the poor. Rhee notes that Chrysostom led multiple churches in Antioch, including the Great Church, to "organize major relief efforts for widows, orphans, virgins, beggars, homeless immigrants, the sick, and the poor through church-administered orphanages, hostels, and hospitals."[28] Even as he critiques the congregants' focus on church splendor, Chrysostom's homilies also feature descriptions of the Great Church's extensive ministries including a hostel for immigrants, a hospital for the incurably sick, and four dining halls where widows had regular meals.[29] The organizational support behind these services was rigorous. There was a register of widows and "the priest or deacon charged with these lists was responsible for ensuring that no unworthy widows, or others who could live from their own means, tainted the table of the poor."[30]

Beyond Antioch, there is extensive evidence of Christian churches serving as a social safety net for the poor in the fourth and fifth centuries. A particularly moving example (to me, anyway) comes from fifth-century papyrological memos between Egyptian churches. The content of the memos open a window into the day-to-day, administrative logistics of this safety net for the poor. In one of the memos, an unidentified Christian requests a coat for a widow named Sophia from the steward of Saints Cosmos and Damian church. "[The steward] is assumed to have a store of coats ready for just such a request. This is not surprising; churches are known to have stockpiled clothes for charity."[31] The writer of an essay on these findings, Adam Serfass, goes on to describe how civil officials inventoried the possessions of one North African church in the early fourth century and found 82 women's tunics and 47 pairs of women's shoes. "These items were surely meant for distribution to widows supported by the church."[32]

Such memos and findings are powerful reminders of how closely aligned service has always been to Christian identity and worship. Here, one finds ancient precedent for winter coat drives with all the administrative memos and storage issues that come right alongside it. Alongside the theological treatises and powerful homilies that remain from this period, these memos requesting specific aid, inventories of shoes and winter cloaks, and descriptions of a registrar of widows, speak to another aspect of ancient Christianity that is oftentimes forgotten. Unlike Clement's disdain for the "unworthy poor," and some current church leaders' distaste for churches becoming overly engaged in what they snub as social work, such evidence reveals the way a practical focus on "the least of these" (with memos and inventories and all) has always been at the heart of this faith.

Chrysostom's story has a disturbing end, an undoing deeply connected with his characteristic bluntness, his focus on "the least of these," and the now intertwined hands of church and empire.

In 398, Chrysostom was unexpectedly called from Antioch to Constantinople to be ordained patriarch. As was the case in Antioch, Chrysostom began forcefully preaching against abuses of wealth and power, although in Constantinople he now did so in the shadow of the Roman Emperor Arcadius's court and clergy. Helen Rhee notes that "the combination of his brutal honesty, asceticism, tactlessness, and uncompromising intensity for reform, joined with the enmity of the Patriarch of Alexandria and empress Eudoxia, brought about his downfall."[33]

As he had done in Antioch and at the Great Church, Chrysostom insisted the church change its priorities and focus its energies on the poor. Chrysostom modeled this by cutting the budget of the bishop's household and by using those funds to support existing hostels and hospitals. He soon began making plans to build several more hospitals in Constantinople.[34] As he was making these plans, he ran headlong into a version of fourth-century form of NIMBY-ism (Not In My Backyard): forceful opposition from wealthy estate holders to his proposal for building a leper colony just outside the city. The landed proprietors whose villas adjoined the proposed colony objected to the idea of having lepers so close.[35]

What happened next is a little unclear. Chrysostom was suddenly deposed in 403, just five years after he had arrived in Constantinople. He was then recalled, only to be deposed again, and was subsequently exiled to Armenia. Tellingly, upon his exile, construction work on the leper colony ceased.[36] [37] When it became clear to all that Chrysostom was still able to argue his cause through correspondence, he was sent even further away, to Pontus at the eastern end of the Black Sea. He died during the journey in 407, essentially starved to death.[38] While I've never seen him described as such, to my mind this makes him one of the earliest martyrs of the church to have died at the intertwined hands of church and empire, a particularly shameful milestone in the story of the Christianity's relationship to wealth and power.

As is so often the case, it was only after his death that Chrysostom's reputation began to be restored. Thirty-one years after being exiled to Pontus and dying of starvation along the way, Chrysostom's relics were brought back to Constantinople and ceremoniously received by Emperor Theodosius II, the son of Emperor Arcadius and Empress Eudoxia.[39] This is quite literally a case of the church celebrating in death someone it martyred in life.

Discussion Questions

John Chrysostom's writings and complicated legacy still leave faith leaders with challenging questions about the purposes of institutional wealth today. How does one go about reconnecting the "golden cups" with "cups of water," the bespangled altar cloths and ornate vestments with coats for the poor, the chains holding up silver lamps with the chains of prisoners, the altar table with tables of food for the hungry? My critique is not only for the Anglo-Catholic tradition but all branches of the church whose major investments in buildings and liturgy have become disconnected from the needs of "the least of these. With characteristic bluntness, Chrysostom describes how lavish devotion to Christ in the eucharist has become largely disconnected from honoring Christ's body in the least of these, and Chrysostom's preaching urges us still to go about the work of reconnecting the two and prioritizing the latter. How might your community of faith go about this work?

While Chrysostom doesn't outright condemn investments in church property and liturgical objects, he insists on fierce clarity around what actually matters to God and which investments determine eternal salvation. Chrysostom argues that while gifts for building up our institutions may not be explicitly condemned by the gospels, scripture is clear that eternal salvation has to do with whether we—through our individual lives and institutions—are engaged in compassionate care for the least of these. Chrysostom describes a Jesus who would be incensed by "the great gulf" in so-called devotion to Christ's body through liturgical splendor, for it is in acts of charity, service, and justice building that we actually honor the one who comes to us in "the least of these." What do you think about this prioritization in how gifts are used to worship Christ's body?

A Next Step

Budgets are moral documents, and congregational budgets help reveal the values and commitments of communities of faith. Take a moment to look at the largest expense categories listed in your congregation's budgets. If your congregation is like most, you may be surprised to find that the largest expenses are clergy salary and buildings with a significantly smaller portion going toward programs such as outreach.

As revealing as this may be, a first glance at these expense categories only tells a part of the story. Having looked at those lines, reflect on the amount of clergy time that is devoted to serving as a "guardian to all in need" and serving and advocating for the most economically vulnerable members of one's community. If your congregation is comprised of mostly poor and members of economically marginalized communities, that may literally be 100 percent of a clergy person's time! Yet, this is frequently not categorized as "outreach" (and rightly so).

Along the same lines, think about the extent to which your congregation's building and other properties are used as a resource for pastoral care among the poor, acts of charitable service, and advocacy for economic justice. Buildings can be critical resources in serving one's community if they are understood and employed as such.

Endnotes

1 Rhee, *Loving the Poor, Saving the Rich,* loc. 4240-4257 (Kindle).

2 Rhee, *Loving the Poor, Saving the Rich,* loc. 4240-4257 (Kindle).

3 Matthew 25:40.

4 Rudolf Brändle, "The Sweetest Passage," *Wealth and Poverty in Early Church and Society,* ed. Susan R. Homan (Ada, Michigan: Baker Academic, 2008).

5 Arthur J. Droge. *The Journal of Religion,* Vol. 67, No. 4 (Chicago: University of Chicago Press, 1987): 541–542.

6 Droge, *The Journal of Religion,* 541-542.

7 Attwater and John, "John Chrysostom," in *The Penguin Dictionary of Saints,* 194.

8 Rhee, *Wealth and Poverty in Early Christianity,* Introduction.

9 Attwater and John, "John Chrysostom," in *The Penguin Dictionary of Saints,* 194.

10 *Homilies of S. John Chrysostom, Archbishop of Constantinople, on the Gospel of St. Matthew,* translated, with notes and indices (London: W. Smith,1885), hdl.handle.net/2027/mdp.39076002354541.

11 Rhee, *Wealth and Poverty in Early Christianity.*

12 J. N. D. Kelly, *Golden Mouth: The Story of John Chrysostom—Ascetic, Preacher, Bishop* (Ithaca, New York: Cornell University, 1998).

13 Brändle, "The Sweetest Passage," *Wealth and Poverty in Early Church and Society.*

14 Brändle.,"The Sweetest Passage." *Wealth and Poverty in Early Church and Society.*

15 Kelly, *Golden Mouth.*

16 Brändle, "The Sweetest Passage," *Wealth and Poverty in Early Church and Society.*

17 Attwater and John, "John Chrysostom," *The Penguin Dictionary of Saints,* 194.

18 Matthew 14:36.

19 Homily 50, Part 3. *Homilies of S. John Chrysostom.*

20 Homily 50, Part 4. *Homilies of S. John Chrysostom.*

21 Chris De Wet, "John Chrysostom," *Brill Encyclopedia of Early Christianity Online.*

22 Homily 50, Part 4. *Homilies of S. John Chrysostom.*

23 Homily 50, Part 4. *Homilies of S. John Chrysostom.*

24 Homily 50, Part 4. *Homilies of S. John Chrysostom.*

25 Homily 50, Part 4. *Homilies of S. John Chrysostom.*

26 Homily 50, Part 4. *Homilies of S. John Chrysostom,* (Italics mine).

27 Acts 11:20-21.

28 *Wealth and Poverty in Early Christianity,* loc. 454 (Kindle).

29 Brändle, "The Sweetest Passage," *Wealth and Poverty in Early Church and Society,* 130.

30 Brändle, "The Sweetest Passage," *Wealth and Poverty in Early Church and Society,* 130.

31 Adam Serfass, "Wine for Widows," in *Early Church and Society,* ed. Susan Holman (Ada, Michigan: Baker Academic, 2008), 95.

32 Serfass, "Wine for Widows," 95.

33 Rhee, *Wealth and Poverty in Early Christianity*, loc. 455 (Kindle).

34 Rhee, *Wealth and Poverty in Early Christianity,* loc. 455 (Kindle).

35 Brändle, "The Sweetest Passage,"*Wealth and Poverty in Early Church and Society,* 132.

36 Rhee, *Wealth and Poverty in Early Christianity*.

37 Brändle, "The Sweetest Passage,"*Wealth and Poverty in Early Church and Society,* 132.

38 Attwater and John, "John Chrysostom," *The Penguin Dictionary of Saints,* 194.

39 Attwater and John, "John Chrysostom," *The Penguin Dictionary of Saints,* 194.

21 Gregory of Nyssa's Witness Against Slavery

In Lent of 379, the bishop Gregory of Nyssa delivered what is believed to be the only known example of a church father preaching a full-throated denunciation of the Roman institution of slavery. Gregory of Nyssa's homily stands out because, "no other ancient text still known to us—Christian, Jewish, or Pagan—contains so fierce, unequivocal, and indignant a condemnation of the institution of slavery."[1]

According to John McGuckin, whose writings on Christianity and slavery and translation of Gregory of Nyssa's homily were foundational to this chapter, Christian discussions of slavery were rare because the practice was so ubiquitous, and Christians were generally accommodating of this economic institution. McGuckin notes,

> Even if early Christianity could have imagined the abolition of slavery on the basis of its new philosophy of inestimable individual worth, it could not explain how it could bring this mysterious reality about. For such reasons it rarely did imagine such a thing and took centuries before it could advocate it as a "good idea"; and meanwhile, even in its foundational scriptural sources (the New Testament Pastoral Letters), it generally commended patience and long-suffering to the enslaved, and lauded their obedience as a virtue that aided in stabilizing society.[2]

Christian acceptance of slavery had ancient Greco-Roman roots. Aristotle theorized that whereas some were born free by nature, others were born degenerate and were natural slaves.

He said, "Knowing the ends of humanity, [God] knows as well who is capable of them and who, deficient in nature, must serve as 'a living tool.'"[1] Augustine of Hippo argued similarly that God had created some people to be enslaved on account of their particularly sinful nature, and held slavery as beneficial punishment for broad swaths of people: "God decreed their condition as a punishment, and God's judgment cannot but be right. Slavery is no evil, but justice, and must certainly not be abolished."[2] Even Basil of Caesarea, Gregory of Nyssa's older brother, could never bring himself to voice the same level of a critique of slavery as his younger, less tactful brother. Basil stated that some are slaves because of a war, others because of poverty, and others thanks to "an ineffable economy/administration" that clearly came from God, "for the worse were commanded to serve the better, which is not even a condemnation but a beneficence."[3] Against this backdrop, Gregory's insistence that slavery was an unnatural and evil institution stands out.

Gregory of Nyssa preached his Fourth Homily on Ecclesiastes during the season of Lent so as to prepare his congregation for Easter, a time in which wealthy Christians traditionally emancipated a few of their slaves. In this homily, Gregory encourages members of the congregation to continue this custom, one that had been around since the Emperor Constantine had made the manumission of slaves by Christians legal in 312.[4] But then Gregory presses the point further, and his homily transforms into an argument for valuing human beings solely on the infinite value they have in the eyes of God.[5] He makes the theological case:

> The image of God, that is, any human, a rational creature endowed with *logos* (and the Logos of Christ), can be bought at no price. God made each human the owner of the whole cosmos; no amount of money could buy a person. Every human is free, *qua* the image of God who is free and powerful *par excellence*.[6]

Gregory argues that as each person is created in the image of God, they are therefore both equal to one another and are born for freedom. Even God, he preaches, chose to not enslave creation insomuch as God allows people to continuously make all kinds of choices for themselves—some healthful, others not so much. Therefore, Gregory contends that for the average, sinful, wealthy Christian to take up the role of master over another human being is not only an act of arrogance but an unnatural act of evil.

One can imagine the uncomfortable shifting in the assembly as the gathered slave masters realized that Gregory was moving well beyond the typical recommendation to free a few of their slaves but was arguing for something more fundamental. For many Christians, a world without slavery was unimaginable.

Gregory of Nyssa was born at Caesarea in Cappadocia c.335 to a distinguished Christian family that included his older brother Basil and sister Macrina. Tutored by Gregory of Nazianzus, he is often described as the most mystical and philosophical of the three Cappadocian fathers (the collective name given to Basil of Caesarea, Gregory of Nazianzus, and Gregory of Nyssa). He began his life as a teacher of rhetoric and was possibly married but was prevailed upon by his former teacher Gregory of Nazianzus to enter a life of service to the church, which he did in 360.[7]

Gregory's older brother Basil appointed him bishop of the small city of Nyssa in 372 to retain control of that area amidst an ecclesiastical, jurisdictional skirmish. Basil made this appointment despite believing Gregory was frequently too impolitic for his own good. Gregory remained there until his death in 395 and became well-known for his theological writings, specifically "defending Nicene orthodoxy and articulating what would become the classic Trinitarian doctrine with the divinity of the Holy Spirit, which was ratified at the second ecumenical council, the Council of Constantinople, in 381."[8] The person who comes across in his writings has a rare combination of qualities: an empathetic personality, a probing philosophical mind, and an eloquent writing style, as well as a boldness that borders on tactlessness. The combination of these traits led him to echo prior theologians' statements on the equality of all people as made in the image of God and follow them to their logical conclusion in the face of the ubiquitous brutality of Roman slavery.

An estimated 50 percent of the ancient Roman population was enslaved, and the Roman Empire's desire for slaves grew with each expansion of territory.[9] McGuckin notes, "Roman imperial society was such a vast war machine that there never was a chance of slave stock being exhausted. Slaves in the Roman system bred slaves. If ever numbers threatened to drop, there were more than enough wars to supply new populations." Indeed, "The Roman Empire, and the extensive civilizations that grew in and out of it, could not have existed on any other economic basis."[10]

Roman slavery has often been presented as a more amiable institution than the system of chattel slavery of the American South. Scholars have pointed to the possibility of manumission, the literary depictions of relatively well-off slaves in urban centers, and instances in which the enslaved purchased their freedom or had it purchased by their masters, as evidence of this. Thankfully, classics scholars like the Dominican-born Dan-el Padilla Peralta, who is a descendant of enslaved peoples, are helping to see the evidence of the brutality of Roman slavery with new eyes. A *New York Times* article explores Padilla's work in the historically white field of classics:

> Enslaved people in ancient Rome could be tortured and crucified; forced into marriage; chained together in work gangs; made to fight gladiators or wild animals; and displayed naked in marketplaces with signs around their necks advertising their age, character, and health to prospective buyers. Owners could tattoo their foreheads so they could be recognized and captured if they tried to flee. Temple excavations have uncovered clay dedications from escapees, praying for the gods to remove the disfiguring marks from their faces. Archaeologists have also found metal collars riveted around the necks of skeletons in burials of enslaved people, among them an iron ring with a bronze tag preserved in the Museo Nazionale in Rome that reads: "I have run away; hold me. When you have brought me back to my master Zoninus, you will receive a gold coin."

While literary descriptions have often depicted the lives of urban domestic slaves, the vast majority of the enslaved population worked on plantations and farm factories under incredibly brutal conditions. Indeed, the other rare instances of Christian critique and resistance to slavery tended to come from more rural regions where bishops lived in greater proximity to plantations and farm factories. Those bishops were more keenly aware of the brutal living and working conditions of the enslaved.[11]

If the sheer pervasiveness of slavery prevented Christians from critiquing this as an institution, a second powerful reason was the horrific punishment that would have been enacted upon anyone who did so. To have critiqued this fundamental aspect of the Roman economy would have been perceived as fomenting anarchy, with the full force of Roman punishment subsequently following. This is partly why Paul and many others after him took a softer approach of instead advising slave masters to practice kindness toward the enslaved and refrain from sexually exploiting them. In his letter to Philemon, Paul writes of sending the runaway slave Onesimus back to his slave master and even alludes to the possibility that Philemon may let him keep Onesimus for himself. Paul's acceptance of slavery, in addition to the household codes scattered across several of Paul's other letters with lines such as "slaves obey your masters" (Ephesians 6:5 and Colossians 3:22), served to justify Christian acceptance and endorsement of slavery across millennia.

This accommodationist stance grew as Christians went from being comprised of slaves and poor people who were former slaves and instead became the religion of propertied slave owners, including quite a number of slave-owning priests and bishops. One example of Christianity's evolving approach can be seen in the canons from the Council of Elvira (c.306), already mentioned in a prior chapter for its rigorous position on usury. Canon 5 discusses the case of a Christian slave owner who had whipped her enslaved maidservant to death:

> If a woman in a fit of rage whips her maidservant so severely that she dies a horrible death within three days, and it is not certain whether she killed her on purpose or by accident: provided that the required penance has been done, she shall be readmitted to communion after seven years if it was done on purpose, and after five years if by accident; if she becomes ill during the prescribed time, let her receive communion.[12]

Although this might have represented more of a punishment than what would have been the norm for Roman society, this canon still reflects the horrific reality of a Christian slave owner beating her maidservant to death. It's notable that the discussion is not about whether Christians should own slaves but what the appropriate terms are for punishing a community member who had beaten their slave to death whether by accident or on purpose.

The danger and threat of violence upon the enslaved—whether by their Christian slave masters or by the state—was ubiquitous and overwhelming. Although sporadically enforced, Roman imperial authorities made it known that any slave found to be fomenting rebellion would be executed by crucifixion, and in those instances in which a slave rebellion resulted in the death of a slave master, the entire household of slaves were to be executed in this same fashion for having been complicit in the crime.[13] This gruesome fact leads to an insight about the liberative nature of Jesus's life and death, for it's striking that his execution at the hands of Roman imperial authorities was the very same one as a slave—a *doulos*—who had fomented rebellion against his master. Perhaps it was in recognition of Jesus's becoming a slave (Philippians 2:7) that Christian slave owners traditionally freed some of their enslaved at Easter, a practice that speaks to the profound connections between resurrection and emancipation from slavery.

The ubiquity and overwhelming cruelty of an economy based on slavery must have been weighing on his mind, then, as Gregory of Nyssa prepared to preach his fourth homily on Ecclesiastes during that Lent of 379. With owners of slaves gathered in the assembly, Gregory took as his starting point the second chapter of Ecclesiastes in which an arrogant man lists the many vanities he had indulged in over the course of his life. After exploring pleasure, laughter, and wine, the rich man proceeded to creating great works for himself, including houses and vineyards. These included "gardens and parks" and "all kinds of fruit trees" and "pools from which to water the forest of growing trees" (Eccesiastes 2:5-6). Continuing in these vanities, the man also purchased slaves:

> I bought male and female slaves, and had slaves who were born in my house; I also had great possessions of herds and flocks, more than any who had been before me in Jerusalem. I also gathered for myself silver and gold and the treasure of kings and of the provinces; I got singers, both men and women, and delights of the flesh, many concubines. (Ecclesiastes 2:7-8)

For Gregory, the fact that Ecclesiastes included purchasing slaves among the man's many vanities serves as his opening for critiquing Roman society's conceits but especially the unnatural act of the wealthy being able to purchase other human beings. "Can you see here that pride originates false pretensions?" Gregory states. "This kind of person abrogates to himself what belongs to God and attributes to himself power over the human race as if he were its lord. What arrogant claim, transgressing human nature, makes this person look upon himself as different from those he rules over?"[14]

For Gregory, the act of purchasing and ruling over another human being was an act of placing one's self in the position of Lord over God's creation. There were two basic beliefs underlying this statement. First, Gregory understood all humans as having been made in the image of God and therefore created for freedom. The second, which flowed from the first, is that insomuch all of us have been made in the image of God, humans are fundamentally equal to one another and this essential equality makes it immoral and "transgressing human nature" for the wealthy to purchase, own, and then rule over others.

These two beliefs, which are repeated over and over again in this homily, come together again in a remarkable passage in which Gregory points out that even God refrains from curbing the freedom of God's creation:

> What price would you set on that nature that God himself has crafted? It was God who said, "Let us make man according to our image and likeness" (Genesis 1:25), and since we are created according to the divine likeness and are appointed to rule over the whole earth, then tell me: who is that person who can buy and sell others? Only God can do this. But such a thing is not appropriate even for him, for "the gifts of God are irrevocable" (Romans 11:29). You see, God called human nature into freedom though it had become addicted to sin, so he would never subject it to slavery again. God's dominion is incontestable, and he refuses to subject freedom to slavery.[15]

As Bentley Hart points out in "The 'Whole Humanity': Gregory of Nyssa's Critique of Slavery in Light of His Eschatology," Gregory's homily is unique because it "leaves no quarter for pious slave owners to console themselves that they, at any rate, are merciful masters, not tyrants, but stewards of souls, generous enough to liberate the occasional worthy servant but responsible enough to govern others justly."[16] Rather, Gregory preaches:

> You are condemning to slavery humankind, who is both free and self-determinative. You are contradicting God by perverting the natural law in this way. Like a sinner and a rebel against the divine commandment, you have put man himself under the yoke of servitude, when he was created as lord over the earth.[17]

Gregory goes on to meditate on the essential equality of all people:

> Do not all these things belong to both slave and master? Do they not both breathe the same air and look upon the same sun? Does not food serve to nourish them both? Do not they have the same insides? Do not they both become dust when they die? Is there not one standard for all? Is there not a common rule and a common hell? So, how can you who are equal in all things claim such a superiority that though being a man, you consider yourselves a man's ruler and say: "I have servants and maidens as if they were goats or cattle?"[18]

This belief in people's equality and dignity as made in the image of God proved essential to both Gregory's views on both enslaved peoples as well as the poor. Elsewhere, in the first of two homilies entitled "On the Poor," Gregory critiques the pious fasting of the wealthy whose rampant avarice he saw as the source of poverty itself. "With self-control, avoid two contrary evils: your own gluttony and the hunger of your brother and sisters."[19] He again insists that the poor—like the enslaved—are not only equal to the wealthy as made in the image of God, but are, in fact, favored by a God who said he came to humanity in the "least of these:" "Do not despise these people in their abjection; do not think they merit no respect. Reflect on who they are and you will understand their dignity; they have taken upon them the person of our Savior."[20]

Tragically, Gregory's homily on slavery proves to be the exception rather than the rule. On the whole, Christianity maintained a qualified acceptance, if not outright condonement, of slavery during the first five centuries. This single homily pales in comparison to the later voices of Ambrose of Milan (339-397) and even more so Augustine of Hippo (354-430), who viewed slavery as a regretful outcome of humanity's fallen nature but who also actively quashed Christian efforts to liberate slaves. Even so, I believe it is important to study Gregory's witness because it helps open up a discussion about contemporary Christians' relative silence on the issue of modern slavery in the world today.

Slavery is alive and well both in the United States and around the globe. Indeed, largely as a result of population growth, it is believed more people are enslaved today than at any other point in human history.[21] This stunning fact alone merits much more attention and discussion than it receives in most churches today.

The International Labour Organization's 2017 report, "Global Estimates of Modern Slavery: Forced Labour and Forced Marriage," offered a conservative estimate of 40.3 million people around the globe living in modern slavery—that is "being forced to work against their will under threat or who were living in a forced marriage that they had not agreed to."[22] Of the 40.3 million people enslaved in 2016, the majority—an estimated 24.9 million—were in some form of forced labor. This means:

> They were being forced to work under threat or coercion as domestic workers, on construction sites, in clandestine factories, on farms and fishing boats, in other sectors, and in the sex industry. They were forced to work by private individuals and groups or by state authorities. In many cases, the products they made and the services they provided ended up in seemingly legitimate commercial channels. Forced labourers produced some of the food we eat and the clothes we wear, and they have cleaned the buildings in which many of us live or work.[23]

The Polaris Project, a nonprofit organization addressing human trafficking in the United States, estimates that the majority of enslaved people working in the United States are domestic workers. Their 2019 report, "Human Trafficking at Home: Labor Trafficking of Domestic Workers," noted that of the 8,000 cases reported between 2007-2017 to their National Human Trafficking Hotline, "the highest number of cases—almost 23 percent—involved domestic work. In human trafficking prosecutions, the highest number of criminal and civil cases for labor trafficking in 2017 were domestic work-related."[24]

The ACLU recently shared a series of anonymized portraits of formerly enslaved people that merit careful reading for they highlight the interconnections between human trafficking, unjust immigration laws, and debt bondage.[25] These include the story of Fainess who was brought to the United States under a special visa to be the domestic worker of a Malawian diplomat, and who was starved, raped, and forced to work in the diplomat's household in Silver Spring, Maryland. "The whole time I was suffering, nobody saw me. I remember shoveling snow in my trafficker's driveway, without gloves, boots, or warm clothes, watching cars pass as everybody missed those red flags."[26] This same collection also shares the stories of Carlos, Sam, and Melanie who came to the United States from the Philippines through an employment agency. Their stories include going into debt to pay their employment agency, cleaning places like country clubs, and working in chicken factories for little or no pay, being held captive and threatened with deportation by their employers and employment agencies.

As is so often the case in the United States, the historical legacy of America's chattel slavery system looms large over these stories. The Polaris Project notes:

> People in slavery cleaned, cooked, cared for children and otherwise provided the scaffolding for life as it was known in the American south during slavery. Following the abolition of chattel slavery, empowering domestic workers was deemed likely to change the racial dynamics of that era and not pursued. Over a century later, the legacy of slavery is still playing out in ways both tangible and less so. The exclusion of domestic workers from protections under certain US labor laws is an example of a tangible hangover from the slavery and Jim Crow eras as those laws were purposefully crafted to block former slaves from amassing power to hold employers accountable. [27]

The church's current approach to modern-day slavery is disturbingly similar to ancient Christianity's relative silence on this issue. While no one condones or endorses the idea of 40 million people being enslaved today, it is rare to hear mention of modern slavery and the ways in which we are all implicated. The prevalence of modern slavery suggests we do not "see" the people who are enslaved around us. Many of us know enslaved people are cleaning our homes, making our food in restaurants, changing the bed sheets at hotels, and building the parts of the technology we use every day. Enslaved people are still supplying our sexual needs too, as 2021 saw investigations into the ties between human trafficking, the enslavement of women and girls across the globe, and websites such as PornHub, a site visited more times per month than Netflix, Yahoo, or Amazon.[28] And yet somehow we fail to fully recognize the full humanity of the 40 million, and I wonder if part of the reason is the centuries of Christian thought that has taught us that enslaved people are less than human.

Significantly, it is believed that a majority of people who are enslaved in forced labor are being held through forms of debt bondage. As noted in the stories above, in the United States, such debt bondage is frequently accompanied by threats of deportation by the very employment agencies to whom workers are indebted.[29] Slavery and debt are literally linked, in these cases, which is all the more reason why the church needs to speak out more forcefully on modern slavery and recover its abhorrence of the ways debt and predatory lending are means of enslavement of the poor.

At the heart of slavery is an economic interest in denying the equal humanity and dignity of those who are enslaved. John McGuckin writes that Roman slavery was, as it always is, about making vast profits as quickly as possible. Our twenty-first century economy has in many ways perfected this principle by spreading culpability and ownership across many interconnected systems.[30] Consider the iPhone and the factory tags on one's clothes. Who is driving this enslavement? Who are the enslavers of today? And the abolitionists?

As a Christian who is enmeshed and complicit in this same global system of modern slavery, it is significant to me that Gregory chose to preach this homily during the season of Lent—a season that calls for repentance and transformation. This suggests that to live as we do—in such a wantonly exploitative and consumerist manner—is to act with much of the same vanity and arrogance that Gregory of Nyssa was critiquing when he preached this rare homily during Lent of 379.

Gregory preached that it was not enough for the wealthy to simply release a few enslaved people every now and then but argued that Christ's overcoming the power of death required emancipation from death-dealing systems. Further, he contended, Christians are called to work for change so as to ensure freedom for enslaved peoples. Christianity's tendency to dream too small, to accommodate itself to enslaving economic systems, and to fail to imagine a world in which exploitation of the poor isn't simply the way it is, lingers with us still. We must join Gregory of Nyssa in daring to stand out in our own time for calling and acting for an end to modern slavery.

Discussion Questions

Historian John McGuckin notes, "Even if early Christianity could have imagined the abolition of slavery on the basis of its new philosophy of inestimable individual worth, it could not explain how it could bring this mysterious reality about." He therefore seems to suggest that Christianity's reticence to call for the emancipation of enslaved peoples was as much a failure of the imagination as it was of fear of reprisal. Do you see similar dynamics at play in how Christians think and speak about the economy today?

Ancient Christianity recognized the linkages between Easter and emancipation of the enslaved (however partial that might have been). There was, then, a recognition that Christ's resurrection had economic implications for the poor and the enslaved. Do Christians today still recognize these linkages? What are the economic implications of Easter?

Gregory's call to end slavery is grounded in a belief in the inherent dignity and equality of all people as made in the image of God. His was a rare voice, then, amidst a culture that implicitly and explicitly embraced the view that some people were assigned by nature and/or fate to serve others. To what extent do you see these same dynamics at play in modern society?

While no one condones or endorses the idea of 40 million people being enslaved today, it is rare to hear mention of modern slavery and the ways in which we are all implicated in the Church today. Why do you think that is?

A Next Step

The ACLU shared a series of portraits of people who had been trapped in modern slavery. These included the story of Fainess who was brought to the United States under a special visa to be the domestic worker of a Malawian diplomat, and who was starved, raped, and forced to work in the diplomat's household in Silver Spring, Maryland. She states in her profile "The whole time I was suffering, nobody saw me."

To Fainess's point above, many—if not most—are simply blind to the reality of modern slavery taking place right before their eyes. Take time to read and discuss with your faith community stories of modern slavery, including those of formerly enslaved domestic workers such as Fainess, Carlos, Sam, and Melanie.[31] According to the US Department of State, modern slavery across the globe includes sex trafficking, child sex trafficking, forced labor, bonded labor or debt bondage, domestic servitude, forced child labor, and the unlawful recruitment of child soldiers.[32] Learn more about the different categories of modern slavery and which are prevalent in your state and nation.

Endnotes

1 Hart, D. Bentley, "The 'Whole Humanity': Gregory of Nyssa's Critique of Slavery in Light of His Eschatology," *Scottish Journal of Theology,* Vol. 54, No. 1 (2001): 51.

2 McGuckin, *The Path of Christianity*, 1060, 1058.

3 Bentley, "The 'Whole Humanity,'" 54.

4 Ilaria Ramelli, "Gregory of Nyssa's Position in Late Antique Debates on Slavery and Poverty, and the Role of Asceticism," *Journal of Late Antiquity*, Vol. 5, No. 1 (2012): 91-92.

5 This is a paraphrasing of statement found in Ramelli's "Gregory of Nyssa's Position in Late Antique Debates on Slavery and Poverty, and the Role of Asceticism," 95.

6 Bentley, "The 'Whole Humanity,'" 52.

7 McGuckin, *The Path of Christianity*, 1064.

8 Bentley, "The 'Whole Humanity,'" 99.

9 Edward R. Hardy, "Saint Gregory of Nyssa," *Encyclopedia Britannica.*

10 Rhee, *Wealth and Poverty in Early Christianity*, 472.

11 McGuckin, *The Path of Christianity*, 1063.

12 McGuckin, *The Path of Christianity,* 1058.

13 McGuckin, *The Path of Christianity,* 1059.

14 Bartosz Zalewski, "If a Maidservant 'Dies a Horrible Death:' Canon 5 of the Synod of Elvira in the Light of the Norms of Roman Criminal Law," *Studia Iuridica Lublinensia,* Maria Curie-Skłodowska University, Poland, Vol. 30, No. 1 (2021).

15 McGuckin, *The Path of Christianity,* 1067.

16 Gregory of Nyssa's Homily on Ecclesiastes, *The Path of Christianity*, tr. McGuckin, 1083-1085.

17 Gregory of Nyssa's Homily on Ecclesiastes, *The Path of Christianity*, tr. McGuckin, 1083-1085.

18 Gregory of Nyssa's Homily on Ecclesiastes, *The Path of Christianity*, 1083-1085.

19 Gregory of Nyssa, "On the Love of the Poor," *Wealth and Poverty in Early Christianity,* ed. Rhee, 71.

20 Gregory of Nyssa, "On the Love of the Poor," *Wealth and Poverty in Early Christianity*, 71.

21 Kate Hodal, "One in 200 People Is a Slave. Why?" *The Guardian*, February 25, 2019.

22 "Global Estimates of Modern Slavery: Forced Labour and Forced Marriage," International Labour Organization, September 19, 2017.

23 "Global Estimates of Modern Slavery: Forced Labour and Forced Marriage."

24 "Human Trafficking at Home: Labor Trafficking of Domestic Workers," Polaris: Freedom Happens Now and National Domestic Workers Alliance, July 2019. polarisproject.org.

25 "Behind Closed Doors: The Traumas of Domestic Work," ACLU, aclu.org/news/immigrants-rights/behind-closed-doors-the-traumas-of-domestic-work-in-the-u-s/.

26 "Behind Closed Doors: The Traumas of Domestic Work," ACLU.

27 "Human Trafficking at Home," July 2019.

28 Nicholas Kristorf, "The Children of Pornhub," *The New York Times*, December 4, 2020.

29 "Behind Closed Doors," ACLU.

30 McGuckin, *The Path of Christianity,* 1057.

31 "Behind Closed Doors," ACLU.

32 "What Is Modern Slavery?", U.S. Department of State, state.gov/what-is-modern-slavery/.

22 Jerome on Sex, Money, and the Holy Poor

Nineteenth-century American abolitionist Frederick Douglass wrote, "When men oppress their fellow men, the oppressor ever finds, in the character of the oppressed, a full justification for his oppression."[1] In Jerome, one finds "the most learned of the Latin fathers of the church and among the greatest of biblical scholars" disparaging the character of the poor as "full of raging lust" and redirecting donations toward a new spiritual elite of scholarly ascetics he calls "the holy poor." As I will describe below, Jerome's focus on "the lust of the poor" was aimed at gaining financial support for the intellectual endeavors of scholarly monks, a troubling fact that reveals the long and intertwined relationships in Christianity between asceticism, knowledge creation, sexuality, wealth, and power.

Jerome's scholarship on behalf of the church required patrons, extraordinary leisure, and vast sums of money, and so he invested his time and significant intellectual abilities in making a biblical case that the "holy poor" such as himself were more worthy recipients of donations than the materially poor whose character he disparaged. This decision was largely driven by the practicalities of scholarship. MacCulloch notes,

> Traditionally [scholarship] had been an occupation associated with elite wealth, and even in the case of this monk in Bethlehem it was backed up with an expensive infrastructure of assistants and secretaries. Studying and writing, he insinuated, were as demanding, difficult, and heroically self-denying as any physical extravagance of Syrian

monks, or even the drudgery of manual labor and craft which were the daily occupations of monastic communities in Egypt."[2]

MacCulloch continues by noting that if Jerome had not been as successful in making this argument, "it might have been far more difficult for countless monks to justify the hours that they spent reading and enjoying ancient texts, and copying them out for the benefit of posterity. Ultimately the beneficiary was Western civilization."[3]

Be that as it may, it is the economically poor whose character is impugned and who get left behind in the dust as Jerome helped Christianity "find in the character of the oppressed, a full justification for [their] oppression."

Jerome (c.342-420) is often considered "the most learned of the Latin fathers of the church and among the greatest of biblical scholars," yet he could just as easily be remembered for his fraught and contradictory relationship with sex, money, and power.[4] Born to wealth in the hinterlands of the Roman Empire, Jerome has been described as the type who "had a seven-point plan for rising to power, taking in the papacy along the way."[5] He began executing this plan after studying in Rome when he traveled to Syria in 374 and spent several years among the desert hermits east of Antioch. It is likely in Syria that Jerome formulated his famous argument that the intellectual labor of scholarship was equal to, if not greater than, the manual labor of the monks of Syria and Egypt he was observing.

Jerome's embrace of both the poverty of asceticism and a life of scholarship set up a financial contradiction that any scholar and theologian engaged in research will recognize. This is because "a monk such as Jerome both claimed to be an advocate of total poverty and at the same time spent his life in the shadow of great libraries. He was tied irrevocably to wealthy persons who paid for the libraries on which his literary endeavors depended."[6]

Therefore, when Jerome traveled back to Rome after Syria, he presented himself to Pope Damasus as an ascetic, one wholly dedicated to poverty but whose scholarly work nevertheless required "profound leisure, hard work, and much money."[7] He would eventually receive that leisure and money both from his patron Pope Damasus as well as from a circle of wealthy women, including the widow Paula. His close relationship to Paula and other Roman women raised a collective eyebrow among Jerome's many critics who would later accuse him of preying on wealthy widows.

In 382, Pope Damasus called on Jerome to begin work on a new translation of the Bible from Greek into Latin in order to replace conflicting Latin translations from prior centuries.[8] The scope of this project expanded, and the fruit of his scholarly labor eventually became known as the Vulgate. This massive work occupied Jerome for many years, including past the turning point of Pope Damasus's death in 384.

It is clear from his writings that Jerome fully expected to become pope upon Damasus's death. Never one to be particularly charming or humble, Jerome would later write that he had been robbed of this position as all of Rome had been behind him: "Before I came to know the palace of holy Paula, all Rome was enthusiastic for me. In the judgment of almost all, I was worthy of the rank of highest bishop. My stylish pen gave voice to Damasus himself."[9] Yet Jerome had seriously misjudged the situation. His rigor, his tendency to lambaste critics, and his relationship with Paula and the circle of women patrons, resulted in Jerome having many powerful enemies. No longer under the protection of the pope, he had to leave Rome quickly and was never to return.

Jerome traveled to Bethlehem and was eventually followed by his patron Paula and her daughter Eustochium. In Bethlehem, Paula set up a large home—a fortified palace, in fact—for Jerome and other scholarly ascetics. She equipped the palace with a library and took "charge of Jerome's personal welfare, which she found no light undertaking."[10] It was there, in the house Paula built, that Jerome completed the Vulgate and wrote treatises against his many critics, including his most abusive treatise aimed at the intriguing figure of Vigilantius.

This treatise—*Contra Vigilantium*—was a bristling response to a priest from Gaul who questioned Jerome and other ascetics' admiration of virginity, the cultic adoration of the bones and ashes of Christian apostles and martyrs, the crude transmission and trading of these bodily bits, and the practice of all-night vigils spent in front of expensive golden vessels in which these relics were displayed. Significantly, Vigilantius had also criticized Jerome's fundraising efforts on behalf of ascetic communities in Jerusalem because of the way this distracted the wealthy from making contributions to the local church and the local poor. Historian David Hunter notes, "Vigilantius voiced concerns that were widespread among the Gallic clergy of his day and that his views may not have been far out of the mainstream of clerical opinion."[11]

As representative as Vigilantius's voice might have been, however, it is clear from the strident tone of Jerome's response that the animus between himself and Vigilantius was also personal: Jerome and Vigilantius knew one another, including through an awkward incident that occurred ten years prior.

The first time Vigilantius's name appears in Jerome's writings was the result of a visit Vigilantius made to the Holy Land during the summer of 395 wherein he attempted to join Jerome's ascetic circle. Afterward, Jerome referred to Vigilantius as a "holy presbyter" but discreetly flagged that Vigilantius had to scurry back to Gaul after a scandalous incident that Jerome, at that point, chose not to describe in detail. More than ten years later, however, in *Contra Vigilantium*, Jerome told how the monastery had been startled awake by an earthquake, and the brothers had discovered Vigilantius praying naked.[12] Addressing Vigilantius directly, Jerome wrote that unlike Adam and Eve who experienced shame at their nakedness, "you, who were stripped alike of your shirt and of your faith, in the sudden terror which overwhelmed you, and with the fumes of your last night's booze still hanging about you, showed your wisdom by exposing your nakedness in only too evident a manner to the eyes of the brethren."[13] This (interesting!) anecdote occurs as part of Jerome's browbeating Vigilantius for what he considered the priest's libertine views on sexuality and wealth.

After being found naked, Vigilantius fled the monastery before sunrise and joined his fellow Christians in Gaul in arguing against the ascetic insistence on celibacy as a requirement for clergy. Vigilantius maintained this ascetic disparagement of sex, which extended even unto sex within marriage, was profoundly unhealthy. Vigilantius argued that deacons and priests should be married before they were ordained and should not have to remain continent within that marriage. A furious Jerome concludes his treatise against Vigilantius by saying, "I will keep vigil for a whole night on his behalf and on behalf of his companions (whether they be his disciples or masters), who think that no man is worthy of Christ's ministry unless he is married and his wife is pregnant."[14]

The discussion of Vigilantius's nakedness and the debate over celibacy is relevant to this discussion of wealth and poverty because the rise of asceticism had linked sexuality and money by the late fourth century in important ways. Jerome argued that the sexual purity of monks and nuns meant that these "holy poor" were more deserving of donations than the common poor whose character he disparaged. This linking of sexuality and money is especially apparent in Jerome's line of attack on Vigilantius around donations to the ascetic communities in Jerusalem.

For in addition to questioning celibacy, Vigilantius also critiques the wealthy of his area for sending financial gifts to ascetic communities in Jerusalem and argues it would be far better for those monies to have been kept closer to home.[15] Clergymen like Vigilantius "resented the drain of gifts that were made by the rich to support ascetics, especially ascetics settled at the far end of the Mediterranean. They preached that the local rich should use their wealth to give to the local poor and to the local churches."[16] Vigilantius also advises that Christians shouldn't give all they owned at once but should instead give larger and larger amounts to the local church and local poor from their wealth's gradual increase.

In *Contra Vigilantium*, Jerome forcefully argues that the sexual purity and poverty of ascetics like himself meant there was a new spiritual elite he termed "the holy poor." These sexually chaste and scholarly "holy poor" merited the wealthy's gifts all at once, not gradually over time. Jerome writes,

> As for his argument that they who keep what they have, and distribute among the poor, little by little, the increase of their property, act more wisely than they who sell their possessions, and once for all give all away, not I but the Lord shall make answer: If you will be perfect, go sell all

> that you have and give to the poor, and come, follow Me.
> He speaks to him who wishes to be perfect, who, with
> the apostles, leaves father, ship, and net. The man whom
> you approve stands in the second or third rank; yet we
> welcome him provided it be understood that the first is to
> be preferred to the second, and the second to the third.[17]

Jerome also addresses Vigilantius's argument that wealthy patrons'
money should be kept for the local church and the local poor in Part
14 of *Contra Vigilantium*: "You will reply that every one can do this in
his own country, and that there will never be wanting poor who ought
to be supported with the resources of the church." Jerome then pits the
local poor against the "holy poor" who are members of the household
of faith: "And we do not deny that doles should be distributed to all
poor people, even to Jews and Samaritans, if the means will allow. But
the apostle teaches that alms should be given to all, indeed, especially,
however, to those who are of the household of faith."

Significantly, Jerome turns to the parable of the unjust steward to argue
his case. As you will recall, in this parable Jesus enigmatically advises
his followers to make friends for themselves by means of dishonest
wealth, so that when the money is gone, those friends might welcome
them into eternal homes. Jerome questions who these friends are,
disputes the notion that the common poor could ever be such friends,
and questions how the destitute could ever have such eternal homes:
"What! Can those poor creatures, with their rags and filth, *lorded over
as they are by raging lust*, can they who own nothing, now or hereafter,
have eternal habitations?"[18]

For Jerome, the answer is clearly "no." It is inconceivable to Jerome
that the common poor—"lorded over as they are by raging lust"—
ought to be the primary recipients of wealthy patrons' support. In this,
he joins Clement of Alexandria in disparaging the character of the
poor and insisting that when the gospels extol the poor as blessed,
they must have actually meant something else. He then contrasts the
lust-filled poor with the scholarly labor of chaste ascetics like himself,
members of the new spiritual elite who were seriously engaged in the
life of the mind. He writes:

> No doubt it is not the poor simply, but the poor in spirit,
> who are called blessed; those of whom it is written,
> Blessed is he who gives his mind to the poor and needy;

> the Lord shall deliver him in the evil day. But the fact is, in supporting the poor of the common people, what is needed is not mind, but money. In the case of the holy poor, the mind has blessed exercises, since you give to one who receives with a blush, and when he has received is grieved, that while sowing spiritual things he must reap your carnal things.[19]

Jerome's disparaging views of the poor, alongside his praise for the sexual purity and the life of the mind of "the holy poor," cinches his argument for the wealthy to continue directing their gifts to Jerusalem in support of ascetic communities rather than their local churches and the local poor. Jerome then cites Paul's Jerusalem Collection to add historical precedent to his argument. Christians have sent their money for generations to the Holy Land in support of the "holy poor," he argues, and these gifts were not sent to the generally poor but rather to fellow believers: "Might [Paul] not have distributed in some other part of the world, and in the infant churches which he was training in his own faith, the gifts he had received from others? But he longed to give to the poor of the holy places who, abandoning their own little possessions for the sake of Christ, turned with their whole heart to the service of the Lord." In doing so, Jerome equates support for "the saints" of Jerusalem who were experiencing famine with "the holy poverty" of ascetic scholars.

Like a skilled and unscrupulous development officer, Jerome makes an argument for why his community is more deserving of receiving the contributions of the wider church and ends up disparaging the poor in the process. Brown summarizes Jerome's position as one in which "Only by giving to holy monks in the distant Holy Land—and not to the faceless and unsavory poor of their own region—could the rich engage in a 'spiritual exchange' that was certain to place their treasure in heaven."[20]

Brown is unsparing in his assessment of the long-term impact of this argument on the life of the church, for through Jerome and other ascetics, "the poor" are eventually replaced with "the holy poor" of monks and nuns, a shift he describes as bringing to a close an ancient form of Christianity:

> In this way, monks gradually came to eclipse the poor as the privileged others of the Christian imagination. The monks

alone had become the "holy poor." In a contemporary monastic rule, lay gifts were instantly sanctified and made effective by being brought into the chapel to be prayed over by the nuns or monks. It is a solution whose high-pitched emphasis on the "holy poor"—on monks and nuns to the exclusion of the real poor—as the only truly reliable, because truly other recipients of alms for the safety of the soul would have struck a fourth-century Christian as vaguely Manichaean. With this shift from the poor to the monks as the primary intercessors for the sins of all Christians, an ancient Christianity died.[21]

Vigilantius has been called a "Protestant of his age," and this feels especially accurate when it comes to Vigilantius's critiques on relic piety.[22] In addition to his reasonable views around sex and money, Vigilantius is recognized for making "the only frontal attack on the cult of saints to appear in Latin Christianity," an attack directed at the splendor of shrines "with their shimmering mosaics, altars sheathed in imperial purple, and vast candelabra in which oil lamps burned day and night."[23] Vigilantius's critique once again touches on the intertwined themes of sex, money, and power. He critiques the placement of relics in expensive vessels and the lighting of tapers during the day and night, and questions what really went on during those all-night vigils. He also discourages the then-growing practice of Christians elaborately greeting relics—acts "self-consciously modeled after the imperial *adventus*," a ceremony that celebrated the arrival of a Roman emperor in a city.[24]

An exasperated Jerome defends these liturgical practices against Vigilantius by saying that when respect is paid to idols, such ceremony is rightly to be abhorred; yet insomuch as it is now the martyrs who are being venerated, these elaborate and expensive rituals should be embraced.[25] Importantly, he justifies the expense of such veneration by invoking the story of the woman with the alabaster jar who poured oil and fragrance on Jesus's body (Matthew 26:7,Mark 14:3,Luke 7:37), an argument for liturgical splendor still regularly used today. He writes:

> Once upon a time even the apostles pleaded that the
> ointment was wasted, but they were rebuked by the
> voice of the Lord. Christ did not need the ointment, nor
> do martyrs need the light of tapers; and yet that woman
> poured out the ointment in honor of Christ, and her
> heart's devotion was accepted.[26]

Jerome's use of the story of the woman with the alabaster offers an
opportunity to address what has tragically become Christianity's
most well-known statement about the poor. In addition to telling
the apostles they should stop complaining about the supposed waste
represented by the woman's expensive gift, Jesus then goes on to say
the fateful line: "For you always have the poor with you, but you will
not always have me" (Matthew 26:10-11).

What I find profoundly appalling is that of all the scriptural
statements about wealth and poverty in the Old and New Testaments,
only some of which have been mentioned in this book, this single
utterance has become by far Christianity's most well-known teaching
on the poor. In *Always With Us? What Jesus Really Says About the
Poor*, Liz Theoharis tells of how the preacher Jim Wallis regularly
conducts a Bible quiz with American audiences and asks them to
name the most famous Bible passage about the poor. "Every time,
he receives the same answer: 'The poor you will always have with
you.' People quote 'the poor you will always have with you' as a
way to discredit antipoverty organizing, justify the foreordination
of poverty, and support the idea that charity is the best response
to poverty."[27] Theoharis notes the tragic irony this represents:

> The Bible—a text replete with calls for economic justice
> and denunciations of the scourge of indifference to the
> poor—has been misused and cynically politicized to
> suggest that poverty is a result of the moral failures of
> poor people sinning against God, that ending poverty is
> impossible, and that the poor themselves have no role
> to play in efforts to respond to their poverty. Biblical
> texts, especially "the poor you will always have with you,
> are used to justify the inevitability of inequality and to
> provide religious sanction for the dispossession of the
> majority for the benefit of the few.[28]

While Jerome may be the first to cite the story of the woman with the alabaster jar as justification for both liturgical splendor and neglect and disparagement of the poor, he certainly isn't the last. The Matthean version of this story has become such an important cornerstone for contemporary Christians' neglect of issues of economic justice and the poor that it needs to be studied and preached on regularly in congregations. What does this passage really mean? How should we understand Jesus's statement in light of everything else he says about the rich and the poor in the gospels? I greatly appreciate Liz Theoharis and The Poor People's Campaign's work in using the passage as a starting point for larger conversations on what the entire scriptural tradition says about wealth and poverty. As tragic, disturbing, and ultimately misrepresentative of Christianity as this one line is, it is in the back of the many people's minds and therefore represents an opening for broader engagement on what the Bible actually says on issues of wealth, poverty, and economic injustice.

This fact brings us back to Frederick Douglass's insight about the oppressor ever finding, in the character of the oppressed, a full justification for that very oppression.[29] "The poor you will always have with you" is our contemporary version of what Jerome was doing when he disparaged the common poor as "full of raging lust." Partly because of Jerome, the transition from the Gospel of Luke's Beatitudes that proclaimed "blessed are the poor" and "woe to you who are rich" is almost complete, and the *Magnificat's* dream of reversal has begun to feel like a distant memory.

Discussion Questions

Tragically, Jerome ultimately elevated the so-called "holy poor" by disparaging the destitute whom he described as full of raging lust and unable to engage in the life of the mind that set ascetic scholars like himself apart. This strikes me as another example of Christians finding in the character of the oppressed a full justification for their continuing oppression. To what extent do you see Christians disparaging the character of the poor today?

What do you think of Vigilantius's criticism of the wealthy in his area for sending monies in support of new ascetic communities in Jerusalem, and his belief that it would be far better for that money to be directed to the local churches and the local poor? What financial obligations do Christians have to the local poor? What financial obligations do they have to the wider church?

Jerome's arguments helped to establish the funding sources for ascetic scholarship, without which "it might have been far more difficult for countless monks to justify the hours that they spent reading and enjoying ancient texts, and copying them out for the benefit of posterity."[30] What does it mean that Jerome's argument for financial support of this work was made by pitting the life of the mind over and against contributions to the local poor? Are there implications for Christian scholars, researchers, and educational institutions today?

A Next Step

Carefully study and reflect on the full story of the racist and
politicized myth of "the welfare queen," a figure popularized during
Ronald Reagan's 1976 Presidential Campaign. Brian Covert's 2019
article "The Myth of the Welfare Queen" in *The New Republic*
goes beyond the stereotype and into the complex life of the actual
person—Linda Taylor—who was transformed into a racist stereotype
and who was used by both President Reagan and President Clinton
to undermine the welfare system. Explore why this remains such
a powerful trope in society today. Where does this myth still
come up today? Finally, reflect on what it means that Jesus states,
unequivocally and without caveats, "blessed are the poor."

Endnotes

1 Frederick Douglass as quoted by Ibram X. Kendi, *Stamped from the Beginning: The Definitive History of Racist Ideas in America* (Bold Type Books, 2016).

2 MacCulloch, *Christianity*, 295.

3 MacCulloch, *Christianity*, 295-296.

4 Attwater and John, "Jerome," 181-182.

5 Attwater and John, "Jerome," 181-182.

6 Brown, *Through the Eye of the Needle*, 275-276

7 Jerome, Prologue, Origen on the Song of Songs, as referenced in Peter Brown's *Through the Eye of a Needle*, 589.

8 MacCulloch, *Christianity*, 294.

9 Brown, *Through the Eye of the Needle*, "Jerome," Letter 45.2.2, 54.1:324.

10 Attwater and John, "Paula," 261.

11 David G. Hunter, "Vigilantius of Calagurris and Victricius of Rouen: Ascetics, Relics, and Clerics in Late Roman Gaul," *Journal of Early Christian Studies,* Vol. 7, No. 3 (1999): 401, 403.

12 Hunter, "Vigilantius of Calagurris and Victricius of Rouen," 405.

13 *Contra Vigilantium*, 11, New Advent. newadvent.org/fathers/3010.htm.

14 *Contra Vigilantium*, 17.

15 Hunter, "Vigilantius of Calagurris and Victricius of Rouen," 401-430.

16 Brown, *Through the Eye of a Needle*, 280-282.

17 *Contra Vigilantium*, 14.

18 *Contra Vigilantium,* 14. Italics mine.

19 *Contra Vigilantium*, 14.

20 Brown, *Through the Eye of a Needle*, 280-282.

21 Brown, *Through the Eye of a Needle*, 517.

22 The English historian Edward Gibbon says this, as noted by David G. Hunter, "Vigilantius of Calagurris and Victricius of Rouen," 420.

23 Brown, *Through the Eye of a Needle*, 280-282.

24 Hunter, "Vigilantius of Calagurris and Victricius of Rouen," 420.

25 *Contra Vigilantium*, 7.

26 *Contra Vigilantium*, 7.

27 Theoharis, *Always with Us?* 36.

28 Theoharis, *Always with Us?*, 36.

29 Frederick Douglass as quoted by Ibram X. Kendi, *Stamped from the Beginning.*

30 MacCulloch, *Christianity*, 295-296.

23 A Pelagian Monk Says Enough Already

De divitiis (On Riches) was written in the early fifth century by an unknown monk long associated with the enigmatic name of "the Sicilian Briton."[1] That monk—whoever they were—wrote a treatise on wealth that is not well-known because it has oftentimes been considered a dangerous and heretical text, an inspiration for both Christian socialism and an example of the heresy of Pelagianism gone wild.

However, I suspect that another reason this text has been sidelined is because the unknown author has such a clear and compelling voice on the evils of economic inequality. The author asks:

> Does it seem just to you then that one man should have an abundance of riches over and above his needs, while another does not have enough even to supply his daily wants? That one should relax in the enjoyment of his wealth while another wastes away in poverty? That one man should be full to bursting-point with expensive and sumptuous banquets far in excess of nature's habitual requirements, while another has not even enough cheap food to satisfy him? That one man should possess a vast number of splendid houses adorned with costly marble statues in keeping with the instincts of his vanity and pride, while another has not even a tiny hovel to call his own and to protect him from the cold or the heat? That one should maintain countless possessions and enormous expanses of land, while another cannot enjoy the possession even of a

small portion of turf on which to sit down? That one man should be rich in gold, silver, precious stones and all kinds of material possessions, while another is harassed by hunger, thirst, nakedness and all kinds of poverty? Add to this the fact that we can see evil men abounding in excessive wealth and good men struggling with need and destitution, which makes us even more suspicious of the unfairness of this thing called riches.[2]

To my mind, the author articulates the essential question about wealth and poverty: does this vast inequality seem just and fair to you? I mean, truly. This matter of "the unfairness of riches" and the devastation of poverty should haunt people of faith every day. In addition, the fact that this paragraph, written in the early fifth century, could just as easily apply to the city block I live on in the twenty-first, speaks to the ongoing relevance of what the author explores so powerfully.

Tragically, many Christians have concluded this inequality has been foreordained by God and that there is little that faithful people can or should do. They wield Jesus's statement in the Gospel of Matthew, "The poor you will always have with you," as their support (Matthew 26:11) while ignoring the broader biblical witness that has much to say about economic justice and denounces indifference to the poor. The author of *De divitiis* represents the exact opposite view. They are unsparing in their attack on the wealthy as engaged in injustice and evil, and they skewer a society that claims to be Christian but has forgotten that Christ himself was poor and taught in his earthly life that the poor are blessed:

Note carefully, I beg you, what a great sign of arrogance and pride it is to want to be rich when we know that Christ was poor, and to take upon ourselves any of the power that comes with lordship, when he took on the outward form of a servant…I shall say no more about material fortune; but let us see if the rich man's way of life has any similarity with that of Christ. There is none that I can see: the one is haughty, the other downcast; the one is proud, the other humble; the one is full of fury, the other of gentleness; the one is angry, the other long-suffering; the one is boastful, the other self-effacing; the one abhors the poor, the other embraces them, the one abuses them, the other extols them.[3]

The writer goes on to say that all wealth—including inherited wealth—ultimately has its roots in injustice: "But what else is the chief source of riches but extortion and robbery?"[4] They also describe a causal relationship between the wealth of the few and the destitution of the many: "the few who are rich are the reason for the many who are poor."[5] They urge the church to stop its imaginative attempts to deny the meaning behind "the eye of the needle" and instead face the fact that Jesus calls all Christians—not just ascetics—to sell their possessions and give their wealth away to the poor so as to follow Christ and gain eternal life.

To be clear, these are challenging statements, and one can see why a faith tradition bent on building its own wealth and power would seek to bury this particular text beneath the labels of Christian socialism and Pelagianism. Yet if you've managed to make it through all of this book's prior chapters, you know by now that these views are fairly common both within scripture and among those theologians formed within the ascetic tradition. Even the boldest and most infamous line of *De divitiis*—"Get rid of the rich and there will be no poverty"—is simply a sharper expression of what other ascetics have said regarding the Christian call to live with just enough and give everything beyond that point to the poor. A broad spectrum of ancient Christian thinkers, including Evagrius of Pontus, John Chrysostom, Basil of Caesarea, and even the ornery Jerome, all made similar (albeit more roundabout) versions of this same statement.

What *De divitiis* does that feels new and unique is gather all of these ideas together in one place—a veritable bouquet of ascetic attacks on wealth—and manages to do so with a memorably moving, sharp, and even occasionally funny voice. A significant portion of the treatise, for example, is devoted to refuting one creative rationale after another for disregarding Jesus's command to the rich man/ruler. Referring to one of the most common arguments, the author writes, "'But,' you will say, 'it is his sins that he has to sell, not his property.' And where will he find a purchaser stupid enough to buy them—unless, perhaps it be the person who understands the passage in such a sense?"[6]

But I'm here for more than just the quips. The questions *De divitiis* raises are strikingly relevant to conversations that are taking place today around sources of wealth and limits on riches, particularly in light of climate change and calls for racial justice reparations. *De divitiis* asks readers to reflect on the sources of wealth in our world and what should be done with wealth made through injustice and exploitation. Amidst climate change, it also raises questions about what it means to live with just enough—that is with *sufficientia* versus in excess and *superfluitas*.

To understand the messages contained in *De divitiis*, historians contend that one has to go back to the Pelagian ascetic movement that the anonymous author is widely thought to have been a part of.[7] This requires getting to know the shadowy figure of Pelagius, a monk best known for having been labeled a heretic by Augustine and through Augustine's anti-Pelagian writings.

The monk Pelagius was born in Britain c.354 and baptized in Rome at some point between 380 and 384. He became one of the most listened to ascetic voices of his time and place and, ironically, worked very closely with the wealthy families of Rome.[8] Despite his popularity, who Pelagius really was and what he actually believed remains elusive in part because his thoughts are known almost exclusively through the writings of his detractors, especially Augustine of Hippo. Through Augustine, we hear of Pelagius as a heretic for what he deems Pelagius's overly positive view of human nature, his belief in the power of human will to overcome sin, and his insistence on the need for Christians to dispossess themselves of wealth and property.

Unlike Augustine, who held that humanity was born into a fallen state and was saved by God's grace, Pelagius and his followers appear to have understood human nature to be fundamentally good insomuch as it was God's creation. This meant that "human nature was created by God with the possibility of fulfilling his commandments, and this ability is still in the possession of human beings."[9] To explain the reality of evil they saw all around them, including the injustice of wealth inequality, Pelagians argued that human will had become distorted over time by both individual sin and the way these individual sins congealed into evil, societally accepted customs.[10] The sin of extreme inequality and general acceptance of modern slavery come to mind as forms of socially acceptable evils that most people, including Christians, don't really get too upset about.

While profoundly difficult, Pelagius believed that people and society could draw closer to God despite these societally ingrained customs by reshaping their will through prayer, discipline, and good works. On the sin of avarice, Pelagius and his followers understood Jesus to be calling his disciples to take radical steps to break free from these demonic customs. The author of *De divitiis* writes, "For just as a man possesses avarice because of riches—if, indeed, an avaricious man can be said to possess rather than to be possessed—so he seeks riches because of avarice, and riches are able to continue in existence only so long as they are protected by their mother, as it were, that is, avarice."[11]

Pelagians, including the writer of *De divitiis*, point to the parable of the rich man/ruler as the prime example where Jesus states followers of Christ have to take radical action to gain eternal life. This action includes giving their wealth to the poor to join the disciples in following Christ (Matthew 19:16–30, Mark 10:17–31, Luke 18:18–30). As noted above, a significant portion of *De divitiis* amounts to the writer refuting (and occasionally ridiculing) all the fifth-century techniques for ignoring the literal meaning of this passage. Some of these are humorous—*But the word "camel," you will say, refers to the gentiles...*—whereas others represent refutations of arguments still being made today.

Referring to the argument that the rich should retain their wealth so as to continue to be able to give donations to the poor, an argument we heard Clement of Alexandria make in the second century, the author vehemently denies that this idea appears anywhere in scripture: "Thus you say, 'If I have become poor, how can I give alms?'—as if you were ever bidden to give alms when you have nothing, or to possess superfluous riches so as to be able to be always giving them."[12] The Pelagians, including the writer of *De divitiis*, are unrelenting in their insistence on a literal interpretation of this story in the gospels. They seek to move church and society toward radical divestment.

Augustine disagreed, to put it mildly. He railed against the Pelagians' positive views on human nature and understanding of sin, as well as this literalist interpretation of Jesus's encounter with the rich man/ruler. Instead, Augustine followed the by then well-established practice of quoting only the Gospel of Matthew's version of the story, which is the only one that includes the phrase "if you wish to be perfect": "Jesus said to him, 'If you wish to be perfect, go, sell your possessions, and give the money to the poor, and you will have treasure in heaven; then come, follow me'" (Matthew 19:21). This qualifier becomes an escape hatch for wealthy Christians and their apologists, for it means that dispossession is not required of everyone but a teaching only intended for those strange monks and nuns who wish to go that extra mile.

Augustine's "big tent" approach—one that offers hospitality to both the rich and ascetics in the church—reveals an aspect of Pelagianism that contemporary appreciators of this movement need to bear in mind. MacCulloch warns those (including myself, admittedly) who relish the rigor and piercing observations of a writer like the Pelagian author of *De divitiis*:

> Pelagius's views have often been presented as rather amiable, in contrast to the fierce pessimism in Augustine's views of our fallen state. This misses the point that Pelagius was a stern Puritan, whose teaching placed a terrifying responsibility on the shoulders of every human being to act according to the highest standards demanded by God. The world which he would have constructed on these principles would have been one vast monastery.[13]

Ironically, Augustine, whose theology is grounded in an unshakable belief in humanity's depraved nature and fallen state, ends up emphasizing the themes of God's love and forgiving grace. He holds that everyone—both the wealthy and those ascetics who seek perfection by giving their wealth to the poor—ought to practice greater humility as all are sinful creatures standing in the need of God's merciful grace. This insight proves key in helping to build a church that is inclusive of rigorous ascetics such as the author of *De divitiis*, as well as the rest of us who fall far short of Jesus's high expectations.

Even so, in a society that is generally unbothered by egregious inequality, one in which the church seems just as invested in pursuing institutional wealth and power as any other, and in a culture where people are reduced to credit scores, corporations are considered people, and people have transformed themselves into (God help us all) "brand ambassadors," *De divitiis*'s passion, force, and clarity about how wealth distorts society is refreshing. *De divitiis* speaks to how Christianity can be, at its heart, a religion that is profoundly out of step with the ways most people think about wealth and poverty. Indeed, the author speaks movingly of Christianity as a faith that causes confusion:

"But," you will say, "it will be a source of confusion, if the man who has been accustomed to give to others now receives from them." If you were afraid of confusion, why were you so willing to give your allegiance to one whose mysteries are a source of confusion to this world? For his birth and Passion and the whole course of his life after taking upon himself human form cause more than a modicum of confusion to unbelievers. [14]

Most Christians, the author concludes, are actually ashamed by Christ and his followers' poverty and are "confused by [Jesus and the disciples'] humility, poverty, shabby clothing and cheap and simple fare, by their mean treatment at the hands of this world, the abuse, the derision, the insults, by all those things, in fact, which we know to have been a cause for rejoicing not only to Christ himself but also to his apostles."[15]

De divitiis lays out a vision of a Christianity in which the gospels stand as a source of confusion to a horrifically unequal, exploitative, and consumerist society and which urges the faithful to strive to break free of the ingrained patterns of avarice and sin.

De divitiis continues to inspire healthy confusion around the question of what it means to live simply and with just enough. In spite of Christianity's long history of accruing for itself institutional wealth and power, there has also been a concurrent strand of thought about the limits of wealth. In *Economics in the Church Fathers*, Hennie Stander writes, "The concept of sufficiency versus superfluity runs like a golden thread throughout all the literature of the patristic authors…" and "Sufficiency of wealth was acceptable, while superfluity was perilous since it could lead to sin."[16]

On the question of living with just enough, the author of *De divitiis* divides the world into three categories: the rich who have more than necessary; the poor who do not have enough; and those who live righteously with just enough, possessing no more than was absolutely necessary.[17] The term the author uses for enough is *sufficientia*, an idea that doesn't derive from Greco/Roman culture ("enough" was hardly a virtue) but from Proverbs 30:8, which states, "Give me neither poverty nor riches; feed me with the food that I need."[18] The author makes the case that all Christians, and not just ascetics, should be focused on learning how to live with just enough and should give all wealth beyond this basic level to the poor. This standard also means he believed that retaining more than just enough— superfluity—was akin to hoarding that which was intended by God for the common good.

This principle reflects the fact that, in the view of the author of *De divitiis* as well as other Patristic writers, the rich and poor were tightly bound to one another in an economy of limited resources. The accumulation of wealth by one member was a sin because it always resulted in many others' poverty. "In his view, the distribution of wealth and poverty in society was the result of an unforgiving zero-sum game. Those who went beyond the measure of sufficiency could do so only by taking from the poor."[19] The conclusion *De divitiis* comes to is among its most infamous lines: "Get rid of the rich and you will not find the poor. Let no man have more than he really needs, and everyone will have as much as they need, since the few who are rich are the reason for the many who are poor."[20]

Although the author of *De divitiis* is perhaps more direct than other ascetics of the time, what he is saying is not so very different from what many others had been saying all along, albeit more elegantly. John Chrysostom (c.349-407), for example, believed it was impossible to acquire wealth through just means, even when it came through inheritance. Chrysostom writes,

> It is true that somebody might argue that he had inherited his wealth from his forefathers, but that would merely mean that his forefathers had stolen it from somebody. The root or origin of this wealth will necessarily be injustice. Nor can one argue that wealth is good merely because the possessor is not greedy, or because he or she practices charity. The fact remains that a rich man cannot explain why he alone has accumulated possessions which the Lord has meant to give to all in common.[21]

A similar understanding of wealth can be found in Gregory of Nyssa's first of two homilies entitled "On the Love of the Poor," wherein he writes,

"All things belong to God, our common Father. We are all of the same stock, all brothers and sisters. And when people are siblings, the best and most equitable thing is that they should inherit equal portions. The second best is that even if one or two take the greater part, the others should have at least their own share. But if one man should seek to be absolute possessor of all, refusing even a third or a fifth to his siblings, then he is a cruel tyrant, a savage with whom there can be no dealing, an insatiate beast gloatingly shutting his jaws over the meal it will not share.[22]

Similarly, the focus on living with just enough echoes what Evagrius Ponticus writes in the fourth century as he instructs his fellow monks on how to combat the demon Love of Money. Evagrius advises complete dispossession, both of one's material wealth as well as of the inner desire for financial security. His advice goes well beyond a generalized simplicity (or a minimalist aesthetic, for that matter) and even extends to being against holding onto wealth so as to avoid poverty in old age: "Against the soul that seeks more than food and clothing and does not remember that it entered the world bare and it will leave it naked. For we brought nothing into the world, so that we can take nothing out of it; but if we have food and clothing, we will be content with these (1 Timothy 6:7-8)."[23] Monks are thereby instructed to practice extreme economic vulnerability and give all their surplus wealth to the elderly monks who were the poor of their monastic communities.

This emphasis on living with just enough has particular resonance with a growing strand of "environmental asceticism" today. In very particular corners of the internet, there is an emerging movement of environmentalists, philosophers, and economists who argue that society needs to place limits on excess wealth so that gains beyond that point can be redirected toward eliminating global problems, including extreme poverty and climate change. This limitarian movement is making similar arguments to what the author of *De divitiis* did in the fifth century—namely, that there needs to be some form of criteria around what constitutes "enough."

In "What, If Anything, Is Wrong with Extreme Wealth?," philosopher Ingrid Robeyns lays out the basic idea of economic limitarianism:

In a nutshell, economic limitarianism holds the view that
no one should hold surplus money, which is defined as the
money one has over and above what one needs for a fully
flourishing life. Limitarianism as an ethical or political view
is, in a certain sense, symmetrical to the view that there is
a poverty line and that no one should fall below this line.
Limitarianism claims that one can theoretically construct a
riches line and that a world in which no one would be above
the riches line would be a better world.[24]

In other words, "Get rid of the rich and you will not find the poor.
Let no man have more than he really needs, and everyone will have as
much as they need, since the few who are rich are the reason for the
many who are poor."[25]

Augustine ultimately wins the day, of course. What *De divitiis* proposed
proved far too radical for the big tent, inclusive church that would go
about building up its own wealth and power as the Roman Empire
fractured into chaos and decline. Pelagius was ultimately deemed a
heretic, and the term "Pelagian" has become a derogatory term for
an overly positive view of human nature that sees us as capable of
working toward our own salvation through righteous actions and
practices. Even so, a Pelagian text like *De divitiis* should be more well-
known and more widely read particularly as a provocation to critical
thought around issues of wealth inequality today.

What *De divitiis* offers Christians is the opportunity to think about
how vast inequality shapes our lives. The author joins the likes of John
Chrysostom, Jerome, Basil of Caesarea, and others in questioning
whether wealth can ever be innocent. *De divitiis* argues that wealth is
almost always the result of exploitation and injustice, and that the act
of accumulating riches is a form of withholding from others what God
intended for the common good. This is an important topic for both
individuals and institutions with endowments to consider. Indeed,
much about what he says rings both true and valuable still today.

In addition, the writer is clear that the iniquity of riches weighs not
only on the generation that made this wealth but also on its inheritors.

Whereas Clement of Alexandria cannot imagine assigning any culpability to the inheritors of wealth—"What is to be condemned if God, who gives life, places a child in a powerful family and a home full of wealth and possessions?"—*De divitiis* maintains that an inheritance is a dangerous thing to pass on to one's loved ones: "What then are we saying? That you should completely disinherit your sons? Far from it! Rather, that you should leave them no more than their nature requires. For how can you be said to love them, if you are seen to confer on them something which will only harm them?"[26]

Such statements can provoke wealthy families and institutions, including church institutions, to reflect on the sources of their wealth and raises the possibility of making reparations for the original injustices that this wealth was built on. It also opens a conversation on the ways that wealth is currently growing, including discussions on socially responsible investing.

Finally, *De divitiis* explores what constitutes "enough" in a more pointed way than most other Christian writers. The author of *De divitiis* comes closer than many in defining sufficiency as retaining only what is absolutely needed. This feels strikingly relevant today, especially as the earth is rapidly warming as a result of carbon emissions. What would it mean for Christians—both as individuals and institutions—to enter into a serious conversation about this ancient emphasis on living with just enough? This is a conversation that the earth itself is requiring us to have, and in the broader ascetic tradition as well as in *De divitiis*, the church has a multitude of sources to draw on to lead this discussion in an authentic way.

Discussion Questions

The author of *De divitiis* asks one of the most essential questions about extreme inequality: "Does it seem just to you then that one man should have an abundance of riches over and above his needs, while another does not have enough even to supply his daily wants?" The writer clearly believes this to be an injustice, but others have argued that even extreme inequality is "just," insomuch as wealth and poverty correspond to what is earned and/or owed. What do you think?

De divitiis speaks to how Christianity can be a religion that is profoundly out of step with the ways most people think about wealth and poverty, and the author speaks movingly of Christianity as a source of confusion in a wealth-obsessed world. What does it mean for Christianity to be a source of confusion in a world that is comfortable with extreme inequality?

De divitiis divides the world into three categories: the rich who have more than necessary; the poor who do not have enough; and those who live righteously with just enough, possessing no more than was absolutely necessary.[27] The idea of *sufficientia* is derived from Proverbs 30:8, which states, "Give me neither poverty nor riches; feed me with the food that I need."[28] What would it mean for you to live with "enough" and share anything beyond this with the poor? What would it mean for our institutions to live with "enough" and share anything beyond this with the poor?

A Next Step

The author of *De divitiis* believed that even in spite of profoundly ingrained societal customs, including the widespread acceptance of extreme inequality, followers of Jesus could draw closer to God by reshaping their will through prayer, discipline, and good works. To do this, many monastic communities developed a Rule of Life to help them make such a radical break with society. What are some rules or practices that you or your community might take up as a way of trying to create some space between yourself and an economically unjust society? What are some small examples of this? What are more radical ways of doing this?

Endnotes

1   As an increasing number of scholars advise against using this name, I'll drop it from here.

2   *De divitiis* 8.1. *Pelagius: Life and Letters,* tr. B.R. Rees, (England: Boydell Press, 2004).

3   *De divitiis* 6.1-6.2, *Pelagius: Life and Letters,* tr. Rees.

4   *De divitiis* 7.2, *Pelagius: Life and Letters,* tr. Rees.

5   Brown, *Through the Eye of a Needle,* loc. 7,573 (Kindle).

6   *De divitiis* 9.2, *Pelagius: Life and Letters,* tr. Rees.

7   This assumption is being challenged today. "Kessler proposes to take a new look at 'criticism of riches' as displayed in [*De divitiis*] and other contemporary writings, and its relation to 'Pelagianism.' He rejects the traditional view that criticism of riches is an element of a 'Pelagian doctrine.' It is difficult, he argues, in historical-theological terms to define precisely what that 'Pelagian doctrine' might be, since the works traditionally grouped together as 'Pelagian' offer a variety of theologies, apart from the fact that for some of these texts questions have been raised, whether they can be called 'Pelagian' at all. There is still no undisputed criteriology for the definition of 'Pelagian' texts." *Reichtumskritik und Pelagianismus. Die pelagianische Diatribe de divitiis: Situierung, Lesetext, Übersetzung, Kommentar,* (Paradosis, 43.) by Andreas Kessler; Review by: Josef Lössl, *The Journal of Theological Studies,* New Series, Vol. 51, No. 2, (October 2000): 739-741. jstor.org/stable/23968442.

8   V. Grossi, "Pelagius (c. 354-c.427)," in *Encyclopedia of Ancient Christianity,* ed. Angela Di Berardino and Thomas Oden, InterVarsity Press, 8

9   Giulio Malavasi, "Pelagius," *Brill Encyclopedia of Early Christianity Online.*

10 Brown, *Through the Eye of a Needle,* loc. 7,402 (Kindle). "Society as a whole was held in the grip of evil customs. These customs were the mute deposit of past ages of willful sinning by individuals."

11 *De divitiis* 2, *Pelagius: Life and Letters,* tr. Rees.

12 *De divitiis* 10.2, *Pelagius: Life and Letters,* tr. Rees.

13 MacCulloch, *Christianity,* 306.

14 *De divitiis* 14.1, *Pelagius: Life and Letters,* tr. Rees.

15 *De divitiis* 14.1, *Pelagius: Life and Letters,* tr. Rees.

16 Stander, "Economics in the Church Fathers," 29.

17 Brown, *Through the Eye of a Needle,* loc. 7,546 (Kindle)

18 Brown, *Through the Eye of a Needle,* loc. 7,567 (Kindle)

19 Brown, *Through the Eye of a Needle,* loc. 7,555, 7,565 (Kindle).

20 Brown, *Through the Eye of a Needle,* loc. 7,573 (Kindle)

21 Chrysostom, Homily on 1 Timothy, as quoted by Stander, "Economics in the Church Fathers."

22 "On the Love of the Poor," *Wealth and Poverty in Early Christianity,* tr. Rhee.

23 "Concerning the Love of Money," *Talking Back,* 97.

24 Ingrid Robeyns, "What, If Anything, Is Wrong with Extreme Wealth?," *Journal of Human Development and Capabilities,* Vol. 20, No. 3 (2019): 251-266.

25 Brown, *Through the Eye of a Needle*, loc. 7,573 (Kindle)

26 *De divitiis* 20.2, *Pelagius: Life and Letters,* tr. Rees.

27 Brown, *Through the Eye of a Needle,* loc. 7,546 (Kindle).

28 Brown, *Through the Eye of a Needle,* loc. 7,567 (Kindle).

24 Augustine, the Good Steward of Wealth and Power

As this is this book's final chapter, I want to return to the original vision of God's reversal. There, it is the lowly who are lifted up, the rich and powerful who are brought low, the poor who are declared blessed, and the rich who are sent away weeping. The long-suffering Lazarus and the rich man have their fates flipped, and it is the rich man who must endure in eternity the hell that Lazarus suffered during his lifetime. In Matthew 25, we are told that God's coming judgment hinges on how each of us has treated the most vulnerable in our lives; Jesus says that he comes to us every day in "the least of these"—the poor, the thirsty, the homeless, the immigrant—a momentous statement about the very fabric of reality that Christians ignore far too often.

The beloved role of the prudent steward and the idealization of stewardship as a Christian virtue also experience a reversal in the Gospel of Luke. In the parable of the unjust steward, we hear of a steward—a first slave—who has spent his life diligently working on behalf of his master, extracting wealth by exploiting other slaves, tenant farmers, day laborers, and through the domination of the land. Accused of financial misdealing, the unjust steward finds his salvation by releasing his master's wealth back to the enslaved and exploited—that is, by reversing the flow of wealth—and by halving the debts of the slaves and field workers he had overseen and exploited so efficiently. Jesus concludes this story about this "first slave" by saying that no one can have two masters; ultimately, all of us have to choose between serving God or serving wealth. If there is a form of Christian stewardship to be emulated, then, it is one in which

God, not wealth, becomes one's master, and wealth is redirected and repurposed toward the liberative release of the most vulnerable from the enslavement of poverty, particularly through the freeing of those entrapped in debt.

Elsewhere, other positions of power and authority are turned on their heads. When the disciples argue about which among them is the greatest, Jesus states that although "The kings of the Gentiles lord it over them; and those in authority over them are called benefactors... the greatest among you must become like the youngest, and the leader like one who serves. For who is greater, the one who is at the table or the one who serves? Is it not the one at the table? But I am among you as one who serves" (Luke 22:25-27). The Gospel of Matthew's version of this story takes this one step further, as Jesus states that whoever wishes to be first must become a *doulos*—literally, the slave laborer of both then and now. Similarly, Paul also regularly refers to himself as a *doulos*.

These images of reversal and liberation are important to hold onto when encountering the writings of Augustine of Hippo, a brilliant bishop and theologian who was a highly effective steward of the church's wealth and power. Augustine's views on wealth and poverty, as well as on the uses and abuses of institutional power, have vastly overshadowed the gospels' themes of reversal. González argues that "to understand the later course of Christian views on issues of faith and wealth, we must see their source in Augustine" for "he brought together many different strands of thought and wove them into a system that entirely dominated Christian theology at least until the thirteenth century and has continued to be influential to this day."[1]

Augustine's reflections on wealth and power remain enthralling in no small part because he lived at a time that feels remarkably similar to our own. He stood "between the classical world and a very different medieval society, sensing acutely that the world was getting old and feeble..."[2] Writing and preaching as the Roman Empire crumbled all around him, Augustine stewarded the church's wealth and power, served as an ardent defender of both Catholic unity and societal order, and bears the dubious distinction of having been the first Christian theologian to call down state violence on heretics in the name of maintaining unity and order. His teachings on the purpose of wealth and poverty, on the usefulness of the poor, his firm defense of slavery, and his prioritization of pastoral care for the rich, all helped the church to grow and grow.

Augustine (354-430), Doctor of the Church in the West and "by far the most extraordinary Latin theologian in early Christianity and beyond," is regularly spoken of as second only to Paul in shaping the warp and woof of the Christianity we know today.[3] Born in Thagaste in North Africa, in what is now Algeria, he lived, preached, and ministered amidst the collapse of the Roman Empire. Indeed, the collapsing empire served as the backdrop of most of his ministerial life and theological writings. Augustine lived through the sack of Rome in 410 and died during a siege of Hippo by the Arian vandals, and so his 113 books and treatises, more than 200 letters, and more than 500 sermons can be read as revolving around the question: "How could God's providence allow the collapse of the manifestly Christian Roman Empire, especially the sack of Rome by barbarian armies in 410?"[4] For "In one of the greatest disappointments ever experienced by the church, the Western Roman Empire of the 390s which had promised to be an image of God's kingdom on earth, disintegrated into chaos and futility."[5]

Augustine's monumental work, *City of God*, was begun in earnest in 413—that is, just three years after the sack of Rome by barbarian armies. It took him thirteen years to write and meditate on the earthly versus the heavenly city amidst the great disappointment of the Western Roman Empire's decline.[6] Augustine wrote that "the earthly city glorifies in itself, the Heavenly City glories in the Lord" and all institutions formed part of a struggle between these two cities, a struggle which ran through all world history.[7] This understanding of two cities struggling throughout history greatly shaped Augustine's perspective on wealth and poverty as well as on what he viewed as the regrettable but necessary institution of slavery.

Augustine's writings about wealth, poverty, and slavery are scattered across many sermons, letters, and other writings, and so I am especially grateful for the compilation organized by Helen Rhee in her book, *Wealth and Poverty in the Early Church*.

Augustine "found himself preaching to the rich (who enjoyed the leisure to take religion seriously) and to the upper layers of the populus—to artisans, to members of the guilds, to small landowners, and to minor town councillors,"—that is, the "relatively prosperous members of the populus who, nonetheless, still saw themselves as permanently at a disadvantage in comparison with the rich."[8] Ensconced among the wealthy, he articulates what remain deeply held truths for much of Christianity: namely, that the moral value of wealth is primarily determined by its use; that the passing down of wealth from one generation to another is fine provided a portion of that inheritance is allotted to the church; that God ordered the poor to remain in poverty so as to aid in the salvation the rich; that slavery was fine provided slave masters act with humility; and that wealth and power are well-used when directed in the defense of the Catholic faith and toward maintenance of good social order.

Augustine's views on wealth stewardship resonate with Clement of Alexandria's second-century understanding of wealth as a neutral tool, wherein wealth's moral value is ultimately determined not by its source but rather by its use. Nuancing this view, Augustine adds that "virtue consists in enjoying (*frui*) proper objects of love for their sake and using (*uti*) proper objects of instruments well without loving them, whereas vice involves mixing up and reversing the order."[9] When preaching to the wealthy, he speaks of wealth and power as tools given by God to be used—but not enjoyed for their own sake— and argues that good people are responsible for using both wealth and power to good ends.[10]

This view is neatly captured in his letter, "To Proba" (c.412), wherein Augustine writes, "People become good not by having such goods, but having become good otherwise, they make these things good by their good use of them."[11] Similarly, on the issue of seeking higher positions of rank and authority, "Certainly, it is proper for them to wish for these things, not for the sake of the things themselves but for another reason, namely, that they might do good by providing for the welfare of those who live under them."[12] As we will see, "providing for the welfare of those who live under them" meant first and foremost maintaining good order at a time when the empire was crumbling all around him. Augustine therefore urges the rich and powerful to use their resources and positions of power with greater humility and social responsibility.

One way he does this is through a unique interpretation of the parable of Lazarus at the gate of the rich man (Luke 16:20-31), an image of societal reversal if ever there was one. Jesus's parable famously details the differing fates of Lazarus, a man covered in sores who begs at the gate of a rich man, and the rich man who feasts sumptuously every day insulated from the suffering of the poor. In death, the fates of Lazarus and the rich man are reversed.

In his "Letter to Hilarius," Augustine zeros in on the detail that when Lazarus dies, he is received into the bosom of Abraham, a patriarch who is described as having had great wealth, property, and many slaves. He argues that it therefore could not have been Lazarus's poverty that resulted in his being received into God's paradise: "And if the poor man's merit had simply been his poverty, not his goodness, he surely would have not been carried by angels into the bosom of Abraham who had been rich in this life."[13]

Augustine concludes that the parable of Lazarus and the rich man was not about material wealth and poverty but rather about how God rewarded both the rich (here symbolized by Abraham) and the poor (Lazarus) who lived with inner humility and in righteousness. He writes that it wasn't material wealth that led the rich man to hell but rather the rich man's pride and arrogance: "It was his pride, not his riches, that brought the rich man to the torments of hell, because he despised the good poor man who lay at his gate, because he put his hope in uncertain riches, and thought himself happy in his purple and fine linen and sumptuous banquets."[14]

One can imagine how pastoral a message this was to the wealthy and powerful families Augustine found himself preaching regularly to. He offered "a view of society where the inequalities created by wealth could be accepted as long as they were softened by the abandonment of the toxic by-products of wealth—arrogance, violence, and the abuse of power."[15] Such a pastoral approach extended to Augustine making a case for the general usefulness of the poor.

González notes that Augustine regularly "speaks of the function of the poor in giving others an opportunity for charity and service,"[16] and therefore, in his theology, "the poor appear to be no more than stepping stones—in Augustine's categories, instruments to be used—toward the goal of salvation."[17] So many Christian mission trips still operate from Augustine's view that, like money and high position, the poor exist to be used by the rich for good and holy ends. González observes that this view serves to reinforce societal order and discourages any act of a deeper questioning of the way things are for, in Augustine's own words, "God made the poor to test the human in them, and made the rich to test them through the poor. God has done everything properly…and we must believe that it was good, even though we do not understand why it was done."[18]

As shown by his interpretation of Lazarus and the rich man, Augustine is especially concerned about the sin of pride and the value of spiritual humility. Brown notes, "In Augustine's preaching, pride, not wealth, was the true Last Enemy of the Christian," and the "real division of the world was not between the rich and the poor. It was between the proud and those who were enabled by God's grace to be humble before God and before their fellows."[19]

In stark contrast with the rigorous and judgmental Pelagians, Augustine writes,

> Let the rich listen to this: "What is impossible for mortals is easy for God." Whether they retain riches and do their good works by using them, or enter into the kingdom of heaven by selling them and distributing them to provide for the needs of the poor, let them attribute their good works to the grace of God, not their own strength." [20] [21]

Every person, Augustine argues, rich or poor, ascetic or otherwise, should recognize with humility their need for God's grace.

In this same vein, Augustine goes on to accuse those ascetics who have given up all their wealth as having become guilty of the sin of pride, and he rails against their judgmentalism toward the rich: "However, if they are truly the poor of Christ, and if they store up, not for themselves but for Christ, why should they pronounce punishment on their weaker members before they have attained to the seats of Judgment?"[22] He also relishes calling out ascetics' hypocrisy and writes that these so-called "holy poor" are very often financed by the very people they go around critiquing: "I think that some of those who babble these ideas without restraint or reason are supported in their needs by rich and religious Christians."[23] In a critique that stings, Augustine calls out the so-called holy poor who "condemn the very ones at whose expense they live by."[24]

In contrast, Augustine argues for the building up of an inclusive church, one that recognizes that the rich and poor, powerful and powerless, stand equally before God in need of God's mercy and grace. Augustine sees this emphasis on humility and on all of humanity's equal reliance on God's forgiveness and grace as essential for creating a more inclusive church, a "big tent" as it were, for the rich and poor, the ascetics and otherwise, as well as slaveowners and slaves.

And yet, however nuanced, graceful, and inclusive Augustine's theological position may be, when it comes to brass tacks, he has a way of ensuring that wealth and power always end up on top. This is especially clear in the tactics he employs and the practical decisions he makes as bishop.

In one instance, we hear Augustine defending himself against the (seemingly valid) accusation that he had stolen church properties from the heretical Christian sect of the Donatists.[25] Augustine refutes this by saying that on account of their heresy, the Donatists could not retain any property as this would have constituted an abuse—rather than proper use—of wealth. Summarizing Augustine's position on these property matters, historian Hennie Stender writes,

> To use property in the right way means to use it to the
> glory of God. Rightful use, then, requires right faith. On
> this basis, Augustine argues that only the church can
> be regarded as a rightful property owner, since only the
> church has true faith. This approach would imply that
> the Catholic Church was the only rightful owner of all
> property, including the property of sects.[26]

Perhaps smarting from a Donatist-led attempt on his life, Augustine
writes of the Donatists that, "Those who use their wealth badly
possess it wrongfully, and wrongful possession means that it is
another's property."[27] Both on the grounds of divine and human law
(for Augustine describes the church as the emperor's), Augustine
concludes that the Donatists, "being outside the communion of the
Catholic Church, usurp to themselves the name of Christians and are
not willing in peace to worship the Author of peace, may not dare to
possess anything in the name of the church." [28] [29]

González explores the vast implications of this position, a view that
brought together right faith (the Catholic Church) and power, in what
Augustine unabashedly calls "the Communion of the Emperor."[30]

> From this text, it is clear that, according to Augustine,
> not only has God made some poor and some rich,
> but also God has done this through the civil order. The
> result is that there is no moral authority to which the
> Donatists can appeal, for the emperor's authority is
> derived from God, and things belong to whomever those
> laws assign them.[31]

This philosophy will have major implications for how Augustine views
moments of unrest and rebellion as the empire crumbles.

Augustine also cleverly stretches the very definition of "poverty'"
to great institutional effect. He is fairly shameless amidst a church
building campaign in his efforts to replace "the poor," as the term
is generally understood, with the needs of the institutional church.
Augustine makes himself and the church "the real poor" when he
writes, "Your bishop may not lack for clothes or need of a roof above
his head [like the poor]. But perhaps he is building a church. You
cannot see into the empty coffers of your leader; but you certainly can

see the empty shell of his building as it goes up… May God grant that I do not say this in vain."[32]

He thereby makes the now fairly common argument that a gift to the church is the same in God's eyes as to a gift to the poor. Indeed, he urges the wealthy to make their gift to the poor through the church and not think too hard about where it goes. "Put it in the hands of the poor; give it to those in need; what does it matter to you how it reaches there? Will I not deliver what I receive?"[33]

Augustine later compares the church to a machine whose internal workings are obscured from plain sight. If you wish to give to the poor, he argues, it is best to make one's donation to the church, for in the same way oil poured into a machine trickles down through pipes unseen and emerges in unexpected places, so too a gift made to the church will reach the poor. Augustine argues that it is not the donor's place to see how that happens or where exactly it ends up. "You cannot see how, but you may trust me; I am the builder."[34]

Finally, in his "Exposition on Psalm 38," what starts out sounding like a traditional critique of wealthy Christians for how wealth is made eventually becomes an appeal to give to the church. Speaking to the rich, he first addresses the exploitative sources of their wealth and the common justifications that the wealthy use for accumulating such riches: "You are shrewd; you use every act you know to add coin to coin and to shroud your growing wealth in jealous secrecy. Robbing others, you are anxious not to be robbed yourself; you fear to suffer the wrong [you do to others], though your suffering does not atone for your sin." He later adds, "To screen your iniquity you make a plea of paternal love—the excuse of injustice. 'I am storing if for my children.'"[35] He goes on to offer a riveting critique of this common excuse for building wealth but then subsequently asserts that all will be forgiven if they remember to include the church in their will: "You have children, you answer. Number one more among them; let one portion be Christ's."[36]

When speaking of views of wealth and poverty, I believe one has to mention Augustine's view of human property—namely, the institution of slavery. McGuckin notes that both Augustine and Ambrose of Milan regularly wrote as "elite defenders of a colonial status quo" and justified the institution of slavery on two grounds: the old pagan argument "that some men (sic) could not be free by nature and so do better when they are mastered by others" and that the continuation of slavery was "better for society than the revolutionary unrest that would ensue if all were treated equally and afforded freedom."[37] If these arguments sound familiar, it's because they would prove exceedingly useful as Christian justification for the trans-Atlantic slave trade. But even in their own time, Augustine and Ambrose stood out as more vocal proponents of slavery than many of the non-Christian philosophers before them.[38]

Augustine's pattern of having a nuanced theological position but brutal *modus operandi* continues on the issue of slavery. In his theological writings, Augustine considers slavery to be reflective of humanity's fallen nature and holds that slavery would not exist in the ideal society of the City of God. Nevertheless, insomuch as humanity does not live in this ideal world but rather in a fallen state, God has entrusted good people with wealth and power to maintain societal order and ensure the welfare of those who God has placed under their care, including slaves. The enslaved, Augustine argues, are being punished by God for their sins, and therefore it is just and in keeping with God's will to keep them enslaved.[39] This is Augustine's "realistic politic" that does "not seek to establish perfect conditions as much as defensible and attainable standards" and therefore leads him to argue that, "to abolish [slavery], though it resulted from sinful alienation from the standards of love, would cause too much social unrest. In the present state of a deficient world, it ought to be endured."[40]

Augustine instead urges slave masters to practice kindness toward their slaves and moderate their violent beatings and sexual exploitation. Augustine says that though harsh commands and insults may be justified to preserve good order ("Male serve!" and "You lousy slave!"), the slave master must never allow those harsh words to affect their inner soul. "[The master] says this under the pressure of a need to keep his household in order. But let him never say it inwardly. Let him never say it deep down in his heart."[41]

If there was any hint of restraint and regret in Augustine's advice on slavery, there is less nuance in his discussion of practical matters. This is striking as the crumbling of the Roman Empire all around

Augustine was resulting in a *kairos* moment, a time of both crisis and opportunity. Cracks were suddenly beginning to appear in the previously firm institution of slavery. The heretical Donatists, for instance, were at the forefront of calling for the abolition of slavery in the fourth century. McGuckin notes, "The Donatist country bishops, where the scandal of slave farm factories loomed as a major aspect of daily life, led the way for a call to finally end the practice of slavery in the Christian empire."[42] They were taking direct action and had begun "torching slave-owner plantations and forcibly liberating slaves."[43]

Augustine's response to the Donatists is fierce and unequivocal. He "eventually advocated bringing in the state police to put down the Donatist movement by force of arms" and therefore bears the distinction of being the first Christian theologian to call down state violence on heretics (and abolitionists) in the name of preserving good societal order. "When the Donatists tried to burn slave plantations to the ground, Augustine preferred to suppress them in the cause of preserving a 'peaceful' state order."[44] He famously justifies this act by citing Jesus's command to "compel the people to come in" (Luke 14:23), arguing that using state violence to preserve good order and bring the Donatists back into line constitutes a right use of God-given power.

Augustine's first use of Jesus's command to "compel them to come in" would prove highly useful in later centuries as the church employed state violence against many other groups. Slavery, in Augustine's theology, might have been an unfortunate outcome of fallen humanity, but in the midst of a crumbling Roman Empire and as the church was ascendent in its own wealth and power, preserving order was much preferable to the anarchy that would come if the slaves working on the farm factories and plantations managed to attain their freedom.

Augustine was right in at least one respect: none of us are perfect and everyone stands in need of God's grace when it comes to Jesus's high expectations, and the issues of wealth, poverty, and money are areas where this feels especially so. And yet, Augustine's views on what constitutes the right use of wealth and power has helped to build a

Christian church in which Mary's call for reversal—"to bring down the powerful, lift up the lowly"—and Luke's version of the Beatitudes now oftentimes feel profoundly out of place.

In addition to advocating a vision of God's grace freeing us from our debt of sin, Augustine also ends up voicing one of the subtlest (and therefore most useful) defenses of wealth, power, unity, and good societal order, and his view comes to define the church's position on these matters through the thirteenth century and still today. In this respect, I think of Augustine as one who saw God's radical grace as freeing us from our debts of sin, whilst simultaneously building up the church's wealth and power at every turn.

Of course, in Jesus's parable of the unjust steward, that "first slave" finds his redemption by eventually doing something else—indeed, the very opposite of what he was expected to do.

As I write in 2022, I'm struck by the many parallels between the fifth century and the twenty-second, both times when life in our respective empires feels threatened, feeble, and on the verge of a collapse. Cracks are appearing in all sorts of institutions, including in the highly exploitative, low-road version of capitalism that has been America's *modus operandi* since the stealing of indigenous people's lands and the institution of chattel slavery.[45] And so, I think faith leaders today have a choice. Will we be among those who decide to use wealth and power to buttress a crumbling unity and order, or will we seize this *kairos* moment and finally heed the call to move beyond the old logic of stewardship and send wealth and power flowing in reverse, toward the alleviation of debt, the freeing of people enslaved by debt, the release of people held in the captivity of everyday poverty?

Discussion Questions

Augustine offers a nuanced understanding of the usefulness of wealth and power. In his letter, "To Proba," Augustine writes, "People become good not by having such goods, but having become good otherwise, they make these things good by their good use of them."[46] Similarly, on the issue of seeking higher positions of rank and authority, he writes, "Certainly, it is proper for them to wish for these things, not for the sake of the things themselves but for another reason, namely, that they might do good by providing for the welfare of those who live under them."[47] What are the strengths and weaknesses of this view of responsible use of wealth and power? Are there aspects of Jesus's teachings that get lost in this perspective?

Augustine argues that the parable of Lazarus and the rich man was not actually about material wealth and poverty but rather about how God rewarded both the rich (symbolized by Abraham) and the poor (Lazarus) who lived with humility and in righteousness. The wealthy, he argued, could indeed be saved provided they avoid the toxic by-products of wealth—arrogance, violence, and the abuse of power. What do you think of this perspective on the parable of Lazarus and the rich man?

As John McGuckin notes, "When the Donatists tried to burn slave plantations to the ground, Augustine preferred to suppress them in the cause of preserving a 'peaceful' state order."[48] Slavery, in Augustine's theology, might have been an unfortunate outcome of fallen humanity, but in the midst of a crumbling Roman Empire and as the church was ascendent in its own wealth and power, preserving order was much preferable to the anarchy that would come if the slaves working on the farm factories and plantations managed to attain their freedom. How and where do you see a similar argument about the need to preserve good order being made today?

A Next Step

Read the parable of the unjust steward one more time. It can be found in the Gospel of Luke 16:1-13. Imagine yourself in the role of the steward. What are you feeling? What are you doing at each point in the story? Spend time reflecting on what you think this perplexing parable could possibly mean.

Endnotes

1 González, *Faith and Wealth*, 214.

2 MacCulloch, *Christianity*, 311.

3 Rhee, *Wealth and Poverty in Early Christianity*, loc. 494 (Kindle).

4 MacCulloch, *Christianity*, 305.

5 MacCulloch, *Christianity*, 3.

6 Brown, *Through the Eye of a Needle*, 348. "The grand theme of the unity of the City of God grew out of Augustine's ceaseless "dialogues with the crowds" in the 400s and 410s. It was only later spelled out with monumental certainty in the pages of his City of God."

7 MacCulloch, *Christianity*, 305.

8 Brown, *Through the Eye of a Needle*, 345.

9 Rhee, *Wealth and Poverty in Early Christianity*, loc. 508 (Kindle).

10 González, *Faith and Wealth*, 216. "Although things are intended to be used, not every use is appropriate to them. Improper use Augustine calls "abuse." … Therefore, those who abuse, or do not use well, do not really use at all."

11 Augustine 130: "To Proba" Parts 3 and 12, *Wealth and Poverty in Early Christianity*.

12 Augustine 130: "To Proba" Parts 3 and 12, *Wealth and Poverty in Early Christianity*.

13 Augustine 130: "To Proba" Section 23, *Wealth and Poverty in Early Christianity*.

14 Augustine 130: "To Proba" Section 26, *Wealth and Poverty in Early Christianity*.

15 Brown, *Through the Eye of a Needle*, 394.

16 González, *Faith and Wealth*, 218.

17 González, *Faith and Wealth*, 217.

18 Psalm 124:2, Quoted in *Faith and Wealth*, González, 218.

19 Brown, *Through the Eye of a Needle*, 349.

20 MacCulloch, *Christianity*, 307.

21 MacCulloch, "Augustine, Letter to Hilarius," Section 28, *Christianity*.

22 MacCulloch, "Augustine, Letter to Hilarius," Section 37, *Christianity*.

23 MacCulloch, "Augustine, Letter to Hilarius," Section 37, *Christianity*.

24 MacCulloch, "Augustine, Letter to Hilarius," Section 38, *Christianity*.

25 González, *Faith and Wealth*,220.

26 Stander, "Economics in the Church Fathers," 27.

27 MacCulloch, "Augustine 153: to Macedonius (c.414)," Section 38, *Christianity*. .

28 MacCulloch, *Christianity*, 304.

29 Augustine Tractates on the Gospel of John 6:25.

30 MacCulloch, *Christianity*, 304. The Catholic Church was in fact what Augustine was not afraid to call "the communion of the emperor."

31 González, *Faith and Wealth*, 220.

32 Brown, *Through the Eye of a Needle*, 355.

33 Augustine, "Exposition on Psalm 38," Section 12.

34 Augustine, "Exposition on Psalm 38," Section 12.

35 Augustine, "Exposition on Psalm 38," Section 11.

36 Augustine, "Exposition on Psalm 38," Section 12.

37 McGuckin, *The Path of Christianity*, 1074.

38 MacCulloch, *Christianity*, 116.

39 Ramelli, "Gregory of Nyssa's Position in Late Antique Debates on Slavery and Poverty, and the Role of Asceticism," 91-92.

40 McGuckin, *The Path of Christianity*, 1087.

41 Brown, *Through the Eye of a Needle*, 351.

42 McGuckin, *The Path of Christianity,* 1069.

43 McGuckin, *The Path of Christianity*, 1069.

44 McGuckin, *The Path of Christianity*, 1069.

45 Desmond, "In Order to Understand the Brutality of American Capitalism, You Have to Start on the Plantation."

46 Augustine 130: "To Proba," Parts 3 and 12," *Wealth and Poverty in Early Christianity,* tr. Rhee.

47 Augustine 130: "To Proba," Parts 3 and 12," *Wealth and Poverty in Early Christianity,* tr. Rhee.

48 McGuckin, *The Path of Christianity*, 1069.

Conclusion:
A Retelling of the Parable
of the Unjust Steward

Clement of Alexandria does it. Basil of Caesarea does it. Jerome and Augustine too. As noted in each of their respective chapters, all four of these theologians offer their own creative perspective on Jesus's perplexing parable of the unjust steward, a story which has played a recurring role in forming how the church thinks about wealth and poverty. Therefore, I have decided to conclude this book by offering my own imaginative retelling of this parable. Like those theologians listed above, I take many creative liberties in my interpretation.

Death Comes for the Unjust Steward

The owner of the plantation was known to be a capricious, angry, and violent man, but for some reason he had always held a soft spot for his first slave, the person he would come to call his good and faithful steward. The owner had spotted him when he was just a child and had raised him up to be the "first slave" of his estate. That young slave proved to be surprisingly bright and gifted with money. Seeing this, the master gave the young man more and more responsibility. Soon "the good steward" was not only managing the plantation fields surrounding the estate but also two nearby farm factories. The steward therefore managed and oversaw a vast operation of fellow slaves, tenant farmers, and migrant field workers.

That is not to say that being a good steward was easy work. No, the workers he oversaw frequently stalled and resisted, and this required harsh punishment. He also noticed that many of his workers slowed down as their time on the plantations wore on. Even the most efficient of laborers were quickly broken and worn out, he observed. Many others simply died of exhaustion and disease. After several years of carefully tracking this, he came up with an accounting model that factored in workers' rapid exhaustion, an approach that vastly expanded hiring laborers and purchasing new slaves so as to make up for those who were being used up so quickly.[1]

His model was controversial at first but soon became a widely replicated practice. When there was bad press about workers taking their own lives, the good steward issued a statement noting that the suicide rate had not, in fact, exceeded the normal average for the region.[2] The public's concerns were assuaged, his non-anxious leadership was praised, and the clamor especially died down when everyone realized how quickly and cheaply their goods were now being made. *The New York Times* eventually featured him in their regular column "Corner Office" because his new management method had rendered unimaginable profits.

The good steward dutifully reported these profits to his master each quarter. His master, in turn, became one of the wealthiest people on the planet. The master grew so wealthy, in fact, that he built a rocket and took an eleven-minute joyride into space. When his master landed back on the earth, the first thing he did was thank his good and faithful steward, as well as all the workers whose toil had helped him to see the stars.[3]

But seeing the stars did not stop the master from being a capricious and violent man. One day, seemingly out-of-the-blue, the master became fixated on his steward's new clothes and nice new home and became convinced that his first slave was stealing from him. This was the beginning of the end. The steward knew his time was up when he received an irate phone call from his master accusing him of theft. He had seen his master turn on others before, and it always meant humiliation, abandonment, and even death. The steward thought about all the years he had faithfully served to build his master's wealth, but he knew none of that meant anything now.

That evening, the good steward went home and considered the strange arc of his life. Born to nothing, he had been picked out as a young man by fate and his master's capricious kindness. When his master gave him a little responsibility, he had been sure to outperform all the others. It bothered him at first that this meant betraying his people—that is, his fellow slaves, his fellow workers, the very families and land that he had come from. Over time, however, the steward had learned to silence that part of himself. He became skilled, efficient, and highly capable at performing those legal but highly exploitative acts that were necessary for keeping his position and growing his master's wealth. Over time, he also cultivated the virtue of *verecundia* at cocktail parties and in meetings before his betters—the delicate art of knowing one's place and staying in one's lane. And yet, knowing that it was all coming to an end, he was now filled with deep regret.

The next day, the good steward rose early to perform a series of acts he knew society would see as immoral. He still had the keys, the passcodes, and all the account information at his fingertips, and he knew he had just a small amount of time to do something to make up for the pain he had caused his people throughout his life.

He personally knew the families who were enslaved by debt to their master. He knew which villages and communities would forever be paying off their debts. He knew of several parents who'd had to sell their children into slavery to feed their families. He knew the women who were at the master's beck and call for sexual exploitation. He knew all these people well because he had dutifully managed their enslavement.

As quickly as he could, the good steward began acting unjustly by canceling debts and sending families money to purchase their own and loved ones' freedom. Each time funds were transferred, he called the families to give them as much time as possible so they could try to make their escape. He continued doing this until he heard a clamor outside his window and his master's new "good steward" burst into the room, and he was hauled away.

In his final moments, the steward saw a vision of a place unlike anything he had ever known in his lifetime: a kingdom without slaves, without debt, without the violent cruelty of masters, and without the exploitative efficiencies of good and faithful stewards. He saw the families he had hurt set free, parents embracing children who had been sent to faraway lands, and even a master whose need for cruelty and violence had been miraculously healed. Even the Earth looked different. The poisonous snow falling finally stopped. The fires died down. Winter returned. When he died, it was with the hope that the God he had abandoned—the God of the Poor—would be gracious and merciful in his judgment, and that what the steward had done in those last few hours of his life would be enough.

At the conclusion of the actual version of this parable (Luke 16:1-13), Jesus makes several observations about wealth and poverty that remain among his most perplexing:

> And I tell you, make friends for yourselves by means of dishonest wealth so that when it is gone, they may welcome you into the eternal homes.

> Whoever is faithful in very little is faithful also in much; and whoever is dishonest in very little is dishonest also in much. If then you have not been faithful with the dishonest wealth, who will entrust to you the true riches? And if you have not been faithful with what belongs to another, who will give you what is your own?

> No slave can serve two masters; for a slave will either hate the one and love the other, or be devoted to the one and despise the other. You cannot serve God and wealth.

Despite the fact that Jesus states, "no slave can serve two masters," Christianity has oftentimes sought to do both—claiming to serve God while maintaining a servile fascination with both wealth and power. In this, we have been unjust stewards of one of the most important messages of the gospel, a dream of reversal and economic justice wherein unjust wealth is turned toward liberative ends. To begin to turn from being stewards of institutional wealth and power to stewards of humanity requires recovering the voices of those who have been advocating for liberation and economic justice throughout Christian history.

This transformation is more important now than ever. Strange and seemingly apocalyptic things are happening. A pandemic has unmasked the deadly consequences of rampant inequality. Climate change is driving a refugee crisis that is being met with rising nationalist and fascist hatred across the globe. The United States is undergoing a racial reckoning, and workers long exploited through too much labor and too little pay are leaving their workplaces in droves. The earth itself is groaning with the too-muchness of our species. And in the midst of this, the Gospel of Matthew 25 is calling the church to account for our treatment of "the least of these" and has found the Christians profoundly complicit in these systems of injustice.

Faith leaders have hard choices about what to do next. Will Christianity forever be the cringing, obsequious stewards of wealth and power? Will we always scrape and bow before the wealthy and powerful, serve as chaplains to the rich, shore up a crumbling order, and counsel patience instead of liberation? Or will we learn to align ourselves differently and do something else entirely in our treatment of "the least of these"? I certainly hope so, and I believe that the well-being of the church and our earth depends on this transformation.

My hope is that we will do something we should have done long ago: return home to our people, use the "unrighteous mammon" we've gained along the way to make friends among those who've been exploited for so long, and hear anew Jesus's concluding words that "You cannot serve both God and wealth."

Endnotes

1 "Amazon and the Labor Shortage," *The New York Times*, podcast, December 1, 2021.

2 Brian Merchant, "Life and Death in Apple's Forbidden City, *The Guardian*, June 18, 2017.

3 Tim Murphy, "Jeff Bezos Thanks Amazon Workers and Customers for Making Him So Rich He Can Go to Space," *Mother Jones*, July 20, 2021.

About the Author

Miguel Escobar is executive director of Episcopal Divinity School at Union Theological Seminary (EDS at Union). There, he works with the Very Rev. Kelly Brown Douglas, dean of EDS at Union, in the formation of social-justice faith leaders for the Episcopal Church. Previously, Escobar served as managing program director for leadership, communications, and external affairs at the Episcopal Church Foundation (ECF). He earned a master of divinity from Union Theological Seminary in 2007 and served as the communications assistant to then-Presiding Bishop Katharine Jefferts Schori from 2007 to 2010.

Escobar is the former chair of the board of directors of Forward Movement and serves as secretary of the board of directors of Episcopal Relief & Development. He grew up in the Texas Hill Country and attended Our Lady of the Lake University in San Antonio, Texas, where he studied the Roman Catholic social justice tradition, Latin American liberation theologies, and minored in Spanish. Escobar divides his time between two partnered parishes in Brooklyn, New York: All Saints, Park Slope, and San Andres in Sunset Park. He lives with his husband, Ben, and dog, Duke, in Brooklyn.

About Forward Movement

Forward Movement inspires disciples and empowers evangelists. While we produce compelling resources like this book, Forward Movement is not a publishing company. We are a discipleship ministry. We live out this ministry through creating and publishing books, daily reflections, studies for small groups, and online resources. People around the world read daily devotions through *Forward Day by Day*, which is also available in Spanish (*Adelante Día a Día*) and Braille, online, as a podcast, and as an app for smartphones.

We actively seek partners across the church and look for ways to provide resources that inspire and challenge. A ministry of the Episcopal Church since 1935, Forward Movement is a nonprofit organization funded by sales of resources and gifts from generous donors.

To learn more about Forward Movement and our work, visit us at ForwardMovement.org or VenAdelante.org. We are delighted to be doing this work and invite your prayers and support.